A FAN'S GUIDE:

EUROPEAN FOOTBALL GROUNDS

★★★★
GATE 26

STUART FULLER

First published 2008

ISBN 978 0 7110 3286 6

Published by Ian Allan Publishing

an imprint of Ian Allan Publishing Ltd, Hersham, Surrey
KT12 4RG
Printed in England by Ian Allan Printing Ltd, Hersham,
Surrey KT12 4RG.

Visit the Ian Allan Publishing website at
www.ianallanpublishing.com

Front cover: Brøndby Stadium, Copenhagen

Contents

Contents

ABOUT THE AUTHOR

Stuart Fuller was born into a footballing family in the early 1970s. As a mark of defiance he actually turned against his West Ham-supporting family and followed Arsenal. All that changed on a Trevor Brooking goal in 1980 and he has never looked back, following West Ham since. He has watched football in over 25 countries and continues to find the most obscure games to see as part of a regular 50 games per season. He became member 1,004 of the 92 Club in 1999. Wherever there is a major tournament in the world, you can be sure he will be there!

ACKNOWLEDGEMENTS

The original idea for a book on European Football travel had been with me for many years. I saw first-hand the number of football fans waiting to board planes in faraway places having just 'popped over' to watch AC Milan, Bayern Munich or Legia Warsaw for the weekend. With the growth of information on the internet it has always been my intention to provide a one-stop shop for such fans to plan their trips as much as possible before they go, to avoid the hidden pitfalls in these faraway places.

Research for such a book is a long and painful process, so please bear with me if one or two facts are out of date – changes in ticket policies often happen as a knee-jerk reaction to events, such as those we saw in Italy last year, and can have a massive effect on travelling fans' plans.

I would like to thank a number of people who have made this book possible though. First, to every fan who has ever expressed an opinion about a stadium, city or airport to me on my travels, as well as those who have filled in my ad hoc requests for surveys and questionnaires. Also, thanks to those people listed in the back of the book who have provided pictures where my own archive has let me down. If I have missed anyone off the list then I apologise unreservedly. The biggest thankyou in this area goes to the fine chaps at Worldstadiums.com who have always assisted when a picture was needed.

A big thankyou must go to Peter Waller at Ian Allan who initially showed interest in the project and chased it through to fruition. He shows remarkable optimism, being a Bradford City and Shrewsbury Town fan, which puts supporting West Ham into perspective! Also, thanks to the team at Ian Allan who have turned my dreams into reality.

Finally, I have to say thankyou to the three people who have really made this project happen: my three little Fullers who have given me the time and support to continue writing into the small hours and have forgiven me for missing the odd family meal, school play or Father's Day (four times and counting).

Introduction

Ever since the first budget airline in the UK spread its wings and sped off down the runway, European football has taken on a new light to us fans in Britain. Those first flights by Debonair, and their 'follow the bear' footprints at Luton Airport, will always be firmly and fondly etched in my mind as I travelled to Madrid hoping to catch a game in the mid-1990s. Without any knowledge of Spanish, or even an idea where the stadium was in the city, I jumped in with both feet to the new world of European Budget Airline Football, and since that warm day in May I have been to over 150 different grounds in 25 countries, 4 continents and 10 major tournaments. Today the internet has opened up a whole new world for the travelling fan. Flights, hotels, restaurants and, of course, tickets can all be booked on-line from the comfort of an armchair. However, there are still some places where it is a bit harder to get all the information you need.

This book is designed to help you on your way. I have attempted to cover the most popular destinations, as well as throwing in a few that are my favourites – for instance nobody could ever say Vaduz is one of the hotbeds of European football but it does make for a cracking trip if stunning scenery is on your agenda. All of the information is first-hand, and where I have had to rely on facts from the club these have been triple-checked.

So go on, treat yourself and book a trip today. Don't just pick a Barcelona or a Bayern Munich; delve into the real heart of Europe and have something really different to talk about in the office on Monday morning when people ask what you did at the weekend.

The Facts

Name: Tivoli Neu Stadium
Address: Stadionstrasse 1b,
                 A-6200 Innsbruck,
                 Austria
Capacity: 30,000 All Seater
Opened: 6th September 2000

■ About Tivoli Neu

As part of the plans to host 2008's European Championships, Innsbruck's modest Tivoli Neu stadium is having a major facelift which has taken the capacity up from 17,100 to just over 30,000 in time for the for big kick-off in June 2008. The stadium has been developed along the same lines as Salzburg's by removing the roof and adding a second tier although in this case it is only on three sides. The stadium now also features a number of restaurants, a fitness centre and a conference centre. Quite what the club will do with 30,000 seats after the tournament is finished is unsure as currently FC Wacker only average around 5,500 for their home games.

The new stadium opened with a friendly between the Austrian national team and Ivory Coast in October 2007. In June 2008 the stadium will host the following matches:

Match 7 – Tuesday 10th June – 18.00 – Spain v Russia
Match 15 – Saturday 14th June – 18.00 – Sweden v Spain
Match 24 – Wednesday 18th June – 20.45 – Russia v Sweden

■ Who plays there?

The Tivoli Neu is the current home of FC Wacker Innsbruck. They were only formed in June 2002, rising out of the ashes of the bankrupt FC Tirol Innsbruck. However, due to the legal complexities of the situation, the new club have no history prior to June 2002. The club started in the regional leagues of the Tirol region for the 2002/03 season, but soon moved up into the Red Zac Erste Liga, the second level of Austrian football. At the end of the season the club merged with Wattens who had finished 3rd in the league, and thus were allowed to take their place in the Austrian Bundesliga – a situation that would not be allowed to happen in most other European leagues. In 2004/05 the club finished 6th in the 10-team league. The following season they didn't fare much better, whilst last season they nervously looked over their shoulders for long periods before a decision was made only to relegate one team at the end of the season.

Wacker were bottom for periods of the season until Grazer AK went into administration and were docked 28 points, thus condemning them to relegation with a dozen games left to play. Therefore a 9th place finish wasn't impressive but was enough to ensure another season of top-flight football for the club. The current squad is dominated by Austrians, with a sprinkling of overseas players including Nigerian top scorer Olushola Olumuyiwa

Aganum. Whilst the club have not ever had the opportunity to compete for any major honours, their previous entity FC Tirol Innsbruck won the Austrian Championship for three consecutive years from 2000, although this history has been erased from the records.

■ How to get there

Innsbruck is a small city and so the easiest way to reach the stadium is on foot. It is located next to the ice hockey stadium alongside the A12 Autobahn. It is less than one kilometre from the Hauptbahnhof. If you are walking from here, come out of the station, turn left and follow Sterzinger Strasse southwards until it becomes Sudbahnstrasse. After 200 metres it will join Olympiastrasse. Turn left here and follow this road over the railway and the river. After 300 metres turn right into Stadionstrasse. If you want to use public transport then bus lines B, K and J run to the Tivoli stop from the old town and train station every few minutes. For this summer's tournament when the stadium will host a number of games, special buses will run in the build-up to games, and after the matches at regular intervals arriving and departing from the front of the Ice stadium at the north end of the ground.

■ Getting a ticket

If you are here to watch an Austrian Bundesliga game then you should have no issues turning up on the day to watch a game. FC Wacker Innsbruck do sell tickets in advance via http://www.oeticket.com or by calling +43 512 588877-86. Tickets cost €14 for a place in the Nord or Sud Tribune and €18 for a seat in the Ost or West stands. Views are good from any spot although head for the Nord Tribune to get a great view of the Tirol Mountains on a clear day. Tickets for all matches during Euro2008™ were sold out in the public ballot in March 2007.

■ Nearest airport – Kranebitten Airport (INN)

The only airlines that fly direct into Innsbruck from the UK are **Easyjet** and **British Airways** from London Gatwick. Bus route F connects the airport to the central station every 15 minutes and the journey takes less than 20 minutes. The central station has some excellent fast routes to other destinations such as Munich (1 hour 45 mins), Vienna (2 hours) and Venice (4 hours).

Wörthersee Hypo Arena – Klagenfurt (Austria)

The Facts

Name: Wörthersee Hypo Arena
Address: Siebenhügelstrasse
Klagenfurt
Austria
Capacity: 32,000 All Seater
Opened: 7th September 2007 – Austria v Japan

■ About Wörthersee Hypo Arena Stadion

Out of all of the stadiums constructed for European Championships, the new Wörthersee Stadium is the most eye-catching and innovative. It is built close to the lake of the same name, in one of the most beautiful areas of Austria. The complex will also include multi-sports facilities including track and field arenas, fitness centre, as well as training facilities for all year round sports. It is hoped that the stadium will attract a number of high-profile European clubs for their pre-season training camps, as is the fashion nowadays.

The new stadium has 32,000 seats, all offering fantastic views of the action. It has three stands with two tiers, with unusually the main stand being a lower one-tier stand, although it does have a viewing gallery for VIPs. The roof is translucent, allowing plenty of light to enter into the arena. What is unique about this project is that after the tournament parts of the stadium will be removed and transferred to other stadiums in Austria including Linz

and Graz to increase their capacities. The final capacity of the stadium will be reduced to 12,000, making it the first stadium of its kind to be built in this way. The concourse areas are wide and offer plenty of opportunities to get refreshments without missing the action. Also, unusually for a stadium, all areas of the seating are accessed from this concourse, so that both the upper and lower tiers enter at the same turnstiles. The upper tiers offer a good view of the action, although the rake of the stand is very steep.

During June 2008, the stadium will host the following games:

Match 4 – Sunday 8th June 20.45 – Germany v Poland
Match 11 – Thursday 12th June 18.00 – Croatia v Germany
Match 19 – Monday 16th June 20.45 – Poland v Croatia

■ Who plays there?

As of the start of October 2007 the Wörthersee Stadiun became home to SK Austria Kärnten, a club basically created out of the ashes of FC Superfund who had finished 6th in last season's Bundesliga. As it only can be in European football, the need to have a top-flight team was too much for the local council, who went on a shopping spree that Abramovich would be proud of, and simply bought a club and moved them hundreds of kilometres to Klagenfurt. So, as of September the club, complete with new name, kit and history, will start a new era. The original FC Kärnten (known as FC Kelag Kärnten)

Wörthersee Hypo Arena – Klagenfurt (Austria)

based at the tiny Kurandtplatz stadium are currently playing in the Red Zac 1st League (the second tier of Austrian football) must be rubbing their heads in amazement. Their history has been pretty uneventful since their formation in 1920. They did reach the Austrian Bundesliga in the 1960s, after promotion in 1965. They went on to stay in the top division for five seasons.

They returned again for periods during the 1970s and 1980s before finding some consistency in the early part of this century. After winning the 2nd division in 2001, the club went on to win the Austrian Super Cup in May 2001, thus qualifying for the UEFA Cup for the first time although a 4-0 defeat to PAOK Salonika was not the best debut they could have made. However, the following season they made it through again after a 5th place finish in the Bundesliga. This time they managed a victory, beating the Latvians Metalurgs before a 2nd round defeat to Hapoel Tel Aviv. To cap another excellent season in 2003, they reached the UEFA Cup again, losing to Feyenoord in the 2nd round. In 2004 the team were relegated back to the 2nd division where they have remained since, although their 2006 3rd place finish did give the fans hope of a return to the top division right up until the last few games of the season. If they did manage to get promotion this season then expect them also to move to the new stadium. As part of the ramp-up events for 2008, the stadium hosted the national team for the first time in a four-team tournament featuring Switzerland, Chile and Japan in September 2007.

■ How to get there
The stadium is located 3km from the shore of Lake Wörther, and 2km from the city centre. You can quite easily walk to the stadium simply by following Siebenhügelstrasse out of the town centre. It should take no more than 20 minutes. Alternatively you can catch bus number 90 from platform 4 of the bus station in Heiligengeitsplatz, which runs every 30 minutes and takes 10 minutes. A single ticket costs €1.70. After the game buses line up close to the stadium but make sure you get on the right one or you will end up at the park and ride close to Europark which is nowhere near the town centre.

■ Getting a ticket
Tickets to see games at the Hypo Arena will be easy to pick up. Over the past few seasons FC Kelag Kärnten have only managed to average around 1,500 for their home matches, and so it should not be an issue at all turning up on the day of the game and gaining entry. If you do want to buy tickets in advance, then you can book online at http://www.fckaerten.com. Tickets will range in price from €19 for a seat in the main stand, to €16 in any other part of the stadium. At the Sportzentrum Fischl, the club charged €16 for a seat in the main stand, and €10 for a place on the terraces. Tickets for matches at the European Championships 2008 sold out during the public ballot in March 2007.

■ Nearest airport – Klagenfurt Airport (KLU)
The tiny Klagenfurt airport is located 2 miles from the city centre in the suburb of Annabichl. Buses 42 and 45 run at regular intervals to the station close by where you can complete the journey to the Hauptbahnhof in less than 30 minutes with tickets €2 each way. Currently the airport is served by three airlines offering nine routes, the only one from the UK being **Ryanair** from London Stansted.

The Facts

Name: EM Stadion
Address: Aigner Strasse 12,
5050 Salzburg,
Austria
Capacity: 30,000 All Seater
Opened: 25th July 2007 –
Red Bull Salzburg 1 Arsenal 0

■ About EM Stadion

The EM Stadion is completely unrecognisable from just 18 months ago when it was known as the Wals-Siezenheim and home to SV Austria Salzburg. However, with investment both from the local government and from Red Bull, the stadium is now a much expanded 30,000-seater arena and home to the new Red Bull Salzburg club. In fact it is hard to escape from the Red Bull theme on visiting the stadium for a domestic match, with Red Bull-branded everything – including the name which will revert back to the Bullen Arena after the 2008 tournament.

The new look stadium was completed during the summer of 2007 as one of the venues for the European Championships 2008 and was officially opened with a friendly versus Arsenal in July 2007. The stadium is one of a select few that is using the FIFA-approved artificial Ligaturf. The previous 18,200-seater stadium has had an additional tier added to bring it up to the 30,000

requirements as a tournament host. This was achieved by raising the 1,900-tonne roof by 10 metres and slotting in the extra tier.

Views are excellent from any part of the stadium. Whilst the arena doesn't have the scenic surroundings of the Tivoli stadium in Innsbruck, it is much more pleasant than some of the stadiums we have in this country. The stadium has some really unique features such as concession stands that serve fans both inside and outside the stadium from the same points, two huge screens and one of the loudest sound systems in Austria. It also has a lighting system that wouldn't look out of place at a disco. Inside the stadium the concourses are wide and spacious, allowing fans a view of the action whilst they queue. Access to the upper tiers of the stadium is via the scaffolding towers dotted around the stadium. Like the stadium in Klagenfurt, only three sides have two tiers, with the main West Stand having a row of executive seating instead. Come June 2008 the whole area will have been completely transformed into a true football festival. The stadium will play host to the following matches:

Match 8 – Tues 10th June 2007 – 20.45 – Greece v Sweden
Match 16 – Sat 16th June 2007 – 20.45 – Greece v Russia
Match 23 – Wed 18th June 2007 – 20.45 – Greece v Spain

■ Who plays there?

Until the end of March 2005 the Wals-Siezenheim stadium was home to SV Casino Salzburg, the three-times champions of the Austrian Bundesliga. However, in the sweep of a pen on a contract, over 70 years' worth of history were erased when Red Bull bought the club on 6th April 2005. Along with the name change, the club were 'forced' to adopt a new strip and a new management team. The sale of the soul of the club was too much for many of the fans who formed their own club, buying back the original name SV Austria Salzburg and joining the regional leagues of the Salzburg region. In their first season playing in the traditional violet and white strip of the former club they finished top of the league and thus started their long climb back up to the top in a similar fashion to AFC Wimbledon.

SV Casino Salzburg were originally formed under the name Austria Salzburg in September 1933, although they had a pretty undistinguished history until they changed their name to Casino in 1978. Under the new name the team won the Bundesliga in 1994, 1995 and 1997. In 1994 the club also reached the UEFA Cup Final, losing 2–0 to Inter Milan on aggregate. In 1994/95 they reached the group stages of the Champions League, finishing third in a group containing Ajax, AC Milan and AEK Athens. They almost appeared in the group stages again in 1997 when they lost to Sparta Prague in the final qualifying rounds. The take-over certainly alienated most of the fan base as Red Bull published the slogan 'Salzburg – the club with no history'. They appointed Giovanni Trapattoni and Lothar Matthäus as the management team in May 2006 and in their first season the team won the league with five games to spare. With funds available to invest in the team few would bet against them retaining this title in 2007/2008.

How to get there

The stadium is located almost at the end of the runway of the airport, and is less than a kilometre from the terminal building alongside the A1 West Autobahn and opposite the Casino. It is around 3km from the city centre. Bus lines 1, 10 and 18 run from the central bus and railway station to the stadium stop in Stadionstrasse on the east side of the ground. Journey time is less than 25 minutes. Close to the stadium is the Europark commercial centre, which includes an Ikea and a massive shopping centre.

Getting a ticket

Tickets can be purchased from the Bulls shop at the stadium from 9am to 6pm Monday to Friday or until 2pm on a non-match day Saturday. You can also call +43 662 43 33 32 and arrange to collect and pay for your tickets on a match day. The website http://www.redbulls.com has an online ticketing function which you need to register for to use. The stadium before redevelopment was almost full on most occasions, although the new stands mean that tickets should be available for most games. Ticket prices range from €14 in the terraced area behind the goal to €21 in the east or west stand. All seats offer excellent views of the action on the pitch. Tickets for matches of the 2008 European Championships were sold out after the public ballot in March 2007.

Nearest airport – Salzburg Mozart Airport (SZG)

The airport is located close to the German border, and 2 miles from the city centre. To reach the city catch the number 2 bus that runs every 10 minutes from outside Arrivals, which takes 20 minutes and costs €1.80. Currently the following airlines serve Salzburg on a daily basis from the UK. **British Airways** from London Gatwick, **Flybe** from Exeter and Southampton, **Ryanair** from Liverpool, London Stansted and Nottingham East Midlands, and **ThomsonFly** from London Gatwick, Bournemouth, Coventry and Doncaster airport.

The Facts

Name: Ernst Happel Stadion
Address: Meiereistrasse 7,
1020 Vienna,
Austria
Capacity: 49,844 All Seater
Opened: 1931

■ About Ernst Happel Stadion

The UEFA 5-star stadium in central Vienna is currently going through some modifications in time for the start of the 2008 European Football Championships which will see the stadium host Austria's group matches, as well as three knock-out stage games and the Final. The stadium is certainly a favourite with UEFA – it is actually the only sub-50,000 capacity stadium to have a 5-star status and has been used on four occasions as the venue for European Champions League Finals, the last time being in 1995 when Ajax beat AC Milan.

The stadium has been on its present site since 1931 when it was constructed for the Workers Olympiad. It originally had a capacity of over 70,000 and was actually expanded soon after the war to a massive 90,000. The record attendance of 92,000 came during this period in a match versus Spain. The capacity has been slowly reduced since, both for practical reasons (nobody likes playing in front of a half-empty stadium) as well as for safety

reasons, to the current 49,844. By the time the tournament kicks off next summer it will hold just over 53,000.

The stadium is an elliptical shape, with an athletics track separating the fans from the pitch. The seats do not run down to pitch level at the moment – meaning that views are good from all places, although part of the work currently being carried out will involve constructing seating in this area. The roof was added in 1986 and is very similar in design to the AWD Arena in Hannover, or the Gottlieb Daimler Stadion in Stuttgart – appearing to float above the stands.

In June 2008 the stadium will host the following matches in the European Championships:

Match 3 – Sunday 8th June – 18.00 – Austria v Croatia
Match 12 – Thursday 12th June – 20.45 – Austria v Poland
Match 20 – Monday 16th June – 20.45 – Austria v Germany
Match 26 – Friday 20th June – 20.45 – Quarter-final 2
Match 28 – Sunday 22nd June – 20.45 – Quarter-final 4
Match 30 – Thursday 26th June – 20.45 – Semi-final 2
Match 31 – Sunday 29th June – 20.45 – Final

■ Who plays there?

The stadium is used primarily by the national team as their first-choice venue, although in recent years it has also been used by FK Austria and Rapid for their Champions

League matches. Derby matches between FK Austria and Rapid have also been played here over the past few seasons. The main focus is obviously on the 2008 European Championships where the stadium will host seven games in the tournament – more than any other.

■ How to get there
The stadium is located on a large island which separates the River Danube and the Danube canal from the old town of Vienna. It is also an integral part of the Prater Park, and the iconic Ferris wheel can be seen from a number of the seats. The city is currently building a new U-Bahn station close to the stadium on line U2. In the meantime fans should use the U-Bahn station Wien Praterstern on U1

which is only six stops from Südbahnhof. Bus line 80a also runs to the stadium from the old town.

■ Getting a ticket
Tickets for all of the games of the 2008 European Championships sold out after the initial ticket sale by UEFA in March 2007. Tickets will undoubtedly be available on the black market in June 2008, but as the stadium is hosting the home nation, expect them to be expensive. For the national team games in the run-up to the finals, tickets are more readily available via the official site http://www.oefb.at. If you want tickets to see any club games then these will be sold via the official club websites.

The Facts

Name:	Gerhard Hanappi Stadion
Address:	Keisslergasse 6,
	1140 Vienna,
	Austria
Capacity:	18,456 All Seater
Opened:	3rd September 1977

■ About Gerhard Hanappi Stadion

The Gerhard Hanappi Stadion is the second largest stadium in Vienna, and is located in the western part of the historic city centre. Certainly for many visitors who are interested in a number of the more famous sites, the stadium is ideally located close to the Hagenpark (Zoo) and the impressive Schloss Schöbrunn complex.

The stadium is very similar in design to the Stade Gerland in Lyon – even down to the curved roof design. It has four separate stands, the side ones being two-tiered, whilst the ones behind the goals are simple single-tiered with 20 or so rows. Views are very good from all seats, although if you are in the Sud Tribune be prepared for the fact that the seats are very uncomfortable metal ones. The stadium is one of the most atmospheric on matchdays in Austria despite its design. Further development work was put on hold after a decision in 2003 was made not to use the venue for any of the matches in June 2008. The stadium is named after the former Austrian and Rapid

Vienna player of the same name.

■ Who plays there?

The stadium has been home to Sporklub Rapid Wien (more popularly known as SK Rapid Wien) since 1977, although the club first came into existence in 1898 as the Erster Wiener Arbeiter Fussball Club (First Worker's Football Club of Vienna), although they renamed as Rapid less than a year later. The club also have the distinct honour of having actually won league titles in two countries – they won the 1941 German Championship when they beat Schalke 04. The club went on to be the most successful Austrian club side with 31 league titles, and 14 Austrian cups to date. The last of these honours was in 2005 when they broke a ten-year barren spell by winning the league.

The club have also had more success in Europe than any other Austrian team, finishing runners-up in the European Cup Winners' Cup twice – first in 1985 to Everton in Rotterdam, and then again ten years later to Paris Saint Germain. In terms of appearances in the Champions League the club have had moderate success. In 1996 they finished bottom in a group containing Juventus, Manchester United and Fenerbahçe, picking up two points, and in 2005 they lost all six group games when placed with Juventus again, Club Brugge and Bayern Munich.

2006/2007 was always going to be a hard season for the club, trying to compete with the cash-rich Red Bull Salzburg. With a couple of games left in the season there was still a chance of a 2nd place finish. However, the club failed to win a game at relegation-threatened Altach which in the end cost them a place in Europe.

■ How to get there

The stadium is located in the western part of the city centre and is almost opposite Hütteldorf S-Bahn and U-Bahn stations. From the city centre you will need to get a U-Bahn to Westbahnhof before changing onto S-Bahn line 45. If you are coming from the old town then U-Bahn Line 4 terminates at Hütteldorf, although it is not the most direct route. Allow yourself 25 minutes if coming on U4. If you are arriving in town at the SudBahnhof then catch U1 north two stops where it intersects with U4 and then head westwards. A one-day travel pass for all public transport in Vienna costs €6.20 and can be purchased from the red machines at any station.

■ Getting a ticket

Attendances for Austrian football are not great, and if it wasn't for the recent Red Bull-fuelled marketing activity in Salzburg, Rapid would have the honour of the best-supported team in the league. Attendances still average over 13,000 (last season it was as high as 14,572) which is quite impressive considering the modest capacity of the ground. Tickets are therefore quite easy to pick up on the day of the game from the windows along Keisslergasse. Alternatively you are able to buy tickets online from the club's website at http://www.skrapid.at or by phone on +43 1 544 5440. Tickets for the most expensive seats in the Süd Tribune start from €22. For a more neutral view, you can get a seat in the upper tier of the Nord Tribune for €18.

■ Nearest airport – Vienna International (VIE)

Vienna airport is served from London Heathrow by **Austrian Airways** and **British Airways**. The easiest way to reach the city centre from the airport is via train from the airport to WienMitte. Trains run every 30 minutes and costs €3 each way. There is also a fast train running from Mitte, although tickets are more expensive. A taxi should take around 15 minutes and cost less than €20.

An alternative airport is located in Bratislava in neighbouring Slovakia some 45 miles away. Both **Sky Europe** and **Ryanair** fly from London Stansted here on a daily basis. A bus run by Terrorvision meets all inbound flights and transfers customers into Vienna in around 45 minutes.

Jan Breydel Stadium – Bruges (Belgium)

The Facts

Name: Jan Breydel Stadium
Address: Olympialaan 74,
8200 Brugge,
Belgium
Capacity: 29,042 All Seater
Opened: 1975

■ About Jan Breydel Stadium

The Jan Breydel Stadium is named after one of the region's most famous martyrs – and a hero of the Battle of the Golden Spurs. It was opened in 1975 as the Olympic Stadium, despite the fact that the city has never hosted the Olympics. The stadium was redeveloped in the late 1990s after the stadium was chosen for one of the Euro 2000 venues. The stadium hosted a number of key games in the tournament, including the dramatic group decider between Yugoslavia and Spain, France versus Denmark and the quarter-final between Spain and France.
The stadium today consists of four separate stands that have a small lower tier/paddock, and fences around the pitch. The view from the upper tiers is quite good, and is certainly favourable for the neutral fans.

■ Who plays there?

The stadium is home to the two professional clubs in the city – Club Brugge and Cercle Brugge. Whilst the former are certainly the more successful of the two teams, Cercle actually won the Belgian First Division before their rivals in 1911. Cercle have certainly had a more turbulent recent history, bouncing between the top two divisions in the last decade before returning to the Jupiter League in 2003. However, their achievements have been modest to say the least. Since winning their first Belgian title in 1911, they have won just two titles, in 1927, when they actually won the domestic double, and 1930. They also won the 1985 Belgian cup final, which gave them their one and only chance to play in European competition. In the subsequent European Cup Winners' Cup campaign the team went out in the first round, losing on away goals to Dynamo

Dresden. The club have never been known for attracting the best players in Belgium, although they did have the services of Danish legend Morten Olsen for a number of seasons in the 1970s.
Club Brugge on the other hand are second only to Anderlecht in terms of domestic success in Belgium. They have won the Jupiter League on 13 occasions, although they only recorded one victory before 1973. The club were originally formed in 1891 and played for many years in the amateur leagues, before turning professional at the start of the 20th century. They won their first title in 1920, but had to wait nearly fifty years for a second honour. In the 1970s, under the leadership of Ernst Happel the club won four successive league titles, one Belgian cup and made appearances in the UEFA Cup Final of 1976, and the European Cup Final of 1978, losing to Liverpool on both occasions.
The club continued to enjoy success in the late 1980s and 1990s, providing competition to Anderlecht and their quest to be the best team in Belgium. They won the title in 2003 and 2005 but have had to play second fiddle in the past two years to the likes of Genk, Anderlecht and Gent. They did enjoy some success in the Belgian cup in 2007 when they beat Standard Liege to take the trophy.
Their European pedigree is second to none in Belgium football, although since the change of format to the Champions League they have struggled to break out of the group stages, finishing 3rd in a weak group in 2003/04, and 3rd again in 2005/06 behind Juventus and Bayern Munich.

■ How to get there

The stadium is located to the west of the small city centre, close to the E403 motorway. It is walkable from the city centre – simply follow Gistelse Steenweg westbound out of the city gates. To get to the relevant gate from the Markt, follow Sint-Jakobsstraat northwards, and then turn left into Noordzandstraat. Allow yourself 25 minutes to walk from the city centre. If you want to use public transport then catch bus line 5 or 15 which runs from the railway station to the road to the north of the stadium.

Jan Breydel Stadium – Bruges (Belgium)

■ **Getting a ticket**

If you are in town and want to watch a game you'd certainly have more luck in getting a ticket for a Cercle match where the average attendance is just under 6,000. Last season Club Brugge were the best-supported club in Belgium, pipping Anderlecht and Standard Liege with an average attendance of 25,329. Tickets for both clubs start from €13 for a place in the Nord or Sud paddock areas behind the goals, to €30 for a seat in the main stand upper tier. Tickets can be purchased via email at kaartenverkoop@clubbrugge.be or by phone at +32 50 40 21 35 for Club Brugge, and +32 50 34 32 45 for Cercle Brugge.

■ **Nearest airport – Brussels Zaventeem (BRU)**

Bruges does not have its own airport, although a few years ago Ostend airport some 10 miles away had daily flights from London Stansted with **Ryanair**. Therefore, the easiest way to reach the city is to fly into Brussels Zaventeem airport, which is located around an hour away. The airport is located north west of the capital city and Brugge is a simple train ride away – with a change required at Brussels Nord. Total journey time is 90 minutes. Brussels Nord is also accessible by the frequent Eurostar services from London St Pancras International.

The Facts

Name: Constant Vanden Stock Stadium
Address: Theo Verneecklaan 2,
1070 Brussels,
Belgium
Capacity: 28,000 (21,100 Seats)
Opened: 1918

■ About Constant Vanden Stock Stadium

The current stadium of Belgium's most famous club side could soon be no more. Anderlecht's home since 1917 is tentatively being scheduled for demolition, and a new 40,000-seater stadium built in its place will be named after the major club sponsor Fortis. However, there will be significant local opposition to the move, especially from the fans who have grown to love the closeness of the stands to the pitch, and the enclosed atmosphere created by the low roof. The stadium initially started out as a single wooden stand, built in the Astrid Park area of the city. It was originally named after the club's first real investor, Émile Versé, and it was his money that allowed the stadium to be slowly built over the next few decades.

As the club became more of a force in European football during the 1970s, a complete redevelopment of the stadium began, funded by Club President Constant Vanden Stock. The new stadium opened in 1983, and has remained the same, apart from a few alterations, until the present day. The club were bitterly disappointed in the late 1990s not to be part of the Euro 2000 championships as the organising committee felt it would be unfair to have two stadiums in Brussels being used (the Koning Boudewijn Stadion being the chosen one).

The stadium is very similar in design to a number of British stadiums, with four stands that wrap around to form a complete arena. Each stand has two tiers, separated by a row of executive boxes. Behind each goal there are standing places in the lower tiers, which are closed for European matches. The stadium has been transformed into a multi-purpose venue with the opening of the Le Saint-Guidon restaurant, which is a Michelin Guide one-star restaurant.

■ Who plays there?

Royal Sporting Club Anderlecht (RSC) are the most successful club that Belgium has produced. They have won 29 championships, including the 2006/2007 Jupiter League title, and five European trophies. However, it took a number of years before the club actually won a trophy – their first major honour was the First Division title in 1947, some forty years after they were originally formed. Their real purple period came in the 1970s when the club, inspired by such players as Francky Van Der Elst, Robbie

Constant Vanden Stock Stadium – Brussels (Belgium)

Rensenbrink and Franky Vercauteren became one of the most feared in Europe. The club reached three successive European Cup Winners' Cup Finals from 1976 to 1978, winning twice versus West Ham United and Austria Vienna, sandwiched between a 2–0 defeat to Hamburg in Amsterdam. They also won the 1983 UEFA Cup Final by beating Benfica 2–1, although the following season they lost on penalties in the final to Tottenham Hotspur.

In terms of domestic success, the club were the most dominant team in the Belgium league after the end of the Second World War when they won seven titles in ten years. Despite their dominance in Europe during the 1970s, they only actually won two domestic titles, although they were a permanent fixture in the Belgian cup final – winning it on five occasions. The second rebirth of the club came under the leadership of Raymond Goethals when the team won the Jupiter League four times in six seasons in the early 1990s. Unfortunately the consistency couldn't be maintained, and the latter part of the 1990s were bleak for the club as Standard Liege and Club Brugge took the honours. In the last few seasons the title has arrived on four more occasions, but due to the limitations of the finances in the Belgium leagues, as soon as a promising team is assembled, the bigger European clubs come and snap up the young Belgian talent.

In 2006/2007, a promising squad was put together by former club legend Franky Vercauteren. Despite a stiff challenge from Genk up until the last few weeks of the season, the title returned to Brussels thanks to a team of real united nations – including a Swede, an Egyptian, a Hungarian and a few Argentinians, as well as some home-grown talent such as captain Bart Goor.

Since their success in the UEFA Cup in the 1980s, European football hasn't been too kind to the club. In the Champions League in 2000, they won the group stage pool, beating Manchester United and Dynamo Kiev. Last season they qualified again into the group stages and found themselves in the weakest group in the competition, alongside AC Milan, Lille and AEK Athens. Unfortunately four draws from their six games consigned them to last place in the group. Therefore, it is with some trepidation that the club will approach the 2007 competition.

■ How to get there
From the city centre the easiest way to reach the stadium is by Metro in the direction of Erasmus on Line 1b, alighting at Saint-Guidon. From Gare Centrale it is 9 stops to the stadium – taking around 15 minutes. If you are arriving by Eurostar, then you need to catch a train northwards four stops to De Brouckère where you can pick up the Line 1b. A taxi from the Grand Place will cost around €15.

■ Getting a ticket
Traditionally, Anderlecht have been one of the best-supported teams in Belgium, fighting it out with Club Brugge for the title of the highest average attendance. In the past few seasons they have averaged just over 24,000, although for the games against Royal Antwerp and Club Brugge you can expect an almost full house. The club allow English-based supporters to reserve tickets in advance by emailing them at ticketing@rsca.be or by calling the ticket office on +32 2 529 40 67. A good seat for the neutral is in the upper tiers of the Tribune 2 and 4, behind the goals where you get a good view of the action both on and off the pitch. In 2006/2007 a seat here costs €18. A seat in the main stand costs €30.

Koning Boudewijn Stadion – Brussels (Belgium)

The Facts

Name: Koning Boudewijn Stadion
Address: Marathonlaan 135,
1020 Brussels,
Belgium
Capacity: 50,100 All Seater
Opened: 23rd August 1930 – Belgium 4 Holland 1

■ About Koning Boudewijn Stadion

The Koning Boudewijn stadium may sound a mouthful, but the decision to change its name from its traditional Heysel was a necessity after the stadium disaster here on the 29th May 1985. On that fateful night the stadium was playing host to its seventh European final, on this occasion between Liverpool and Juventus. Prior to the match a disturbance in the crowd between the two sets of fans led to a wall collapsing, trapping and killing 39 people in the ensuring chaos. Despite protestations, the game was played with Juventus winning 1–0. Since then the stadium has been rebuilt and renamed, but still has not been sanctioned to hold major club finals since the 1996 Cup Winners' Cup Final.

The stadium was originally named the Stade du Jubilé, and opened on the 23rd August 1930 to commemorate the 100-year anniversary of the country. After the Second World War it took on the name Heysel, named after the area of the 1935 World's Fair where the stadium was located. It became a real favourite of UEFA for hosting major competitions, and held the European Cup Finals in 1958 as Real Madrid beat AC Milan, 1966 when Real Madrid again captured the title beating Partizan Belgrade and again in 1974 when Bayern Munich beat Atletico de Madrid in a replay. It also hosted the European Cup

Winners' Cup Final in 1964, as well as its most famous night in 1976 when home-town club Anderlecht beat West Ham United 4–2. Four years later Arsenal lost here on penalties to Valencia. Once the stadium was renamed it also hosted the 1996 final between Rapid Vienna and Paris St Germain.

The stadium today has been completely rebuilt from the dark days of 1985. The athletics track is still in existence, but each of the stands has been rebuilt. On three sides they merge together into an oval, with a large lower tier, and a small upper tier almost hanging down from the roof. On the final side a single two-tier stand sits on its own. Views are okay, although the presence of the athletics track does hinder the view from the lower tiers. The stadium was one of the host venues for Euro 2000 and staged games in the group stages (the most memorable being Turkey's defeat of Belgium that eliminated them), as well as the semi-final between Portugal and France.

■ Who plays there?

The stadium was traditionally the home of the national team, although between 1985 and 1995 when the stadium was closed for redevelopment they played mainly at Anderlecht's Constant Vanden Stock Stadium. However, on reopening the team returned and played here until a disagreement arose in 2006 due to perceived safety issues. The games were again switched to the home of Anderlecht across the city, as well as the 2006 Belgian cup final. In November 2006 an agreement was again reached, and normal service returned to the stadium, with the first match being played here being the 3–0 win against Azerbaijan. The 2007 cup final was also played here as Club Brugge beat Liege 1–0.

Koning Boudewijn Stadion – Brussels (Belgium)

■ How to get there

The stadium is located in the north west of the city centre, close to the Atomium and Europark area. The easiest way to reach it by public transport is to catch the metro Line 1A in the direction of Heysel. You can then alight either at Roi Baudoin or Heysel for the stadium. Journey time is around 15 minutes from the Grand Place area of the city.

■ Getting a ticket

Tickets for the national team are sold via the Belgium FA website at http://www.footbel.be. For most internationals, tickets can be booked in advanced and picked up on the day of the game. The best tickets for the neutrals are in the Lower Tribune 3 – which runs down the side of the pitch, and avoids the sunshine that sets in the early evening games. Ticket prices vary according to the opposition. For Belgian Cup Final tickets, contact the participating clubs direct for availability. The Stadium also offers guided tours plus a visit to the museum from €6 for adults on Wednesdays to Saturdays from 10.30am. For more information call +32 2 474 39 40.

■ Nearest airport – Brussels Zaventeem (BRU)

The easiest way to reach Brussels from London and the south east is via Eurostar from London St Pancras International, where trains run every two hours and take 2¹/₂ hours to reach Brussels Midi station. If you want to fly then Brussels Zaventeem airport is served on a daily basis by **BMI** from East Midlands and London Heathrow, **British Airways** from London Heathrow, **Brussels Airlines** from London Gatwick, Manchester and Newcastle, **Eastern Airways** from Cardiff, Durham Valley and Southampton, **Flybe** from Manchester and **VLM Airlines** from London City. A regular train runs from the airport to both Brussels Nord and Midi.

Vasil Levski National Stadium – Sofia (Bulgaria)

The Facts

Name: Vasil Levski National Stadium
Address: Boulevard Evlogi Georgiev 38,
Sofia,
Bulgaria
Capacity: 43,632 All Seater
Opened: 1953

■ About Vasil Levski National Stadium

The Vasil Levski is Bulgaria's biggest stadium, and unsurprisingly classed as the National Stadium. The stadium is named after the Bulgarian national hero who led the struggle against the rule of the Ottoman Empire in the middle of the 19th century.

The stadium was originally opened in 1953, having been constructed on the site of the original stadium used by Levski Sofia. It was originally built with a capacity of 70,000, with fans standing on the terraces of a huge bowl arena. Today the terraces have been converted to smart blue seats, although apart from a small roof over the more expensive seats in the main stand, it still remains roofless which is fine for those warm balmy April evenings, but not so for the cold and wet games in January. Sightlines are quite good though and if you get a chance a visit to the stadium to watch the big Sofia derby between CSKA and Levski it is a memorable experience. Further modifications were made in 2002, giving it UEFA 4-star status, and so become eligible to hold UEFA Cup Finals. Whilst the stadium is used by the national team for their games, Levski play their derby matches versus CSKA and Champions League matches here. Other than these, they play their domestic games at the Georgi Asparoukhov stadium located around 2km east of the Vasil Levski which is basically a bowl with one large stand. This stadium can hold around 30,000 fans. A few hundred yards south of the Vasil Levski is the Stadion Balgarska Armia which is home to CSKA Sofia.

■ Who plays there?

Whilst the Vasil Levski is officially the home of the national side, and the Bulgarian cup final, in recent seasons the success of Levski Sofia has prompted the stadium to be used for Champions League matches. Last season the stadium played host to home matches against Chelsea, Werder Bremen and Barcelona – quite a formidable trio, which unsurprisingly led to three defeats. After winning the championship again in 2007, the club will be hoping for a favourable draw in the qualifying rounds to again compete in the group stages.

Levski's recent success has made them the most successful team in Bulgarian football, overtaking bitter rivals CSKA. They have now won 25 championships and 26 Bulgarian cups including the domestic double on 13 occasions (including 2007). Since 2000 the team have won the championship on five occasions. However, they actually made a slow start to their footballing life. After being formed in 1911 by a group of students, the club had to wait ten years until the formation of the Sofia Sports League before they could compete on a semi-professional stage. The first National Championships took place in 1924 and the club were chosen to represent Sofia. It would be nearly ten years before they won the National Championship though, repeating the feat on five occasions in the 1940s.

In 1949 the club's name was changed to Dynamo on the orders of Stalin who wanted to see all of the top teams in the Soviet empire called Dynamo (hence Dynamo Kiev, Dynamo Moscow, Dynamo Berlin and Dynamo

Vasil Levski National Stadium – Sofia (Bulgaria)

Dresden amongst others). However, once the rule of Stalinist Russia was lifted in 1957 the club readopted their Levski name. The following decade was marked with inconsistency on the pitch as the club invested in its youth policy. These young players started making their mark in the late 1960s as Levski picked up championships in 1965, 1968 and 1970. This conveyor belt of talent continued to come through the youth academy at the club during the late 1970s and 1980s as the team won five more titles up until 1985. In that season, Levski met CSKA in the Bulgarian cup final. In a game marred by crowd trouble, and fighting on the pitch which saw players sent off and clashes with the referee, both Levski and CSKA were forced to change their names (to Vitosha and Sredets respectively) and a number of players from either side were banned for life. The 1985 title was also taken away from the club. These sanctions were overturned within a few months but it wasn't until 1989 that Levski were able to regain their name.

Europe has still proved a bridge too far for the club. They have reached the European Cup Winners' Cup quarter-finals on three occasions, and a similar stage in the UEFA Cup twice. Last season under the leadership of Stanimir Stoilov, the domestic double was delivered with considerable ease. Fans hope that this season they can repeat the feat as well as progress in the Champions League.

■ How to get there

The Vasil Levski Stadium is located close to the Borisova Gardens in the south east corner of the city. It is a pleasant 15-minute walk from the city centre down Graf Ignatiev, although if you want to use public transport trams 2, 12, 14 or 19 run to the stadium. The stadium sits around 100 metres from CSKA's Stadion Balgarska Armia. If you are heading to Levski's Asparoukhov stadion then use buses 78 or 120 which terminate at the Istok bus station adjacent to the stadium.

■ Getting a ticket

As Levski move their derby matches with CSKA and their Champions League matches to the national stadium, getting a ticket for any game has never been a problem. Their home games attract crowds of just over 6,000 on average. If Levski are playing at the Asparoukhov then a ticket in the main stand (Sektor A) will cost 10 lev. At the national stadium expect to pay double that for a seat in the main stand. Tickets can be purchased from the club in advance – at the moment there is no facility to purchase tickets in advance from the website – although on occasions they will reserve you one by emailing them at adv@levski.bg.

■ Nearest airport – Letishte Sofia Airport (SOF)

Sofia Airport is a hub for Bulgaria Air and Hemus Air. The airport's second terminal was officially opened on 27th December 2006. A new city bus line 284 serves the route from Sofia University to Terminal 2, while bus line 84 continues to run to Terminal 1. A single ticket costs 70 stontiki (around 25p). The airport is served by **Bulgarian Air** from London Gatwick, Heathrow and Manchester, **British Airways** from London Heathrow, as well as **Hermus Air**, and low-cost option **Wizzair** from London Luton.

Maksimir Stadium – Zagreb (Croatia)

The Facts

Name: Maksimir Stadium
Address: Maksimirska 128,
100000 Zagreb,
Croatia
Capacity: 38,923 All Seater
Opened: 5th May 1912

■ About Maksimir Stadium

The Maksimir is classed as the national stadium despite not being the newest stadium in the country. That honour sits with Hajduk Split, and their redeveloped Poljud stadium. However, the Maksimir is one of the most atmospheric. Dinamo have played at the stadium since their inception in 1945. The first real redevelopment didn't take place until the mid-1980s when the stadium was chosen to host the World Student Games of 1987.

The stadium today is an odd affair. All four stands are uncovered, with two large two-tier stands, one smaller single-tier stand and finally the original curved bank behind the goal. The stadium suffers by having a running track, meaning that some fans behind the goal are quite a way from the action. The home fans – the Bad Blue Boys – are located in the north stand. There are plans to completely redevelop the stadium, with the inclusion of a new south stand, corner infilling, as well as one of the largest retractable roofs installed anywhere in the world. There are no definite time-scales for this work, and it is expected that Dinamo will continue to play at the Maksimir whilst the work is carried out.

■ Who plays there?

The number one team in the Croatian capital continues to be Dinamo. Formerly known as Croatia Zagreb after independence in 1991, the fans petitioned and protested until 2000 when they were renamed Dinamo and pride was once again restored. The club was formed in 1945 after the merger of a number of teams in Zagreb. They won their first Yugoslavian championship in 1948 and went on to win two further championships in the next ten years as well as the Yugoslavian cup in 1951. All of this was quite remarkable considering that they were competing against Partizan Belgrade, the Yugoslav army team, who could buy and sell the country's best players at will.

The club added Yugoslavian cups on a regular basis in the 1960s, and thus qualified for the European Cup Winners' Cup from inception. In that first tournament in 1960/61 they reached the semi-finals before losing 4–2 to Fiorentina. In 1963/64 they fell at the first hurdle to Celtic, and a year later they went out to Torino in the quarter-finals. Their greatest European moment though came in 1967 when they won the Fairs Cup, beating Leeds United in the final. The team went through a barren run in the 1970s, apart from a couple of UEFA Cup campaigns of insignificance. However, they bounced back in the 1980s with two Yugoslavian cup final wins in 1980 and 1983, sandwiching their fourth league title in 1982. After Croatia gained its independence from Yugoslavia, Dinamo's first title came in 1993. Hajduk took the title in 1994 and 1995 before Otto Baric took over the reigns. With the inspirational coach in charge, Croatia Zagreb won the double in 1996 and 1997. In 1998 Zlatko Kranjcar, the current national-team coach, took over the team and repeated the feat, capturing the double in 1998. The following season the club at last made an impact in the Champions League. After beating Celtic in the qualifying rounds, the team finished second in their group, but did not get one of the two best runners-up spots that would have taken them into the semi-finals.

The following season, with Zajec taking over from Kranjcar and the team containing want-away players such as Mark Viduka, Dario Simic and Maric, they took the title again. Zajec's reign lasted but a few months and he was replaced by Ossie Ardiles in a hope of bringing some glory in Europe. In his first campaign in 1999, the team made the group stages again but finished the winnable group featuring Manchester United, Marseille and Sturm Graz in bottom place, despite starting the campaign with a 0–0 draw at Old Trafford. The disappointing campaign signalled the end of Ardiles's reign and despite the team retaining its title in 2000, its first back under the Dinamo name. Two further Croatian cup finals were won in 2001 and 2002 but this is where the titles ended.

■ How to get there
The stadium is situated to the east of the city centre in the recreation area of the Maksimir Park. The easiest way to reach the ground is to jump on tram line 4 from the central station, alighting at Bukovacka, seven stops and 15 minutes away. If you are coming from the bus station then catch tram line 7. The stadium's main stand is just beside the tram stop.

■ Getting a ticket
With the ground three-quarters of the way to full redevelopment, the stadium is rarely full. Only the big European matches and the Croatian derby between Dinamo and Hajduk raise the average attendance above the 10,000 mark. Tickets can therefore be purchased on the day of the game from the booths to the right of the stadium as you approach it from the tram stop. Traditionally, the hardcore Bad Blue Boys take up residence in the north stand, so it may be worth avoiding this stand if you want to watch the football, and not your back.

■ Nearest airport – Zagreb Plaso Airport (ZAG)
Zagreb Pleso Airport is located 17km south from the city centre. Shuttle buses run to the city centre every 30 minutes. The journey takes less than 30 minutes and costs 25HRK one way. A taxi from the airport should cost less than 150HRK – make sure you negotiate the rate before you start the journey. Currently the only direct flights are offered by **Wizzair** from London Luton, although Zagreb is only an hour or so away from Llubljana in Slovenia which is served by the **Easyjet** on a daily basis.

AXA Arena – Prague (Czech Republic)

The Facts

Name: AXA Arena
Address: Milady Horákové 98,
170 82 Prague 7,
Czech Republic
Capacity: 18,800 All Seater
Opened: 1933

■ About AXA Arena

Formerly the Letna Stadium, the AXA Arena is a perfect example of the Czech attitude to football. Functional but with little thought of ambition. It is amazing to think that the modest AXA Arena is also the home to the Czech Republic team, as this is the biggest football stadium in the country – a country that is currently ranked by FIFA in the top ten in the world! The stadium is a complete box-style stadium, made up of two tiers of seating. The pitch has perimeter fencing and a small moat around to deter pitch invaders. One of the strange aspects of it is that on the main stand (west) upper tier, the concourse runs along the front of the seats, meaning that if you are unlucky enough to be sitting in the first few rows, your view will be constantly obstructed by people walking to and from refreshment stands and toilets.

The ground is located at the top of a hill to the north of the city centre, and opposite the entrance to the huge Letna Park. Next to the stadium is a big McDonald's, which is split on two levels. The lower floor is open to the public from the outside of the stadium, whilst the upper floor doubles up as a concession stand for ticket holders on a match day, linked to the stadium concourse by a walkway. There is very little else around the stadium apart from a couple of car dealerships, so it's best to stick to the city centre for your pre-match enjoyment before heading up to the stadium. Whilst the modern version of the Letna is comfortable enough, you do get the feeling that the stadium has been built for the corporate bucks.

■ Who plays there?

Sparta are one of the perennial clubs that always seem to make the Champions League group stages, before putting up a plucky fight and finishing bottom of their group. The last seasons have been no exception. Drawn in a group with Arsenal, Ajax and FC Thun in 2005, Sparta managed to throw away an opportunity of at least a UEFA Cup spot by drawing their final home match with the Swiss unknown team. Last season the best they could offer was a place in the UEFA Cup. It is also amazing to think that 90% of the best Czech players playing in Europe today have at some point in the past pulled on the famous maroon shirt of Sparta. Players such as Pavel Nedved, Tomas Repka, Petr Cech, Karel Poborsky, Tomas Rosicky and Vladimir Smicer have all won honours with Sparta before going on to ply their trade in the bigger European leagues.

The club was originally formed in 1893 as the Athletic Club Kralovske Vinohrady, although they soon adopted the name Sparta. They adopted the dark-red colours after the then club president travelled to London and saw Arsenal play in the coloured kit they wore during their first season at Highbury. The club took their place in the first Czechoslovakian league in the 1922 and won the inaugural title as well as six more before the outbreak of the Second World War. When football returned to Central Europe in earnest in the early 1950s, Sparta again became one of the power houses. They took the title again in 1952, 1954, 1965 and 1967 along with a few Czech cup wins in that period. As the Cold War was at its peak during the 1970s and 1980s, the club's fortunes suffered dramatically, and they even experienced their only relegation in 1975. However, success soon returned to the Letna stadium when the club captured their first title in 17 years in 1984. From that point onwards they were virtually unbeatable domestically, capturing the Czech league title every year from 1984 to 1993, with just one exception.

Unfortunately Europe provided a bridge too far. They had their most successful campaign in 1992/93 when they finished 2nd in the final qualifying group. This was the last season that the format was like this and the following season this position would have seen them compete in the semi-finals. Repka has returned to his spiritual home with his cult status from his five years at West Ham intact and under the leadership of Michal Bilek they stole the title from their city rivals on the last game of the season, before winning the Czech cup to complete their first-ever domestic double.

■ How to get there
The stadium sits to the north of the river, high above the city centre. By far the easiest way to reach the stadium is to get the Green Metro line A in the direction of Dejuiká to Hradcany. From there you can either get any eastbound tram or walk 5 minutes or so down Milady Horakove for the stadium. A taxi from the city centre will cost around CZK 400 (£9) and take less than 10 minutes.

■ Getting a ticket
The only time the AXA Arena sells out is when the national team are in town playing a big country, or when Sparta host one of Europe's big guns such as Arsenal or Manchester United, as they have in recent Champions League campaigns. Tickets can be bought online, or from a number of ticket agencies in the city centre, as well as from the stadium itself. Ticket prices range from CZK 60 behind the goals to CZK 210 in the main stand. A good bet for the neutral is a place in the Upper Grandstand, whose tickets start from CZK 110.

■ Nearest airport – Ruzyne Airport (PRG)
Ruzyne Airport lies 10 miles north west of the city centre. The easiest way to the city is to catch the regular 112 bus that runs from outside the terminal building to Dejuiká metro line where you can change onto the Green line for services to the city centre. A single ticket costs CSK 20 and covers the journey both by bus and by metro. The main budget airlines that currently fly into Prague are **Easyjet** from London Stansted, Bristol, Gatwick, Newcastle and East Midlands, **Bmibaby** from Birmingham International, Cardiff International, East Midlands and Manchester, **Thomsonfly** from Doncaster Sheffield, and finally **Jet2** from Leeds Bradford. Traditional flag carriers **British Airways** and **Czech Airlines** also fly from London and Birmingham.

The Facts

Name: Brøndby Stadium
Address: Park Allé,
Glostrup, Copenhagen,
Denmark
Capacity: 30,000 All Seater
Opened: 22nd October 2000 –
Brøndby 4 AB Aarburg 2

■ About Brøndby Stadium

Located in the western suburbs of the city, the new Brøndby Stadium holds the title as the best stadium in Denmark. Whilst not as picturesque as Aarhus's stadium, or as big as the Parken, it is certainly the most modern. The stadium reopened its doors to the fans in late 2000 after a period of relocation at the Parken in the north of the city.

The stadium has all the aspects of a great club stadium. A terrace behind the goal – home to the hardcore home fans – literally bounces on match days. The three other stands wrap around with two tiers, with a row of executive boxes on either side of the pitch. The view from all stands is unobstructed and good – although the setting sun in the summer can cause problems for people in the east stand. The concourse areas are wide, and there are BBQ areas where sausages and kebabs are grilled. Outside the stadium, on the east side is the 1964

sports bar, a great place to come and listen to some live music, have a few Carlsbergs and watch whatever game from around the world is on TV. It's open to everyone – although you may need to get there quite early. The site has been home to the club since their formation in 1964 – initially it was simply a pitch with one small main stand. As the club became more successful during the 1980s, the stadium seemed to be a constant state of redevelopment, culminating in the need to move out for a couple of seasons in the late 1990s. Today the stadium is certainly fit for a team who are ready to challenge for European honours – unfortunately no one seems to have told the team!

■ Who plays there?

Despite vying for the position as Denmark's most successful club, it is only 20 years ago since Brøndbyernes Idaetsforening won their first honour, and just over 40 since they were formed. In 1964 the club was formed from a merger of a couple of local teams, and started playing in the Copenhagen regional leagues. The club stayed at this level for nearly twenty years despite some regular funding from the city council keen to see a club from the city make a mark on the European scene. In 1982 the club turned semi-professional and were rewarded within three years with their first honour – lifting the Danish league championship. The next few years saw the club lift two further championships and a Danish cup in 1989 as well as becoming the first Danish club to turn professional.

Brøndby Stadium – Copenhagen (Denmark)

The architect of this success was undoubtedly Finn Laudrup, father of Michael and Brian, who was a player with the team until 1981 when he retired and became the team's coach. He also oversaw a complete overhaul of the coaching, scouting and academy networks – a move that saw the development of such talent as Peter Schmeichel, John Jensen and of course his own sons.

After a brief flirtation with financial ruin when the board decided to purchase a bank (yes – a bank) which soon went under due to its exposure to bad debt, the club bounced back on the pitch and captured back-to-back championships in 1990 and 1991, as well as reaching the semi-final of the UEFA Cup in 1991 – their best European achievement to date. During the 1990s they found themselves with a new rival to hate after the formation of FC Copenhagen in 1991 but that didn't stop the success with a treble of championships captured between 1997 and 1999 as well as a first appearance in the Champions League group stages in 1998. Unfortunately the draw was very unkind to them as they were grouped with three previous winners of the competition in Manchester United, Barcelona and Bayern Munich. Since then, honours have arrived sporadically. In 2002 the club went into the winter break with a 10-point lead, but had to rely on other results to secure the title on the final game of the season. The following season saw the return of Michael Laudrup to the club as coach. Whilst it took him a couple of seasons to revitalise the club, he delivered a first league and cup triumph in the club's history in 2005.

The 2006/2007 season will be remembered though as a disaster. Three coaches failed to deliver any inconsistency and it was no surprise that a 1–0 home defeat to FC Copenhagen in May 2007 delivered the title to their bitter rivals with games to spare, and consigned Brøndby to 6th place – their worst league position for decades. One small consolation was the capture of the Royal League title which had been held by FC Copenhagen for the past two seasons. To make it all the sweeter they captured it against their great rivals in the Parken Stadium.

■ How to get there
The stadium is located out to the west of the city in the suburb of Glostrup. If you are planning on coming via public transport then catch the S-Tog train from any one of the three main stations (Central, Østerport or Nørreport) on line B to Glostrup – approximately 20 minutes away. From here catch one of the special football buses which run to the stadium. It's a 30-minute walk from either Glostrup or Brondbyoyster stations.

■ Getting a ticket
Despite having such a smart new stadium, the club only really sells out one game a season and that is the local derby versus FC Copenhagen. For all other games tickets are available on the day of the game from the ticket kiosks around the stadium, and from the fan shop on the west side of the stadium. You can also buy your tickets from the official website http://www.brondy-if.dk. Ticket prices range from 70DKK in the Faxe (south stand standing area) to 200DKK for an upper-tier seat in the east or west stands. For the Copenhagen game, and for big European games, prices rise significantly – a place in the Faxe costs 200DKK.

The Facts

Name: Parken Stadium
Address: Øster Allé 50,
2100 København,
Denmark
Capacity: 41,600 All Seater
Opened: 9th September 1992 Denmark 1 Germany 2

■ About Parken Stadium

The Parken has been the home of the national stadium since the end of the Second World War. The ground went through significant redevelopment work in the early 1990s and reopened with a friendly against Germany in September 1992. The stadium is, unusually for a national stadium, owned by a club side, FC Kobenhavn, who purchased the rights over the ground for 138 million DKK.

The stadium is built on similar lines to a number of English grounds, with four separate box-type two-tier stands. All of the stands offer unobstructed views of the action. The stadium has a UEFA 4-star rating, and has hosted the Cup Winners' Cup final in 1994 when Arsenal beat Parma, and the UEFA Cup Final in 2000 when Arsenal were the visitors again losing to Galatasaray on penalties. The stadium hosted a sell-out crowd for the friendly with England in 2005. However, its sub-50,000 capacity means it cannot be included in future UEFA Champions League final matches. The stadium has a retractable roof which is used primarily for concerts, such as U2 in 2005 and the 2001 Eurovision Song Contest.

■ Who plays there?

It is hard to believe that FC Copenhagen have only existed since 1992. However, as with a number of other clubs in Scandinavia, their roots are much deeper than this and the club can actually be traced back to 1876. Back then, Kjøbenhavns Boldklub, or KB for short were formed. The team were actually the first Danish league winners and went on to capture 14 more titles before they faded into the background of the lower leagues. The other partner in this new super-club was B1903 who were formed in 1903 (surprisingly enough). B1903 had been Danish league champions on seven occasions and had a spot in the Superliga up until 1992 when the merger took place. All of this tied in with the rebuilding of the Parken National Stadium which naturally became the home of the new team.

In their first season the team won the Danish league, breaking the near-monopoly of their cross-city rivals Brøndby. In doing so they qualified for Europe at their first attempt, losing 6–0 to AC Milan in the opening stages of the Champions League. The momentum, however, couldn't be carried forward. The club finally won a second championship in 2001 under English coach Roy Hodgson, narrowly beating Brøndby to the title on the last weekend of the season. The Blues would have their revenge the following season, pipping FC Copenhagen to the title at

Parken Stadium – Copenhagen (Denmark)

last, but they did reach the Champions League again, narrowly losing to Lazio on aggregate. Another title in 2003 was followed up by the double in 2004. The Champions League group stages still however eluded the team after defeats in the final qualifying match to Glasgow Rangers in 2004, and in 2005 Gorica denied them a lucrative spot in the group stages. Last season the club made some great strides in Europe, competing until the last game in the group stages with Manchester United, Celtic and Benfica. In the league they easily saw off the challenge of rivals Brøndby and won the league with six games to go. The Royal League was a disappointment. After winning the first two competitions, FCK lost the final on home soli to Brøndby.

■ How to get there
The best way to reach the Parken from the city centre is to catch bus 15 from Østerport station. Alternatively the station is just a 15-minute walk from the ground. If you are coming from the central station then bus 1A runs to Trianglen which is a 2-minute walk from the station. The stadium is also easily walkable from the Nyhavn area of the city centre. Just head back towards the city and turn right and follow Store Kongensgade until it runs into Ostergarde – the stadium will be a 25-minute walk away.

■ Getting a ticket
Crowds in Danish football are not known to be too high, and for most games buying tickets in advance for the Parken is not necessary. The biggest game in Danish football is the Copenhagen derby when Brøndby come visiting. For tickets to see FC Copenhagen log onto http://www.billetnet.dk. Tickets for top matches range from 90DKK to 180DKK. There are no real unsafe areas of the ground – the loyal FCK fans tend to congregate in the west lower tier.

■ Nearest airport – Kastrup Copenhagen (CPH)
Copenhagen's main airport is located 8 miles to the south of the city. **Easyjet** are the main budget carrier to fly to Copenhagen. They fly here daily from London Stansted. **British Airways** and SAS also fly here from London Heathrow. **Snowflake**, SAS's budget brand, fly twice daily from London City. **Sterling** fly three times a day from London Gatwick. The fastest way to the city is to catch one of the regular trains that run from below Terminal 3 to the central station.

The Facts

Name: Anfield
Address: Anfield Road,
Liverpool L4 0TH,
Great Britain
Capacity: 45,400 All Seater
Opened: 28th September 1884 –
Everton 5 Earlstown 0

■ About Anfield

Anfield is now in the twilight of its life as a stadium, as plans are now firmly established to move the club to a new 60,000-seater stadium less than a mile away in Stanley Park, thus bringing an end to the 125-year history of the ground. Today the stadium is one of the most atmospheric in European football. It is a UEFA 4-star stadium, and has regularly hosted internationals, including games played by Wales and the Republic of Ireland.

The stadium was originally home to Everton FC who moved here in September 1884, and played here during the inaugural Football League championship in 1888. Three years later a row over rent led to Everton leaving Anfield and setting up home to the north of Stanley Park at Goodison Park. Liverpool FC then became sole owners of the ground and started developing it, adding a main stand in 1895 and completing the Walton Breck Bank in

1897. This stand was renamed the Spion Kop in 1906 in memory for those British servicemen who lost their lives on the Spion Kop hill in the Second Boer War. At its peak this stand alone could hold 30,000 and was one of the single biggest stands in British football.

The stadium has undergone serious redevelopment over the past thirty years as the club have tried to upgrade facilities at the same time as expanding the capacity. The Main stand is the oldest surviving stand, dating back to 1973, although it now looks old and tired. The Centenary stand was opened in 1992, replacing the Kemlyn Road stand and providing the club with some state of the art hospitality and conferencing facilities. The Kop was converted to all-seater in line with the Taylor Report in 1994.

In June 1996 the stadium was one of the venues for the European Championships, and hosted games including the quarter-final between France and Netherlands. Whilst the Millennium Stadium was being rebuilt in Cardiff, Wales played a number of games here. After the original Wembley Stadium closed in 2001, the stadium also hosted three England matches. The stadium is very accommodating for fans, although the Main stand suffers from a real lack of space both in the seating and concourse areas. Other areas of the stadium offer excellent views, and an opportunity to sit on the Kop is still one of the best match-day experiences in football. The club offers regular tours of the stadium and the museum. It is essential that these are reserved in advanced by calling

0151 260 6677. The cost of the combined ticket is £9 for adults and £5 for concessions.

■ Who plays there?

Anfield is home to England's most successful club side, Liverpool FC. The club were formed in 1892 as an offshoot of the Everton football club after a row about the rent due on the ground at Anfield. They were elected into the Football League Second Division in 1893. They went through the following season unbeaten, winning the division before claiming their first First Division title in 1901.

However, it wasn't until the appointment of Bill Shankly in 1959 that the club started to make a real impact on British football. He was responsible for building a team that in 1962 won promotion to the First Division again, where they have remained ever since. In 1964 they won the Championship again, which started a run of success that took in FA Cup Final victories and the UEFA Cup in 1973. In 1974 Shankly retired and was succeeded by his assistant Bob Paisley. Paisley continued this success with seven League Championships, four League Cups – in fact the club went undefeated in this competition for five years – and three European Cups. In fact it was in Europe where their dominance was seen in the European Cup Final victories over Borussia Moenchengladbach in 1977, FC Brugge in 1978, Real Madrid in 1981 and Roma in 1984.

Paisley handed over the reigns to Joe Fagan in 1983, although his tenure will be remembered for the wrong reasons as he was in charge for the European Cup Final in Brussels against Juventus on the night of the Heysel tragedy. Fagan stepped down after this match, and was replaced by the legendary Scottish striker Kenny Dalglish as player-manager. In his first season he captured the domestic double. The club won their last Championship in 1990, and then went through a period of internal upheaval as managers such as Ronnie Moran, Graeme Souness and Roy Evans failed to deliver anything apart from an FA Cup win against Sunderland in 1992. It took the arrival of ex-French coach Gerard Houllier in July 1998 to start the Anfield revolution. He built a team that was on the verge of breaking the Manchester United monopoly on the Premiership. In 2001 the team won an unprecedented five major honours after capturing the FA Cup, Carling Cup, Community Shield, UEFA Cup and European Super Cup – a feat that has never been repeated.

Houllier could not deliver the title though, and after a serious health scare in 2003 he stepped down at the end of the 2004 season. He was replaced by Rafael Benitez who revamped the team, bringing in new talent such as Xabi Alonso, John Arne Riise and Pepe Reina to play

alongside Anfield legends such as Steven Gerrard and Jamie Carragher. In his first season the club won the Champions League by coming back from 3–0 down against AC Milan in Istanbul to win on penalties. In 2006 the team beat West Ham United on penalties again to capture the FA Cup. Last season the team could not break the Chelsea/Manchester United stranglehold on the Premiership, but they did reach the Champions League final again in Athens, losing 2–1 to AC Milan in a repeat of the 2005 final. The 2007 pre-season has seen the club spend significant sums of the recently-invested money from new US owners Tom Hicks and George Gillett Junior. In have come players such as Fernando Torres, Andriy Voronin, Alvaro Arbeloa, Ryan Babel and Yossi Benayoun in what many see is Benitez's final attempt at winning the Premiership.

■ How to get there

The stadium is not well served by public transport from the city centre. Bus number 26 runs from Paradise Street station to the ground, whilst from Queen Square bus station you can catch routes 17B, 17C, 17D or 217. The nearest station is Sandhills, which has a free Soccerbus link to the stadium on match days. Lime Street station is around 2$\frac{1}{2}$ miles away.

■ Getting a ticket

Unless you are a club member or season ticket holder then getting a ticket to see a match at Anfield is almost impossible at the current time. A very small number of tickets are held back for each game and you are able to take your chances in getting these. Exact details of how you can try and get your hands on them are displayed on the official website. You may have a better chance for cup games where season ticket holders may not take up their allocation. Ticket prices range from £35 in the Main or Centenary stands, to £28 in the Kop. To book a ticket then, call 0870 220 2151.

■ Nearest airport – Liverpool John Lennon (LPL)

Liverpool John Lennon Airport is located next to the River Mersey 7 miles south of the city. It is one of the fastest-growing airports in Europe with passenger numbers now 5 million per annum. The airport is currently served by **FlyBe** from Belfast, Jersey and Southampton and **Ryanair** from Belfast and Inverness. The majority of flights that come and go are chartered flights. To reach the city centre catch one of the regular Airport Express 500 bus services that run to Liverpool Queen Street bus station, as well as Liverpool South Parkway station – a single ticket costs £2. A taxi to the city centre should cost no more than £13.

The Facts

Name: Emirates Stadium
Address: Highbury House,
London N5 1BU,
Great Britain
Capacity: 60,432 All Seater
Opened: 22nd July 2006 – Arsenal XI 2 Ajax XI 1

■ About Emirates Stadium

Having played at the cramped Highbury since 1913, the move to the new Emirates stadium has not yet overwhelmed the club. Many of the fans never wanted to see the club move out of the historic stadium – loving the atmosphere, cramped stands and the iconic buildings. However, the new stadium is certainly an impressive structure, built in just two years at a cost of £390 million – half the price of Wembley Stadium. The stadium was built by HOK who also built Sydney's Stadium Australia. So what makes the stadium so special? It has certainly been built for comfort with padded seats in most of the upper tier, lots of leg room and two huge screens that relay action from the pitch.

The roof undulates from corner to corner – supposedly designed to reflect the waves on the Arabian Sea, although it does obstruct the view of the screens in some places. The middle tier of the stadium is designated as the Platinum area with some of the best hospitality facilities in

the world. From the inside, the stadium looks and feels almost identical to Benfica's Stadium of Light. Since the team has moved into the stadium, average attendances have been impressive with an average attendance of 60,043, a huge rise on previous years at Highbury. The old stadium at Highbury is slowly being converted into some exclusive flats – the East and West stand were listed buildings and they are being used as a shell for the new apartments, with the pitch acting as a communal garden.

■ Who plays there?

The Emirates stadium is home to Arsenal FC, one of England's most famous teams. In recent seasons they have enjoyed a position of power within the English game, regularly fighting it out for honours with the other big three teams in England – Manchester United, Chelsea and Liverpool. However, the club had very humble beginnings, actually starting life as the works team from the Royal Arsenal Company in Woolwich, south of the River Thames in 1896. Then, they were known as Dial Square but soon changed their name to Woolwich Arsenal in 1891, and entered the Football League Second Division in 1893. In 1904 they won promotion to the First Division, although found the new competition hard to cope with. In 1913, after relegation back to the Second Division, the club moved to Arsenal Stadium in Highbury, north of the Thames and at the same time dropped the 'Woolwich' from their name. In 1919 they were promoted back to the First Division where they have remained ever since.

The first period of success in the club's history came in 1930 when Herbert Chapman joined the club as their manager. In the 1930s the team went on to win five First Division titles and the FA Cup on two occasions. This was to be their only period of success, however until well after the war years, and the arrival of Bertie Mee as manager in 1966. In 1970 the club won their first European trophy when they won the Inter-City Fairs Cup (the forerunner to the UEFA Cup), following it up in 1971 with the second domestic double that any team had captured in the 20th century. However, the run of success did not last and the 1970s were characterised by near misses, such as the FA Cup Final defeats in 1972, 1978 and 1980. They also lost a penalty shoot-out in the European Cup Winners' Cup Final to Valencia in 1980.

It took the return of former player George Graham in 1986 to revitalise the team. He was responsible for developing a defensive strategy that was both mean, as well as goal-scoring. The club was soon amongst the honours again as they captured the League Cup in 1987, and two seasons later stole the First Division Championship from under the noses of Liverpool at Anfield with the last kick of the season. In the next few seasons with stars such as David Seaman, Tony Adams and Ian Wright playing at their peak the club won two more titles, as well as both domestic cups (by beating Sheffield Wednesday in each one) in 1993. In 1994 Alan Smith's goal in Copenhagen was enough to beat Parma and give them the European Cup Winners' Cup. The following season Graham was sacked after it was revealed he took some illegal payments from unlicensed agent Rune Hauge.

After a short period under Bruce Rioch, the club appointed Frenchman Arsène Wenger in 1996. He revolutionised the club, from the youth academy right up to the coaching staff. In came nutritionists, fitness coaches and the like and as a result the club enjoyed success like it had never experienced before. They won the double again in 1998, repeating the feat in 2002. They won the FA Cup in 2003 and 2005, whilst in the season in between they actually won the Premiership without losing a single match. Since the FA Cup win in 2005 they have not won another trophy, although in 2005/2006 they came close to becoming the first London team to win the Champions League when they lost to Barcelona in the final in Paris. Last season they were too far behind Chelsea and Manchester United to threaten them for any major honours, and suffered another blow at the end of the season when captain and leading scorer for the past few seasons Thierry Henry left to join Barcelona. With a number of other high-profile departures from the club as well as Henry, it will be interesting to see if Wenger is able to wave his magic wand again and recover some of their recent glory in 2007/2008.

■ How to get there

Public transport will take you within a few minutes walk of the ground and clear signs direct you from the stations and bus stops. The stadium has a colour-coding system to signify different areas. Arsenal (Piccadilly Line) is the nearest tube station, around 3 minutes walk from the ground. Finsbury Park (Victoria, Piccadilly Line and Great Northern rail) and Highbury & Islington (Victoria Line, North London Line and Great Northern rail) stations are around a 10-minute walk – these are normally less crowded on a match day. Holloway Road station is exit-only before and after matches with pre-match eastbound trains non-stopping. If you are arriving by bus, then the main bus stops are located on Holloway Road, Nag's Head, Seven Sisters Road, Blackstock Road and Highbury Corner.

■ Getting a ticket

The Emirates Stadium operates an automated access control system – similar to the system used at Upton Park and the City of Manchester Stadium. Everyone who purchases tickets for a game will be issued with a card. The bad news is that demand still exceeds supply for all matches. Tickets go on sale to Priority (Silver) members two months prior to each home match, except cup games. Any remaining tickets will go on sale to (Red) members one calendar month prior to each fixture. If any tickets are left for general sale they will be advertised at http://www.arsenal.com or the information line on +44 207 704 4242.

CARDIFF
CAERDYDD

The Facts

Name: Stamford Bridge
Address: Fulham Road,
London,
England SW6 1HS
Capacity: 42,449 All Seater
Opened: 28th April 1877

■ About Stamford Bridge

Stamford Bridge was dragged kicking and screaming into the 21st century prior to the Abramovich era – although the credit for revolutionising the club will always be given to his Russian roubles. The stadium was for many years a massive wide open ground, with the old stands set back from the pitch and a wide dog track separating the fans from the pitch.

The stadium does hold the record for an attendance outside of a major cup final in the UK when in 1945 a friendly against Dynamo Moscow attracted a crowd of over 100,000. The stadium also hosted the final three pre-Wembley FA Cup Finals between 1920 and 1922. In 1973 ambitious plans were drawn up to revolutionise the ground. The new East stand, whilst one of the most impressive structures in British football when it opened, almost bankrupted the club and further developments were put immediately on hold. In 1982 Ken Bates bought the club for £1, but despite constant offers, could not buy the stadium. The company who owned the stadium went bankrupt in the late 1980s allowing Bates to take over the ground and begin the development work. This started with an investment from Matthew Harding, who had recently joined the board. A multimillionaire in his own right,

Harding clashed with Bates on a number of issues but tragically died in a helicopter crash in 1996 just before the first stand (the North stand) opened. This was subsequently named after Harding. The West stand was next to be developed, with the final part being completed in the early part of this century to take the stadium to the shape it is now.

So does the stadium befit the mega-rich club today? The stadium is certainly atmospheric, with the stands hugging the touchline, and views are good from all stands. However, there is simply no room to expand the stadium any further due to the proximity of the local housing. The average attendance at the ground is just over 41,500.

■ Who plays there?

The stadium is home today to one of Europe's richest clubs, Chelsea FC. Whilst their current situation as one of the elite clubs in Europe is undeniable, their history pre-Roman Abramovich is certainly less impressive. They were originally formed as a pub team in 1905, initially taking the name the Rising Sun (after the pub of the same name located opposite the stadium). Their early history was less than impressive, with a single FA Cup Final appearance in 1915 to show for their efforts before the Second World War.

Under the leadership of Arsenal legend Ted Drake in the 1950s the club at last won their first major trophy – the 1955 Championship. In the early part of the 1960s Tommy Docherty took over the reigns, and he nearly took them to an unprecedented treble in 1965 when they were within minutes of taking the League and the FA Cup to add to the League Cup trophy they had already won. In the early 1970s the club beat Leeds United in a replay to win the FA Cup, and the following year claimed European success, beating Atletico Madrid in a replay in Athens in the European Cup Winners' Cup final.

The remainder of the 1970s and most of the 1980s were simply horrible for the club's fans – hooliganism was a major concern at all matches, and the club spent many seasons in the second tier of English football. The change in fortunes for the club came when Chairman Ken Bates managed to pull a real coup in securing the services of Ruud Gullit as player-manager. Over the course of the next few years Gullit brought in true world-class stars such as Gianfranco Zola, Roberto Di Matteo and Gianluca Vialli. In the space of the next five seasons the club won more honours than they had done in the previous 100 years. The team won the 1997 FA Cup, and then in the following season after Vialli took over from Gullit they won the League Cup and a Zola-inspired European Cup Winners' Cup.

In 2002 Vialli fell out with Bates and he was replaced with Italian Claudio Ranieri. He was responsible for winning the last-ever FA Cup Final at Wembley Stadium when they beat Aston Villa, as well as guiding the club to the promised land of the Champions League. Despite another successful campaign in 2004, Ranieri was sacked by the newly self-appointed owner Abramovich and was replaced by Porto manager José Mourinho who had just won the Champions League in Gelsenkirchen.

And so the ride to the top of the tree started. In 2005 they broke all records in becoming Premier League champions as well as winning the League Cup. The only disappointment was losing in the Champions League semi-final. The cheque-book of Abramovich was opened and players such as Ashley Cole and Didier Drogba joined the team over the next few years as a further Premiership title was added in 2006. The following season they set out with an objective of winning everything. The first part was delivered in March 2007 when Chelsea beat Arsenal in the Carling Cup Final. In the league they had to be content with a 2nd place finish behind Manchester United, although they did get one over on their new enemies by beating them 1–0 in the first FA Cup final at the new Wembley Stadium in May 2007. The real disappointment though was a third successive failure in the Champions League when they lost on penalties to Liverpool in the Champions League semi-final.

■ How to get there

The nearest tube station to the ground is Fulham Broadway which is on the Wimbledon branch of the District Line. You can also walk from West Brompton that is one stop before. There is also a train stop on the Clapham Junction to Watford Junction line. To reach the ground from here, simply turn right and walk through the cemetery – it should take around 15 minutes.

The stadium is in Travel Zone 2 – meaning that a single ticket from anywhere in Zone 1 is £4. A daily travel card is the better option, which would only cost £5.10 for a full day's off-peak travel. Driving is not a viable option as there is almost no public parking close to the stadium, and even if you do find a place, expect to pay well over £10 for the privilege.

■ Getting a ticket

Unsurprisingly, getting a ticket to watch Chelsea play is not a cheap day out. It is also not easy, and the days of simply turning up at the ticket office to buy a seat have long gone. Despite this, tickets are available for most games for the general public – you just need a degree to work out when and where you can apply. Ticket prices start from £50 for a non-member in the Matthew Harding lower stand, rising to £65 for a seat in the West stand lower tier. Most seats are fine for the neutral in the new sanitised Stamford Bridge. For Champions League matches, ticket prices are reduced by £5 across the board. For other cup games ticket prices start from £20.

Tickets will be sold via telephone on 0870 300 2322, from the website http://www.chelseafc.com or by personal callers at the stadium. Tickets for Premiership games go on sale 28 days prior to the match to members only. General sale starts, if tickets are available, one week before the game. For tickets purchased at the stadium, there is a £5 premium per adult ticket (to discourage touts officially) and you cannot pay with cash. Tickets purchased by other methods (phone or internet) attract the usual admin fee of £1.50 per ticket. Chelsea are also part of the Viagogo Ticket Exchange programme, which is accessible from the main website. This allows ticket holders to sell tickets back to the club, who then resell them on to the general public.

The Facts

Name: Wembley National Stadium
Address: Wembley Way
London HA9 0WS
England
Capacity: 90,000 All Seater
Opened: 24th March 2007 – England U21 3 Italy
U21 3

■ About Wembley National Stadium

The hype is finally over. After $6^{1}/_{2}$ years, the new Wembley Stadium finally opened its doors to the paying public in March 2007. Despite years of delays, escalating budgets and enough rumours to fill an edition of a Sunday tabloid, the FA took control of the stadium on 16th March 2007, and promptly set about arranging the necessary warm-up events so that the FA Cup Final between Chelsea and Manchester United on the 19th May 2007 could be hosted.

The original stadium – the Empire Stadium – opened on the 28th April 1923 for the FA Cup Final between West Ham United and Bolton Wanderers when an estimated 200,000 fans squeezed in the 125,000-capacity stadium after building was finished at the last minute by Sir Robert McAlpine. The following year the stadium hosted its first international as England drew 1–1 with Scotland.

In those days the stadium was an oval bowl, with a running track around the outside, and two roofs that ran half way along each side. The stadium continued to host the FA Cup Final, as well as international matches throughout the Second World War – including a crowd of over 80,000 for a game against Scotland when air raids over London were a daily occurrence. In 1948 the stadium was the host of the Summer Olympic Games – having originally been chosen to host the 1944 games. In 1951, possibly the most remarkable games in its short history took place between Pegasus and Bishop Auckland in the FA Amateur Cup Final. What made this so unique was that the crowd was 100,000! In terms of major events though, one football match will continue to dominate the history of the stadium. In 1966 England hosted the World Cup, and through a 'carefully' planned draw, the stadium hosted all of their games. Without ever kicking into top gear, the team got to the World Cup Final, where in front of an estimated 40 million TV viewers, and over 100,000 paying spectators the team beat West Germany 4–2 after extra-time to win their one and only World Cup Final.

Other big games held at the stadium include the European Cup Finals of 1968, when Manchester United beat Benfica, 1977 when Liverpool beat Brugge and 1992 when Barcelona beat Sampdoria. It also hosted the 1965 and 1993 European Cup Winners' Cup. In 1998 and 1999 Arsenal also chose to move their Champions League games to the stadium, although the crowds didn't exactly warm to the venue. The last major match played at the stadium was in October 2001 when Germany's 1–0 win over England forced the hand of Kevin Keegan to resign as national manager.

So what is it like today? The famous white Twin Towers have been replaced by a massive arch which is visible from over 20 miles away. Leg room and sightlines are built to the highest specification. Concourse facilities are plentiful and spacious, although food and drink prices are very high. The stadium has a roof which covers all of the seats if inclement weather is forecast, but does not fully extend over all of the pitch. Outside the stadium is a statue to the late Bobby Moore.

■ Who plays there?
The stadium has been built as a monument to English football, and will be the home venue for all future England senior home matches for the next 20 years. The stadium will also host the major domestic finals, which including the play-offs will number more than ten per season. As of 2008, the stadium will also host the FA Cup semi-finals. The stadium will also host major concerts, such as George Michael (June 2007), as well as other events such as a regular season American football game between the New York Giants and the Miami Dolphins (October 2007).

■ How to get there
Within a 10-minute walk of the stadium there are three stations which carry the vast majority of fans. Wembley Park tube station is on the Jubilee and Metropolitan tube lines. This station allows for a journey from central London (Bond Street) in around 25 minutes or from London Bridge in 35 minutes. The station is a 10-minute walk away up the historic Wembley Way.

Wembley Central station is on the Bakerloo tube line as well as the Silverlink train line. The overground train service links Wembley to London Euston in 15 minutes and is a 15-minute walk away from the stadium. Wembley Stadium station is located just behind the stadium, and has an access ramp direct onto the outer concourse. It is served on the Chiltern mainline link from London Marylebone. The stadium is in Travel Zone 4, meaning a single ticket currently from Zone 1 would be £4. A daily travelcard covering this Zone would be £5.70 off peak for

adults and £1 for children. If you do intend to drive, there are no public car parks within a 15-minute walk from the stadium.

■ Getting a ticket
Ticket availability will depend on the event being staged. For the majority of England home internationals, tickets will be sold initially to the England fans' club members, and then to the general public. Ticket prices for England internationals range from £25 in the family section in the lower tiers to £60 in the middle tier. Ticketing arrangements for the major finals will be handled by the clubs concerned, and so you should check with them on availability – in general you will not have a problem getting a ticket for finals such as the Johnstone's Paint, FA Trophy or the lower league Play-Off finals. All other ticketing will be handled by either Ticketmaster – http://www.ticketmaster.com or by See Tickets – http://www.seetickets.com.

■ Nearest airport – London Heathrow (LHR)
London Heathrow is the busiest airport in the world in terms of passenger numbers. It serves almost every country on earth and so it can be bewildering to the first time visitor. It currently has four terminals, with a fifth due to open in late 2008 which will be dedicated exclusively to **British Airways**. Public transport options include the Heathrow Express, which runs every 15 minutes to Paddington Station (£14.50 single), the underground (Piccadilly Line to central London in 35 minutes, £5 single), Coach (National Express every 30 minutes) or taxi which can take over an hour and cost £50 or more.

The Facts

Name: Old Trafford
Address: Sir Matt Busby Way,
Manchester M16,
Great Britain
Capacity: 76,134 All Seater
Opened: 10th February 1910
Manchester United 3 Liverpool 4

■ About Old Trafford

The 'Theatre of Dreams' as it is more commonly known is the biggest club stadium in the United Kingdom, and one of the biggest in Europe. The stadium has been redeveloped over the past twenty years, initially transforming from standing to all seater, and then the demolition and rebuilding of three of the four stands.

What you see today is a magnificent cathedral of football, with the North stand souring up into the sky as a monument for miles around. The only stand that is still to be redeveloped is the main stand – the South stand. This would prove to be problematic due to the existence of the railway line as well as the changing rooms and press area. However, plans have been submitted to convert this into a two-tier stand which would take the capacity to 82,000, although no date has been set for this work to commence.

The stadium is one of the few 5-star UEFA venues in Europe and was given the honour of hosting a Champions League final when AC Milan beat Juventus in 2004. The stadium was also home to the England team for the most part when Wembley Stadium was being rebuilt, and still hosts the odd FA Cup semi-final. After initially opening as Manchester United's home in 1910, the stadium hosted

the FA Cup Final in 1911 and 1915. In March 1939 the FA Cup semi-final between Wolves and Grimsby Town attracted a crowd of 76,962 which is still (just) the record attendance at the stadium. Bombing during the Second World War closed the stadium from 1941 to 1949 and the club moved in with neighbours Manchester City. Today the stadium is an awesome sight on a match day. Views are excellent from all seats, although those sitting in the upper tier of the North stand may need binoculars. Leg-room is generous, as too are the wide concourses. The noise on a match day is not as passionate as you will find in Barcelona or AC Milan but it is impressive all the same. The stadium has a very impressive museum that is open daily, and can be combined with a half-hourly tour of the stadium taking in the changing rooms, players' lounge, dugouts and a walk down the tunnel all for £9.

■ Who plays there?

Old Trafford is home to one of the world's greatest clubs, Manchester United. Whilst Real Madrid, Barcelona or Liverpool may lay claim to the title, nobody could complain at their title of the best-supported club in the world. This fact is borne out by the constant demand for seats in the Theatre of Dreams, which despite being increased by 40% in recent years, is still not enough to satisfy the potential fans.

The club are also one of the richest in the world today (although since the takeover of the Glazers in 2005 they have lost their top spot) – quite a way from their humble beginnings in 1878 as Newton Heath, a works team from the Lancashire and Yorkshire Railway Company. The club officially changed their name in 1902, and at the same time adopted the famous red and white kit. The club spent its formative years bouncing between the top two divisions after moving into their new stadium in 1910. After the Second World War, Matt Busby was appointed manager of the club and began a revolution that would lay the foundations for the success we see today. In the mid-1950s the club started to produce a string of young players who were destined for greatness, including Duncan Edwards and Bobby Charlton. In 1957 the club won the League Championship and almost stole the double, losing to Aston Villa in the FA Cup Final. The following season they entered the European Cup for the first time, reaching the semi-finals before losing to Real Madrid.

On 6th February 1958 the team had played a European game in Belgrade against Red Star. On a refuelling stop in Munich the plane crashed due to bad weather and a number of these great players perished, including Edwards. The team was decimated and rumours circulated that they may actually fold. The club did go on to finish 2nd in that season though. In the 1960s the team continued to be rebuilt with new stars such as George Best and Denis Law, and they reached their emotional nadir at Wembley in 1968 when they became the first English team to win the European Cup by beating Benfica 4–1. The 1970s and 1980s were a bleak time for the club with few honours won. In 1974 the team were actually relegated for the first time in 40 years.

Managers such as Dave Sexton, Tommy Docherty and Ron Atkinson were brought in to try and revive the club's fortunes, and apart from the occasional FA Cup victories (in 1977 and 1985) the club failed to deliver the major prize. In November 1986 Alex Ferguson was appointed new manager. In his first full season the club finished 2nd in the League, but this was the high point until 1990 when the club at last won some silverware by beating Crystal Palace in the FA Cup Final. This was to be the turning point in the club's history as the following season they went on to win the European Cup Winners' Cup in Rotterdam against Barcelona. The following season, with Eric Cantona installed as the fans' favourite, the team broke their 25-year hoodoo on the title and took their first Premiership title. Since that day in May 1993 the club have gone on to win eight further titles as well as six FA Cups and the League Cup. Their finest season came in 1999 when they won the domestic double and the European Champions League by beating Bayern Munich with two goals in injury time. That team, containing such home-grown talent as Ryan Giggs, David Beckham, Paul Scholes and Gary Neville was probably the finest team that the club has produced.

In the last few seasons the club invested heavily on the back of the takeover by the Glazer family and brought in talent such as Wayne Rooney, Cristiano Ronaldo, Michael Carrick and Louis Saha, although this has been tempered by the ruthless approach of Ferguson in selling stars such as Ruud Van Nistelrooy, David Beckham and Jaap Stam. Last season the team played some of the best football we have seen in decades and were worthy winners of the Premiership, although again disappointed in Europe. Since the final in 1999 they have failed to reach a major European final – something that does not sit very comfortably with the club and supporters alike.

■ How to get there

Old Trafford is located 3 miles south east of the city centre in Salford Quays. However the majority of fans drive to Old Trafford and use the numerous private car parks that open close to the ground on match day and charge between £10 and £20. The Metrolink tram network runs services every few minutes from Piccadilly down to Trafford Bar and Old Trafford which are the nearest stations to the ground. The latter is located next to the cricket ground and is a 5-minute walk to the stadium. Another option is to head for the area around the Imperial War Museum where parking is much cheaper and the stadium is a 15-minute walk away. The stadium has its own station, built alongside the South stand, although queues to get on trains after the match build up very quickly indeed.

■ Getting a ticket

Despite its huge capacity, Manchester United have over 100,000 club members who get priority in booking seats for each game. For a normal league game there are around 10,000 seats made available to club members and so as a neutral you are often better off trying to get a ticket for the away team. Ticket prices are very reasonable with the most expensive seats in the North or South stand centre being £42 and the cheapest in the East and West stands lower being £25 each. If you get a chance to get a ticket then all seats offer a fantastic view, although you are very high up indeed if you are in the North stand upper tier.

Manchester United do offer special packages that include a ticket, hotel for the night and a tour of the stadium for around £199 per person per night. This is often the only way to get to see a league match at the stadium. For Champions League matches the situation is slightly different. Season ticket holders often do not take up their allocation of seats for the group games and these are put on sale via the website.

■ Nearest airport – Manchester International (MAN)

Manchester International Airport is slowly growing to be one of the biggest in Europe. It has over 100 airlines that use it daily, handling around 22 million passengers last year flying to over 200 destinations. It also handles a number of domestic flights including **AirBerlin** from London Stansted, **Air Southwest** from Bristol, Newquay and Plymouth, **American Airlines** from London Heathrow, **BMIBaby** from Heathrow, Glasgow and Edinburgh, **British Airways** from London City, Gatwick and Heathrow, **Flybe** from Belfast, Exeter, Glasgow, Isle of Man, Norwich and Southampton, and finally **VLM** from London City.

The easiest way to reach the city centre is by train. There is a dedicated station at the airport which runs services every 20 minutes into Manchester Piccadilly and onwards. Plans are being considered at the moment for a metrolink extension as well. National Express coaches also stop at the airport and can take you as far away as London. A taxi would cost around £20 to the city centre.

The Facts

Name: Le Coq Arena
Address: Asula 4c,
Tallinn,
Estonia
Capacity: 9,300 All Seater
Opened: 15th May 2001

■ About Le Coq Arena

Just to underline the importance of football to the Estonians it was felt that such a small stadium was more than adequate for the national team's purposes when Le Coq was designed. FC Flora Tallinn, who play their home games here, struggle to get crowds over 1,000 and the national team attracts less than 2,000 unless the visitors are of the likes of Russia or England.

The stadium is an excellent venue to watch football on a long summer's night, as the sight lines and leg room are very good, each stand has a large bar and refreshment areas and the roof offers protection from the occasional Estonian rain shower. The two side stands are identical – resplendent in their green seats. Both are two-tier with the lower tier much larger than the upper one. The concertina-style roof is also unusual as it sits quite a way above the final row of seats. The end stands are set above the action on the pitch by 8 feet, which allows an additional 1,000 seats to be installed in the stadium when demand exists.

The hardcore Estonian fans, if you can call them that, will be located in the lower tier of the south stand. The brand new stadium sits on an old area of wasteland to the south of the city centre, and has very little around it. As the city centre offers so much in terms of hospitality it is much better to stick here until 30 minutes before kick-off before heading down.

■ Who plays there?

FC Flora are the biggest sporting club in Estonia. Since the team was formed in 1990, the club won back-to-back titles in 1994 and 1995, and then a further six titles up until 2003. They have also won the Estonian cup on two occasions. The 2005 season's 4th place finish was the first time ever they had finished outside of European qualification. Last season they were too far behind Trans and Levadia to make an impact on the title, finishing in 3rd place. In terms of European pedigree they have recorded three wins in 28 matches. The club has two well-known past players – Mart Poom, who is now goalkeeper for Watford and still the country's number 1, and Jonatan Johansson who played for Charlton Athletic and Rangers. The stadium is also home to the national team. In the short history of the country the stadium has hosted a few sell-outs, notably against England and Russia in the European Championships 2008 qualifying tournament.

Le Coq Arena – Tallinn (Estonia)

■ How to get there

The stadium is located in the south west of the city, just outside the main ring road. The stadium is easily walkable from the city centre in around 30 minutes. The shortest way is to head south along the Parnu Mnt main road until you reach the elevated bridge over the railway line. At this point, head down the steps on either side of the road and turn right into the residential road. You will then see the unmanned crossing over the railway line. The other option is using tram number 3 that runs down Parnu Mnt from the town to the stadium entrance road every 20 minutes, and takes less than 10 minutes. A taxi should cost £5.

■ Getting a ticket

Assuming you are in town for a league match, simply head down to the stadium and buy a ticket from the table on the corner of the south east stand. For a mere 30EEK you will get a ticket for the main stand and a programme. If you want to sit with the dozen or so hardcore fans in the south stand then a ticket costs 5EEK less. For most of the international games you should not have a problem paying on the gate – however, for the visits of the top nations, buying tickets from touts is your only real option.

■ Nearest airport – Ülemiste Airport (TLL)

Located on the shores of Lake Ülemiste, and just 4km from the city centre, Tallinn Airport is very small with one terminal, a small cafe and a couple of shops. The airport is served by **Easyjet** from London Stansted, and **Estonian Air** from London Gatwick. To reach the city centre catch bus number 2 that leaves from outside the terminal building. A single fare costs 15EEK and travels to the downtown bus terminal outside the Kaubamaja department store. The journey takes around 15 minutes. You can also reach Tallinn from Helsinki via helicopter or fast ferry. The journey is run by http://www.copterline.com and takes around 15 minutes although it is not cheap. The ferry is run by Tallink (http://www.tallink.fi) and costs €49 return for the 100-minute journey.

Stade Felix Bollaert – Lens (France)

The Facts

Name: Stade Felix Bollaert
Address: Avenue Alfred-Maes,
62304 Lens Cedex,
France
Capacity: 41,800 All Seater
Opened: 1st August 1932

■ About Stade Felix Bollaert

There were a few raised eyebrows locally when the decision was made in the early 1990s to expand the stadium to over 40,000, with the population of the town of Lens just 37,000. However, such is the passion and interest locally for the team that the stadium is often full. The stadium is named after the director of the regional coal industry, and the man responsible for building the stadium.

It is a very British stadium, with four steep two-tier stands that are close to the touchline, allowing for a very passionate atmosphere to be generated on most match days. All stands offer unobstructed views of the action. The stadium frequently hosts rugby union internationals, and was one of the venues that was used in the 2007 World Cup finals and in the 1998 Football World Cup, including the key games between Germany and Yugoslavia, England and Columbia and the last-16 game between France and Paraguay. The stadium was in the news again in February

2007 when it hosted the Champions League tie between OSC Lille and Manchester United, after Lille's stadium was deemed unsuitable to hold Champions League matches. Overcrowding in the away supporters' end led to some ugly scenes with the fans and the police, bringing into question again the basic facilities of the stadium to host such matches. In 2009 the south stand is due to be demolished and in its place will rise a new two-tiered main stand, with a casino, shopping centre and access to the new Le Louvre-Lens museum that is currently being constructed.

■ Who plays there?

One of the proudest teams in France, Racing Club Lens were founded in 1905 under the name of RC Lensois. After a few name changes and kits, the club settled on RC Lens in 1923 and adopted the colours of Spain for their first game at the Stade Municipal. In fact such is the link with the local coal industry that pre-Second World War most of the team was made up of local miners. The club's identity has grown over the last 50 years as the fortunes of the region have declined. The team have become a reason for hope for many unemployed coal miners in the region, after the collapse of the industry.

Apart from a couple of runners-up spots in the French Ligue 1 and French cup during the 1950s and 1970s, the club entered the 1990s without a major honour to their name. In 1998, on the back of a real high in French football, the club won its first and only Ligue 1 title to date, pipping AS Monaco under coach Roger Lemerre. The chance of a unique double was in their grasp as well but they lost a hard-fought final 2–1 to Paris Saint-Germain in the Stade de France. The league title gave the club a chance to compete in the Champions League group stages for the first time. Drawn in a group with Arsenal, Dynamo Kiev and Panathinaikos, the team won away at Highbury before a shock 3–1 defeat at home to Kiev eliminated them. In 2002 they again failed to make it out of the group stages after being drawn with AC Milan, Bayern Munich and Deportivo La Coruna. Since then the club haven't been able to make the Champions League, much to their fans' annoyance as local rivals OSC Lille have reached back-to-back group stages in the competition. Since then the team have been a regular in the top six in the Ligue 1 without making a serious challenge for the title. They did win the Intertoto Cup in 2005, but failed to make the final 16 in the UEFA Cup. 2006/2007 was a mixed season for the team, finishing in 5th place and qualifying for the UEFA Cup, although they only actually finished one point off third place which would have been a Champions League spot. In the UEFA Cup they reached the last 16 before losing 4–2 to Bayer Leverkusen. The current squad is a real mix of internationals including Brazilians, Malians, Serbs and of course French. They have a number of high-profile players who recently played in the 2006 World Cup including Eric Carrière, Ivory Coast's Aruna Dindane and Serbian Nenad Kovačević, and have recently been joined by new coach Jean Pierre Papin.

■ How to get there
If you are visiting the town centre, then the floodlights from the stadium are visible from most points, and nowhere in the town is more than a 10-minute walk

away. If you are driving to the stadium then leave A1/E17 at the A21 junction, then follow to the junction of Lens-Ouest, or the A211 at the Bollaert junction and simply follow the signs for the stadium.

■ Getting a ticket
Tickets for most games go on sale three weeks before the match. Whilst the club continually averages over 35,000, it tends to be the games against the big three that sell out (Marseille, PSG and Bordeaux). Prices range from €12 in the Delacourt Niveau lower tier behind the goal to €60 in the main stand, the Presidentielles Lepagnot area. A good bet for neutrals is the Xerces Louis side stand where tickets will cost €28. Tickets for matches can be purchased from the stadium in the Emotion Foot shop, by phone on 0825 862 862 or online at http://boutique.bollaert.fr. Tickets are also sold via a number of large hypermarkets in North France including the Auchan chain in Calais and Boulogne.

■ Nearest airport
Lens is the largest town in the Picarde area of North France. It is not high on the list of places to visit by tourists, as most prefer to divert up to Lille. The nearest major airport to Lens is Charles de Gaulle, which is some 110 miles to the south. The nearest major railway station is Lille – 25 miles away and a major stop Eurostar trains to Brussels. Local services from Lille to Lens run four or five times an hour and take less than 45 minutes. Driving is the easiest option to reach Lens from the UK. The town is 60 miles down the A1 from the Eurotunnel terminal at Calais. Added to the convenience is the proximity of major hypermarkets such as Carrefour and you can see why so many British football fans head south to watch games in Lens.

Stade Gerland – Lyon (France)

The Facts

Name: Stade Gerland
Address: 350 Avenue Jean-Jaurès,
69007 Lyon,
France
Capacity: 43,000 All Seater
Opened: 3rd August 1926

■ About Stade Gerland

The Stade Gerland has been home to Lyon since the end of the First World War – in fact most of the original stadium was actually built by German PoWs at the end of the conflict. Originally it was a multi-purpose venue, hosting athletics and cycling with a capacity of over 50,000. In 1984 the stadium hosted two games in the European Championships, including the semi-final between Denmark and Spain in front of over 47,000.

In preparation for the 1998 World Cup finals, the athletics track was removed from the stadium, and the terracing replaced with seats, reducing the capacity to 42,000. The stadium hosted six games at the finals, including the historic meeting between USA and Iran, and France's game versus Denmark. It was also chosen as one of the hosts of the 2003 Confederations Cup tournament, and was the venue for the ill-fated game between Cameroon and Colombia when former midfield star Marc-Vivien Foé collapsed and died. The venue was chosen to host games in the 2007 Rugby World Cup, including a New Zealand All Blacks and an Australian Wallabies game. The stadium features some classic architecture that has led to parts of the ground being listed. These include the entrance archways and the main stand façade. The views from all parts are unobstructed and very good. Games against local rivals St Etienne or Paris Saint Germain are very lively affairs.

■ Who plays there?

Olympique Lyonnais, or simply OL, represents the new world order in French football after securing their sixth successive league title in 2006. The turnaround in their fortunes has been remarkable – as before 2002 their only honour had been a couple of French cup victories in 1964 and 1967. In fact it wasn't until the early 1990s that the team became firmly established in Ligue 1.

The club as we know it today was formed in 1950 as Lyon Olympique Universitaire, and they soon started on the road to success with a Ligue 2 title in 1951. No further success came until the 1960s when the club managed to beat Bordeaux in 1964 and Sochaux in 1967 to take the Coupe de France. In 1983 the team found themselves back in Ligue 2. During the next few years the club was sold to Jean-Michel Aulas who vowed to the fans to deliver European football to the club within three years. One of his first moves was to appoint current French national coach Raymond Domenech, who wasted no time in getting the club promoted back to the top league.

Within two years Domenech had guided the club to 5th place which meant they qualified for the UEFA Cup – as promised by Aulas. Over the next few years a series of high-profile coaches were employed to try to fulfil the next stage in Aulas's dream – the delivery of the Ligue 1 title. These included Jean Tigana, Bernard Lacombe and Jacques Santini. It was Santini who finally delivered Champions League football to Lyon in 2002 when the club finished as runners-up, and a year later they claimed their first title.

Santini was replaced by Paul Le Guen who commenced a plan to make Lyon one of the dominant teams in Europe. The club were accepted as the only French team in the G-14 power-base, a massive feather in their cap over bigger teams such as PSG. Their best performance in the Champions League came in 2004 when the team won their group and beat Real Sociedad before falling to eventual winners Porto in the quarter-finals. In the 2005/2006 season the team again set an astonishing pace in the domestic leagues as well as waltzing through their Champions League group. In the 2nd round they convincingly beat Werder Bremen on aggregate 10–2, before losing again in the quarter-finals on penalties to PSV Eindhoven.

New coach Gerard Houllier continued the success of the team, with the likes of Sylvain Wiltord, Gregory Coupet and the Brazilian pairing of Juninho and Fred capturing a fifth successive title in May 2006. Again in the Champions League, the quarter-final proved to be a bridge too far, with defeat in the San Siro against AC Milan scant reward for some of Europe's most attacking football. In 2006/2007 the story was almost the same. The title was delivered in April (they ended up winning the league by 17 points), and in the Champions League they lost 2–0 on aggregate to Roma in the 2nd round. However, at the end of the season Houllier announced he was stepping down, to be replaced by Alain Perrin. Coupled with the departure of a number of key players such as Florent Malouda, 2007/2008 could be more open than any of the previous five seasons.

■ How to get there
The stadium is based in the south east of the city and is served by its own Metro stop on Line B – called Stade de Gerland. From the centre of the old town in Perrache, go north on Line A to Bellecour, then change to the eastbound Green Line D, changing onto Blue Line B for four stops at Saxe-Gambetta. From the main station at Part-Dieu you can just head south on Line B for five stops. You can also catch bus number 96 from Perrache for the stadium.

■ Getting a ticket
Tickets go on sale on the website http://www.ticketnet.fr. These tickets can be posted to the UK or collected from the stadium ticket office. Tickets range in price from €45 in the lower tiers behind the goals, to €60 in the Jean Bouin or Jean Jaures stands along the side of the pitch. A good seat for the neutral is in the €40 seat in the Jean Jaures lower tier. Tickets for league cup matches are around 20% cheaper. Tickets for Champions League games are slightly more expensive than normal league games – €20 to €70. Tickets can also be bought from the club shops (Planet' OL) in the city centre and at the stadium, Auchan and Virgin megastores.

■ Nearest airport – Lyon Saint-Exupèry (LYS)
The airport is located 20km to the east of the city and is the major transport hub for the Rhône-Alps skiing area. Currently the best way to reach the airport is via a half hourly bus that runs to Port Dieu and Perrache stations, with a journey time of 45 minutes. The airport also has a high-speed rail link served via the TGV trains en-route from Paris to Marseille. The airport is currently served by **Easyjet** from London Stansted, **British Airways** from London Gatwick, **BA Connect** from Birmingham and Manchester, and **Air France** from London Heathrow.

The Facts

Name: Stade Vélodrome
Address: 3 Boulevard Michelet,
13008 Marseille,
France
Capacity: 60,031 All Seater
Opened: 13th June 1937 – Marseille v Torino

■ About Stade Vélodrome

The Stade Vélodrome is the biggest club stadium in France and certainly one of the most atmospheric even though it only has one side with a roof. The stadium was originally built as a cycling track, hence its name. In 1937 football was added to the list of events it hosted. It wasn't until the late 1990s that the cycle track was actually removed. In 1938 the stadium hosted a number of matches in the World Cup finals, including the semi-final between Italy and Brazil.

Since then the stadium has been developed on a number of occasions, raising the capacity over time to the present 60,000 limit. The most unique feature of the stadium is the huge curved Tribune Ganay that holds above 20,000 supporters. There are currently plans to redevelop both ends of the stadium, and to add a roof to the remaining three sides to take capacity to 80,000. Such a move is interesting as technically the stadium has never sold out – the record attendance being just under 59,000 for a UEFA Cup semi-final versus Newcastle United in 2004.

The views from any part of the stadium are very good – even in the upper parts of the Ganay. Despite its Mediterranean aspect, the uncovered stadium can get very chilly in the winter months as the infamous mistral wind blows in from Africa. The four stands have the names of local celebrities, such as Chevalier Roze who stopped the spread of the Bubonic plague in the 18th century. The hardcore Marseille fans can be found at either end of the stadium in the Virages.

■ Who plays there?

Whilst the ground is world-known as the home of Olympique Marseille, it is the stadium that has gained a reputation as one of the finest arenas in the world for hosting rugby. In fact the French national team are frequently visitors to the stadium, and actually went over 4 years unbeaten here until 2004. The ground was chosen to host a number of matches in the 2007 Rugby World Cup finals. Despite recent problems, the club, Olympique Marseille, are undoubtedly the biggest in France, and some would argue the most successful. They were originally formed in 1899, although success didn't really arrive in the south of France until late 1980s and the arrival of the millions of francs from new owner Bernard Tapie. The club won their first honours in the 1920s, winning successive French cup titles in 1926 and 1927. In 1937 the club won their first title in the new professional era of French football. The following few years saw another couple of French cups, as well as a second championship in 1948. In the 1970s the club became the most successful French team when they won the double in 1972.

In 1986 Bernard Tapie arrived as the new owner of the club, thanks to the money of Adidas and the political power of then mayor Gaston Deferre. He immediately started funding a revolution in French football and success did not take long to arrive as the club won the double again in 1989, followed by championship titles in 1990, 1991 and 1992. In 1991 the club reached the final of the European Cup, losing to Red Star Belgrade on penalties in Bari. Two years later they reached the final of the Champions League where they recorded their finest moment in their history when they beat AC Milan 1–0 in Munich. In 1994 the football world was shocked by revelations of match fixing involving Tapie and the club were relegated to the second division and had their Champions League title stripped. Their exile lasted all of two seasons as they returned to the top division as champions in 1995 – thanks to the goals of Tony Cascarino. The investment in the team was once again forthcoming from Adidas – this time from Robert Louis-Dreyfus. Since then they have failed to match the ambition and investment by Lyon domestically, although in Europe they have managed to reach two UEFA Cup Finals in 1999 and 2004 where they lost to Parma and Valencia respectively. In 2007 they had the chance to win some silverware for the first time in 15 years when they reached the French cup final. However, they lost on penalties to underdogs Sochaux. They can be consoled by a 2nd-place finish in the league, and a return to the Champions League group stages in 2007/2008.

■ How to get there

The impressive Stade Vélodrome is located in the south east part of the city, 4km from the centre. The easiest way to reach the stadium is by Metro, on Line 2 to Ste Marguerite/Dromel which is five stops and 8 minutes journey time from St Charles SNCF station. Exit the station via the Rond Point du Prado exit and you will see the stadium straight ahead. Alternatively you can catch bus 83 from the city centre.

■ Getting a ticket

Whilst Marseille are the best-supported team in France, average attendance in previous seasons at the stadium has rarely broken the 50,000 barrier, meaning that there tends to be on average around 10,000 seats available on the day of the game. Tickets go on sale ten days before the match from the ticket office at the ground, and from the club shop at OM Café Vieux Port, the official Tourist Office at 4 La Canebière and any Carrefour or FNAC store in France. They can also be bought online from the official site at http://www.om.net. Ticket prices range from €30 in the Tribune Ganay which is the huge open stand, to €50 in the Balcon which offers some protection from the elements.

■ Nearest airport – Marseille Provence (MRS)

Marseille Provence airport is located 27km north west of the city centre. To reach the city centre, catch one of the buses that run every 20 minutes to Gare St Charles, costing €8.50 each way. **British Airways** from London Gatwick, **BMIBaby** from Birmingham, **Easyjet** from London Gatwick and Bristol, and **Ryanair** from Bournemouth, Glasgow-Prestwick and London Stansted, flights to Marseille being on a daily basis.

Stade Louis II – Monaco (Monaco)

The Facts

Name: Stade Louis II
Address: 7 Avenue des Catelans,
98000 Monaco,
Monaco
Capacity: 18,500 All Seater
Opened: 11th May 1985

■ About Stade Louis II

The Stade Louis II is one of the most surreal venues at which to watch football in Europe as it sits squarely in the middle of the world's richest playgrounds, where space is at an absolute premium. The club first started playing in the principality in 1919, although they had to wait until 1939 for their first stadium to be constructed on land that had been reclaimed from the sea. In the early 1980s when Prince Rainer III came to power in Monaco he funded the building of a new stadium a few hundred yards away from the existing ground in Fontvielle, overlooking the cliffs of the Cote d'Azur. The new stadium was built with a car park, office space, swimming pool and a gymnasium, all underground, such was the demand for space in the principality.

The stadium opened in 1985 and was named after Prince Rainier's grandfather. Despite its small capacity it was chosen to host the 1986 Cup Winners' Cup final between Dynamo Kiev and Atletico Madrid. Since 1998

the stadium has also hosted the annual UEFA Super Cup match, played between the Champions League and the UEFA Cup winners. The stadium also hosts a number of top athletics competitions every year, including the IAAF World Athletics finals. The presence of the athletics track is one of the only annoyances in an otherwise excellent stadium. The views from the stands are very good, with the prime seats being in the upper tier of the north stand – known as the Tribune d'Honneur.

■ Who plays there?

Association Sportive de Monaco Football Club to give them their full title are quite unique in world football. They are by default a national team, but as Monaco is not affiliated to FIFA they are able to play their games in the national league of France (although technically they could play in any other European league). The club were formed in 1919, although it wasn't until after the Second World War that they turned professional. Their formative years were relatively unimpressive, and it wasn't until the 1960s that they won their first trophy by beating St Etienne 4–2 to capture the Coupe de France. The following season they won their first Ligue championship. Two seasons later they won the championship again, and a few weeks later beat Lyon in the Coupe de France final replay to complete a domestic double.

The club had to wait another 15 years before they captured a third title, starting an impressive run of form that delivered three Ligue 1 titles and two French cup victories in the next decade. In 1997 they won the league again and qualified for the Champions League again. In fact the club's performance in European competition ranks very high with the other teams in Europe. They reached the Champions League quarter-finals in 1989 before being eliminated by Galatasaray, and the semi-finals in 1994 and 1998, before the famous run to the final in 2004. In the Cup Winners' Cup they were losing finalists in 1992, defeated by Werder Bremen, and also reached the semi-final of the 1997 UEFA Cup before losing 3–2 on aggregate to eventual winners Inter Milan.

However, in recent times the club is best remembered for the Champions League 2003/2004 under the leadership of Didier Deschamps. After winning their group containing PSV Eindhoven, AEK Athens and Deportivo La Coruna (which included an amazing 8–3 home victory), they beat Lokomotiv Moscow on away goals to set up a quarter-final against favourites Real Madrid. After a 4–2 defeat in the Bernabau the omens did not look good for Monaco, especially when Raul scored midway through the first half of the second leg to make it 5–2. However, goals by Ludovic Giuly and on-loan Fernando Morientes against his employers saw Monaco go through on away goals. In the semi-final versus Chelsea, Morientes was on fire again and helped the club to a 3–1 victory at the Stade Louis II. Chelsea could not break down a stubborn defence and a 2–2 draw in London was enough to take the club through to the final in Gelsenkirchen against Porto. Unfortunately their run of form deserted them in Germany and the Portuguese won 3–0.

Since then the club have struggled to recapture form as the star players from that team have left. Strikers Morientes, Nando and Prso all left within 12 months, and Giuly was lured by the big bucks at Barcelona. Although they did reach the last 32 of the UEFA Cup in 2006, defeat to FC Basel signalled the end of their European adventures. In the league last season's 9th place finish was very disappointing.

■ How to get there

The stadium is located close to the city centre of Monaco, just south of the Royal Palace. It is a 5-minute walk from the main railway station, or a 3-minute walk from the Heliport from where you can fly direct to Nice airport in less than 10 minutes. Just to the south, past the Heliport, you can see how close the stadium is to the Mediterranean Sea.

■ Getting a ticket

Despite having one of the most affluent supporter bases in the world, crowds don't exactly flock to the Stade Louis stadium on a regular basis. Last season they averaged just over 11,000 and had a best attendance of 17,500 for the match versus Marseille. Therefore tickets can be purchased on the day of the game on most occasions. Tickets can be purchased online at http://www.asm-fc.com, by emailing the ticket office at billeterie@asm-fc.com, by phone on +377 92 053754 or from a number of shops around the region including FNAC in Monaco, Cannes and Nice. Ticket prices start from just €8, with a ticket in the Tribune d'Honneur costing €40, making it one of the cheapest clubs in Europe to watch.

■ Nearest airport – Côte d'Azur Airport (NCE)

Nice airport is the second most important in France, handling over 10 million passengers a year. It is located on the Promenade des Anglais 8km west of the city of Nice. From the UK it is well served with daily flights operated by **British Airways** from London Gatwick and Heathrow, **BMIBaby** from Birmingham, **Flybe** from Exeter and Southampton, **Jet2** from Leeds-Bradford and Manchester, and **Easyjet** from Bristol, Liverpool, London Gatwick, Luton and Stansted as well as Newcastle. To reach the centre of Monaco from Nice you can go the cheap way, which is by the hourly bus from platform 2 which takes 45 minutes and costs €26 each way, or the expensive but much more impressive way by helicopter which is operated by Heliair Monaco (http://www.heliairmonaco.com) and costs €89 each way.

The Facts

Name: Stade de la Beaujoire
Address: Rue de Saint-Joseph,
44300 Nantes,
France
Capacity: 38,500 All Seater
Opened: 8th May 1984 – FC Nantes 0 Romania 1

■ About Stade de la Beaujoire

The Beaujoire was designed in the early 1980s as a replacement for FC Nantes' compact Marcel-Saupin stadium, and to meet the demand for a new west coast stadium for France's bid to host the European Football Championships of 1984. Out went the old steep terraces and basic seating and in came a brand-new stadium full of curves and sweeping stands and a significantly increased capacity at over 53,000.

The stadium hosted its first match in May 1984 when FC Nantes played a friendly against the Romanian national team. Just a few weeks later the stadium welcomed the French national team as they hosted Belgium in a sell-out group match of the Championships. A Platini-inspired performance saw Les Bleus beat their neighbours 5–0. The stadium also hosted Portugal versus Romania, although a 24,000 crowd was disappointing. Fourteen years later, after a multi-million-franc redevelopment which saw the stadium converted into a 38,000 all-seater

ground, the Beaujoire hosted a number of games in the 1998 World Cup finals, including Brazil versus Morocco and the quarter-final between Brazil and Denmark. The stadium is certainly unique in design. Two Tribune stands that sweep upwards in the middle provide a focal point for the stadium, whilst behind the goals the smaller Visage stands are intimate and home to some of the most vocal supporters in France. The main stand, the Jules Verne one, is massive and can be seen for miles around. The views from the top tier here are impressive. Behind the goals the seats are simply plastic backless seats bolted to the original terrace – so don't expect much comfort here.

■ Who plays there?

The stadium is home to FC Nantes Atlantique, who until a few seasons ago were one of the most feared teams in France. Their eight French championships make them one of the most successful teams in the domestic leagues – however, the club went from champions in 2001 to bottom of the table in 2007 – one of the most spectacular falls from grace in French football and ending a near 45-year run in the top flight.

The club won their first honours in 1965 when they captured the French league, repeating their feat a year later. Over the next couple of decades they won four more championships. Between 1976 and 1981 the club set a record for remaining unbeaten at home for 92 matches. In 1995 they captured their greatest championship when they narrowly pipped Paris Saint Germain, Auxerre and

Stade de la Beaujoire – Nantes (France)

Lens to the title, recording 32 games without defeat in the process. The following season they competed for the first time in the Champions League. Drawn in an easy group with Panathinaikos, Porto and AaB, they gained a vital point away in Portugal to go through to the quarter-finals. A 4–2 victory against Spartak Moscow took the Canaries through to the semi-finals where they met the mighty Juventus. Facing a 2–0 deficit from Turin, Nantes put on a brave show back at the Beaujoire and nearly overturned the 2–0 lead, falling just short in a 3–2 win. In 2000 the club were nearly on the receiving end of one of the greatest cup shocks in French history when they narrowly beat the amateurs of Calais in the French cup final at the Stade de France. The club had to wait until 2001 for their final championship – the last time a club apart from Lyon, has taken the title. The following season the club again performed well in the Champions League, winning the first round group against PSV Eindhoven, Lazio and Galatasaray. Unfortunately they could not carry this form into the second stage where draws at home to Manchester United and Boavista were their only points from a tough group.

In 2006/2007, hopes were high for at least a UEFA Cup spot. Unfortunately the team never found any consistency, and by Christmas were close to the relegation zone. In what was planned to be an inspired move, veteran goalkeeper Fabian Barthez was signed from Marseille. Unfortunately, things went from bad to worse and their run of form saw them relegated for the first time in over 44 years.

Occasionally, the national team have played here, although the last time they visited was back in 2001 for a friendly versus Denmark. In September and October 2007 the stadium hosted a number of matches in the Rugby World Cup including the match between England and Samoa. The French rugby team have played a few games here over the years, the most famous game being a French win versus the All Blacks in November 1986.

■ How to get there

The stadium is located in the north west of the city, adjacent to the E62 main road, 7km from the city centre. Around the stadium are some nice wooded areas, and it does feel as if it is in the suburbs with little in the way of bars and cafes in the immediate area. The easiest way to reach the stadium from the city centre is to catch the tramway number 1 to the end stop which is right outside the stadium. The journey from the city centre takes no more than 20 minutes. Be warned that the trams get incredibly crowded. Bus numbers 1, 22, 71 and 76 also make the journey to the stadium. A 24-hour ticket covering either the bus or the tram is €3.

■ Getting a ticket

FC Nantes are one of the best-supported teams in France. With average attendances close to 30,000, getting a ticket still isn't a problem for most matches. Tickets can be purchased from the official website at http://www.fcna.fr. You can also purchase tickets from around the region in the Leclerc stores. Some of the best seats for the neutrals are in the Credit Mutuel Oceane Bas which is one of the side tribunes where tickets are €25. Behind the goal in the Presse Ocean Erdre a seat would set you back €15.

■ Nearest airport – Nantes Atlantique (NTE)

Nantes Atlantique airport is located 15 minutes from the city centre. There is a regular bus that runs to the central station in 20 minutes. Tickets cost €6.20 each way and a taxi €22. The airport's route map is expanding every year, and currently there are a number of options to reach here from the UK. This includes **Aer Arann** from Bristol, Cardiff and Manchester, **GB Airways** from London Gatwick and **Ryanair** from Bournemouth, East Midlands and London Stansted.

The Facts

Name: Parc des Princes
Address: 24 Rue du Commandant Guilbaud,
75016 Paris,
France
Capacity: 49,000 All Seater
Opened: 4th June 1972 – Marseille 2 Bastia 1

■ About Parc des Princes

The Parc des Princes was for so long the jewel in French sports grounds, boasting the biggest capacity and best facilities. Named after the monarch's hunting grounds that it sat in, it was originally opened in the late 19th century as a multi-purpose venue. It hosted athletics, cycling (it has been used for the final stages of the Tour de France), football and rugby.

For long periods of time it was not used by any club side – the current tenants Paris Saint-Germain were only formed in 1970. The ground was chosen by UEFA in 1956 to host the first ever European Cup Final, Real Madrid beating Stade Reims. The stadium has gone on to host the European Cup Final in 1975 when Bayern Munich beat Leeds United and again in 1981 when Liverpool beat Real Madrid, two European Cup Winners' Cup Finals and one UEFA Cup Final. In the late 1960s the local city council wanted to demolish the stadium to make way for the newly constructed Paris ring road. Local opposition saw a

huge demonstration mobilised against the plans and a compromise was found where the stadium was redeveloped by turning the pitch around, allowing a road tunnel to be built underneath.

The new remodelled stadium opened in 1972 for the French cup final between Marseille and Bastia, and the newly formed Paris Saint-Germain moved in in the 1972/73 season. The stadium was modernised again in 1983 as one of the host stadiums for the European Championships the following year, which was won by France by beating Spain in the stadium – possibly the ground's finest moment. In 1998 it also hosted a number of games in the World Cup finals. A year later it hosted group matches for the Rugby World Cup including England's quarter-final defeat by South Africa. The stadium can create an excellent atmosphere on match days. All of the stands are close to the pitch, and all seats in the two-tier stadium offer unobstructed views. The hardcore PSG fans, the Boulogne Boys, are located in the south stand. For games versus their hated rivals Marseille the stadium is whipped up into a cauldron of noise and colour hours before kick-off and is one of the great sights in football. Few stadiums in Europe can match this atmosphere.

■ Who plays there?

Many people associate PSG as the most successful team in France. This fact underlines the power of the media – the team only came into existence in 1970 when two local teams, Racing Club Paris and Saint-Germain Ensoon, merged and gained some favourable decisions from the FFR in gaining firstly a place in the top division, and secondly being given a state of the art stadium on the newly remodelled Parc des Princes.

The early years were less favourable to the team as they struggled to make an impact, although they were up against some very good teams such as the Michel Platini-inspired St Etienne. During the 1980s the club started to make some progress on the field, although they were still struggling to attract the fans. They won their first trophy in 1982 when they captured the French cup and their first championship in 1986, although their debut in the European Cup lasted 180 minutes as they lost to Karvina 3–2 on aggregate. In 1991 they club were technically bankrupt, and it took some huge investment from Canal Plus to keep the team afloat. In 1993 the new-look team featuring stars like Louis Fernandez, George Weah and David Ginola delivered trophies in the golden period for the club. The French cup was brought home in 1993, 1995 and 1997 and they won the championship again in 1994.

European football was next on the agenda for the club and they started with the UEFA Cup in 1993/94. An impressive run of victories over PAOK Salonica, Napoli (with a fit again Maradona) and Anderlecht got them through to the quarter-finals versus Real Madrid. In one of the most famous games in the club's history, PSG turned around a 3–1 defeat from Spain with a 4–1 victory, winning 5–4 on aggregate. In the semi-finals they lost 3–1 to Juventus, despite having a number of opportunities to snatch a winner in the 1–0 second-leg home defeat. After the championship victory in 1994 they gained automatic qualification for the Champions League group stages which put the club in the European spotlight for the first time.

They did not disappoint, becoming one of the first teams to win all six group games against Bayern Munich, Spartak Moscow and a Shevchenko/Rebrov-powered Dynamo Kiev. In the quarter-finals they got a tough draw against Barcelona. However, a 2–1 win in Paris took them through 3–2 on aggregate and into the last four. Unfortunately this turned out to be the club's peak as defeat to AC Milan saw them miss out on the final. Undeterred, Louis Fernandez's team picked themselves up and started an assault on the European Cup Winners' Cup in 1996. The club easily brushed past Molde of Norway, Celtic and Parma to reach their third successive European semi-final. This time they managed to convert their chances and a 2–0 victory over Deportivo La Coruna took

them into the final in Brussels versus Austria Vienna. Winning 1–0 with the goal scored by Bruno N'Gotty, they secured the club's first-ever European trophy. The following season the club set out to retain their title in the European Cup Winners' Cup. They easily beat Vaduz of Liechtenstein in the 1st round, before beating Galatasaray in another classic at the Parc des Princes (overturning a 4–2 first-leg deficit to win 6–4), and then AEK Athens to take a place in the semi-finals for the fourth consecutive year. There, they met Liverpool and in a completely one-sided home leg powered them to a 3–0 lead. Despite some very nervous last few minutes at Anfield, a 2–0 defeat saw them reach the final again in Rotterdam. This time, Ronaldo's penalty was the only difference as Barcelona took the trophy.

Apart from a few brief appearances in the UEFA Cup, European football has gone too as the club slip further behind Olympique Lyonnais in terms of domestic success. A solitary cup final win in 2006 was the first for three seasons. The current team contains a number of young French players, although the most notable player is Portugal's Pauletta. The crowds have at least stayed with the club, averaging over 40,000 for the past five seasons. Last year, under Guy Lacombe, the club started the season poorly, putting pressure on him with a number of defeats to teams they would normally be expected to beat. The team finished the season sixth from bottom – their worst finish for more than a decade.

■ How to get there

The stadium is located to the south west of the city centre, right above the inner ring road. The easiest way to reach the stadium is by Metro on Line 9 to Pont de Sèvres or Line 10 to Boulogne-Porte de Saint-Cloud. The stadium is signposted as you leave either station. You can also get regular bus services to Porte de Saint-Cloud via the 22, 62 and 72 bus routes.

■ Getting a ticket

Tickets are available for most games. The game which is always going to sell out is the one versus Marseille where you will need to buy in advance. Tickets can be bought from the club's megastores at the stadium or in the Champs D'Elysee. The club also sell tickets via http://www.ticketclic.fr. Tickets range in price from €60 for a seat in Sections CD Rouge (upper tier) to €19 in the Boulogne end where the Boulogne Boys are located. A safe bet for the neutral is in the HIJ sections which cost €32.

Stade de France® – Paris (France)

The Facts

Name: Stade de France®
Address: Cornillon Nord,
93216 Saint Denis La Plaine,
France
Capacity: 79,959 All Seater
Opened: 28th January 1998 – France 1 Spain 0

■ About Stade de France®

In 1992 FIFA announced that France would host the 1998 World Cup finals. One of the conditions of awarding them the finals was the provision of a stadium that could hold more than 70,000 fans. Although Marseille's Stade Velodrome was near this capacity, it was almost unheard of for a capital city not to host a World Cup final (only Washington DC has not hosted the final after the USA was awarded the competition), so work started almost immediately on finding a site in Paris to build a state-of-the-art venue. Once a site had been located in the north of the city, and funding put in place, construction started in 1995. What was unique about this project was the amount of resources allocated to the construction meant that less than two years later the stadium was ready and in use.

The stadium has a number of unique features such as the roof that appears to float above the stands – it is actually 42 metres above the playing surface and gives complete cover from the elements to the 80,000 spectators. The lower tier is built in such a way that 25,000 seats can slide back into the middle tier, allowing events such as speedway and athletics to take place without compromising the views for football and rugby. The stadium is one of the best in the world in terms of spectator facilities and the sightlines are excellent. Paris Saint-Germain were given the opportunity to move here, but decided to stay in the south west of the city. For a few games Red Star Paris played here and actually attracted a crowd of over 45,000 for a league game versus St Etienne in 1999.

The stadium not only hosted the famous World Cup final between France and Brazil in 1998, but has also hosted the majority of French football and rugby national games since opening. It has also hosted two Champions League finals – first in 2000 when Real Madrid beat Valencia, and in 2006 when Barcelona beat Arsenal. It also hosted the final of the Rugby World Cup in October 2007. The stadium offers daily tours for €10, including two per day in English at 10.30am and 2.30pm.

■ Who plays there?

The Stade de France® is home to the French national football and rugby teams, and is not used on a regular basis. It also plays host to the two French cup finals in April and May respectively.

Stade de France® – Paris (France)

■ How to get there
The stadium is located in the Saint Denis, and adjacent to the A1 motorway that runs up towards Calais. It is very well served by public transport with the authorities deciding to build access points at either end of the stadium. RER station Stade de France-St Denis is on the Green Line that passes through the city from Creteil in the south, whilst RER station Le Plaine-Stade de France links Paris CDG airport in the north with Orly airport in the south on the Blue Line B.

Both stations are one stop from Gare du Nord and the journey time is 7 minutes. Metro Line 13 also serves the stadium through the stop at St Denis-Porte de Paris. If you want to travel by bus to the stadium then use Lines 139 from Porte de la Villette or 173 from Porte de Clichy. A taxi from the centre of the city will cost around €20.

■ Getting a ticket
The ease of getting a ticket for the stadium depends on the event. Most French rugby internationals are sold out and tickets never go on general sale. Tickets for the French league and cup finals go on sale around four weeks before the event via http://www.ticketclic.fr.

■ Nearest airport – Charles de Gaulle (CDG)
Paris CDG airport is located 25km to the north-east of Paris, adjacent to the A1 motorway. It one of the busiest airports in the world with five terminals in total – although they are split into two hubs, A and B. The airport is connected to Paris by the RER rail line which runs to Gare du Nord and Les Halles in 25 minutes from the station in from Terminal 2B. The station also serves TGV trains to Lille, Lyon and Marseille. The following airlines currently use Paris CDG: **BMI** from Leeds/Bradford and London Heathrow, **BMIBaby** from Cardiff and Nottingham/East Midlands, **Flybe** from Exeter and Norwich, **British Airways** from London Heathrow, **BA Connect** from Birmingham, Bristol, Edinburgh, Glasgow and Manchester, **Air France** from London Heathrow and Manchester, **Brit Air** from Newcastle and Southampton, **CityJet** from Birmingham, Edinburgh and London City, **Easyjet** from Bristol, Liverpool, London Luton and Newcastle, and **Jet2** from Leeds/Bradford.

■ Alternative airport – Paris Orly (ORY)
Orly Airport is located closer to the city than CDG, although journey times tend to be the same. The most direct route to the city is to catch the transit from either Orly Ouest or Orly Sud to Antony station which takes 8 minutes. From there you can then catch RER line B to Les Halles in less than 25 minutes. There is also a bus that runs to Denfert Rochereau in the city in approximately 30 minutes. The airport has two terminals, South and West. The following airlines fly to Orly: **Easyjet** from London Gatwick, **Thomsonfly** from Bournemouth, Coventry and Doncaster–Sheffield, and **Air France** from London City.

■ Alternative airport – Beauvais Tille (BVA)
Whilst being 60 miles north of Paris, Beauvais airport earns the right to call itself Paris as much as Luton or Stansted do to call themselves London airports. The airport was originally a military base until 1956 when it opened to commercial flights. **Ryanair** became the first major airline to start using the airport in 1998. They currently fly here from London Stansted and Glasgow Prestwick. A bus meets all inbound flights, taking 75 minutes to reach the city centre at Port Maillot. Tickets cost €13 each way.

The Facts

Name: Stade Municipal
Address: 1 Allee Gabriel-Piénès,
Toulouse,
France
Capacity: 36,369 All Seater
Opened: 1949

■ About Stade Municipal

The Stade Municipal was originally opened in 1949 as a multi-sport venue, hosting football, rugby and athletics. Today, after going through a number of major redevelopments, the stadium is a classical shape, with two side stands (the Honneur Nord and Sud) and two curved stands behind the goals. The stadium is often used as the venue for some of the big rugby matches played by Stade Toulouse. The venue was also used for matches in the 2007 Rugby World Cup finals.

The stadium was one of the venues in the 1998 World Cup finals, hosting for six games including England's defeat by Romania. Whilst its capacity is relatively small for a major stadium at just over 36,000, it is the biggest in this area of France. The view from most areas is excellent – the curves behind the goal are not as pronounced as traditional athletic-type stadiums so you are not far away from the action.

■ Who plays there?

Apart from the occasional big tournament game, the stadium is used by two teams – Stade Toulousain Rugby Club and FC Toulouse. Whilst there is no argument that the former are most successful – having won rugby's European Cup on three occasions – they actually play all bar their big matches at their own 19,000 Stade Ernest-Wallon close to the airport, north of the city centre. FC Toulouse meanwhile have been playing at the stadium since its construction in 1937. The club has two clear periods of history. From 1937 until 1967 the team played as Toulouse Football Club, winning their only major honour in 1957 when they captured the Coupe de France. However, in 1967 the club 'merged' with Red Star Olympique who were based in Paris and professional football disappeared from the streets of Toulouse as the club were moved lock, stock and barrel to the capital.

In 1970 the club re-formed as Union Sportive Toulouse and entered the second level of French football the following season. In 1977 they were able to reclaim the name FC Toulouse after the demise of Red Star. In 1982 they were promoted back to Ligue 1, and even managed a UEFA Cup spot in 1984. However, history seemed to be on the verge of repeating itself in the late 1990s as the club teetered on the edge of financial meltdown as they plunged down the leagues, ending up in League D2. However, against all of the odds, under Erick Mombaerts the club rose again through the leagues until they returned to the top division in 2004. Last season they capped a remarkable few years by finishing in the Champions League qualification places. The current squad of mainly young French players will undoubtedly find life in the Ligue hard but pride has been returned to the city at last.

■ How to get there
The stadium is located to the south of the city centre, on an island in the middle of the Garonne River. It is easily walkable on a nice day, especially if you have been enjoying a long lunch around Pont Neuf or Rue du Metz. However, if you want to come by public transport then use either Metro Line A to Arenes or Line B to St Michel-Marcel. Both stations are within a 5-minute walk of the stadium. Buses 1, 12, 34 and 52 also drop you off close to the stadium from the city centre.

■ Getting a ticket
In the past few seasons getting a ticket for a game at the Stade Municipal has never been a problem. In fact it was only a couple of seasons ago that Toulouse were in the second level of French football. In 2006 the club averaged just over 19,000. However that rose last season to close to 22,000 as the club challenged for a Champions League spot. Tickets go on sale at a number of points. The club offers internet and personal bookings, as well as bookings over the phone on +33 3940. You can also get them from branches of Virgin Megastore and FNAC in the local area. Tickets range in price from €10.50 in the Visage's to €36 in the Honneur Nord upper tier.

■ Nearest airport – Toulouse Blagnac (TLS)
Toulouse airport is one of the busiest in France, and is also the home to Airbus – you get an excellent view of some of the new huge Airbus planes when you are landing and taking off. The airport is located 20 miles north of the city centre. There is a bus that runs from the airport to the main railway station every 20 minutes from 7.30am. Tickets cost €5.90 return, and the journey takes 25 minutes. The airport is served on a daily basis by **British Airways** and **Easyjet** from London Gatwick. **Easyjet** also fly here from Bristol. **Jet2** have recently starting flying to Toulouse from Leeds/Bradford and Manchester. London Heathrow is served by **BMI** and **Air France**.

The Facts

Name: Olympiastadion
Address: Olympischer Platz 3,
14053 Berlin,
Germany
Capacity: 74,400 All Seater
Opened: 1st August 1936

■ About Olympiastadion

The Olympiastadion is one of the most impressive and historic stadiums in the world. The stadium itself appears almost monumental from the outside – a perfect elliptical structure of finest German limestone. In fact some of the original inspiration of the design was taken from Rome's Coliseum. The original architect, Werner March, designed the stadium with clear input from both Adolf Hitler and his chief architect Albert Speer. It was meant to be a showpiece arena where Hitler could show the world the power of the German state both in terms of athletics and in edifices during the 1936 Summer Olympics.

After the Berlin Wall fell in 1989, and unification gathered pace, the stadium was granted funds to begin to update its facilities. The host club, Hertha Berlin, were invited to join the inaugural German Bundesliga, and redevelopment was necessary to bring the standard of the ground up to those in the west. However, funds were not available to add probably the most important thing for a

spectator – a roof. Berlin is not known for its warm balmy winter's evenings, and so their loyal fans had to endure the elements whilst watching their team.

In 1998 a decision was taken by the state government to begin the complete modernisation of the stadium. The work, which took over four years to complete, saw the whole of the inside of the stadium demolished and replaced piece by piece, as well as the much needed roof being added. All this construction took place with events continuing to take place in the stadium, albeit with a reduced capacity. The redevelopment work included the removal of every limestone block to be cleaned, and then replaced – a job akin to completing a huge jigsaw puzzle. The reconstructed stadium was finally finished in time for Hertha's first game of the 2004/2005 season with VfL Bochum and underlined the venue as one of the most modern stadiums in the world, and a venue fit for the World Cup Final in 2006. The stadium also hosted five other matches, including the quarter-final penalties victory by Germany over Argentina.

■ Who plays there?

Berlin has never been a one-team city, and there is much more to the history of football in the city than just Hertha. After merging with local rivals Berliner Sport Club, Hertha went on to reach an unprecedented six consecutive championship finals, losing the first four before beating Holstein Kiel in 1930, and then 1860 Munich in 1931.

After the Second World War, the club became

homeless as their 'Plumpe' ground had to be demolished due to bomb damage. However, the club were asked to represent Berlin when Germany launched its first professional league in 1963. This in itself caused significant controversy as the winner of the previous three regional championships had actually been Tasmania Berlin and not Hertha. However, Hertha were deemed to be the best team to represent the city, and the invite to take part in the league was too much of a temptation for the West German government to resist. In order to show the strength and power of 'their team', the East German government made the Olympiastadion available for Hertha's home matches.

With a young Otto Rehhagel in the side (later to coach Greece to their improbable 2004 European Championship win), Hertha kicked off in front of 50,000 against Nuremberg in August 1963. However, due to the financial restrictions in place on Berlin following the building of the Berlin Wall, Hertha found it very hard to attract the players needed to compete at this level. The club tried to entice players through bribes, but an investigation in early 1965 found the tell-tale financial irregularities and Hertha were expelled from the league. In the late 1970s there was only one team from Berlin that people were talking about – Dynamo Berlin. As with traditions in Russia, Dynamo was seen as the team of the Stasi, the secret police. Dynamo became the team to beat almost overnight. They won the East German league for the first time in 1979, and went on to hold the title for the next eight years, adding the East German cup to the collection in 1988 and 1989. Come unification in 1989, and the fall in power of the Stasi, Dynamo's influence over the league faded as quickly as it had appeared. The fall of the wall was also a start of a new period for Hertha Berlin. They bounced between the top two divisions for a number of years, although one interesting highpoint was the cup final of 1993, when Hertha's amateur team reached the German cup final before losing 1–0 to Bayer Leverkusen. In the last years of the century, the team managed a 3rd place finish and qualified for the Champions League where wins over Chelsea and AC Milan almost saw then qualify for the quarter-finals. Hertha's 6th place finish in 2006 meant a sixth successive year in Europe for the club, although last season the mid-table finish was seen as a major disappointment.

■ How to get there

The easiest way to reach the stadium is by either U-Bahn on line U2, or by S-Bahn on lines S5/S75. Both of these stations are called Olympiastadion. The U-Bahn station is located to the east of the stadium on Rominter Allee – which will bring fans out onto the huge Olympischer Platz and the view of the famous Olympic towers. A journey from Zoo Station in the west of Berlin takes 15 minutes. The S-Bahn station is located to the south of the stadium, and is 200 yards from the Sudtor entrance. Trains run from Zoo Station, Alexanderplatz and the newly constructed Hauptbahnhof. The journey from Zoo should take 10 minutes.

■ Getting a ticket

Tickets for any event that is being played at the stadium can be booked in advanced via the website http://www.olympiastadion-berlin.de. Hertha also have their own ticket website at http://www.hertha.de. Last season the average attendance at the stadium was only 47,000, meaning that for the majority of matches tickets were available on the day of the game. Tickets range in price from €13 behind the goal to €45 for one of the best seats in the Sud Tribune.

■ Nearest airport – Berlin Schönefeld (SXF)

Berlin Schönefeld airport is located 18km south east of the city centre, in the old East German part of the city. The airport is used by **Easyjet** from Bristol, Liverpool, London Gatwick, London Luton, and Newcastle and **Ryanair** from London Stansted. The airport is linked directly to the city centre on S-Bahn lines 9 and 45. **Air Berlin** currently use Tegel airport to the north of the city. The railway station is a 5-minute walk from the terminal building. S45 runs to Westkreuz in the west of the city, whilst S9 (the 'Airport Express') runs to Zoo Station via Alexanderplatz, taking 30 minutes. The single fare is €2.40. A taxi to the city centre would take around 30 minutes, depending on traffic and cost upwards of €40.

The Facts

Name: Weserstadion
Address: Franz-Böhmert Strasse 1c,
28205 Bremen,
Germany
Capacity: 42,100
Opened: 1909

■ About Weserstadion

The Weserstadion has been the home of Werder Bremen for nearly 100 years, although it has gone through a number of major changes during that time. It is now one of the most distinctive-looking stadiums in Germany due to its unique floodlights and its oval shape. It was originally used as a general sports field in the early part of the century before being developed for political rallies in the early 1930s at the time when the Nazi party was on the rise. The stadium was extensively remodelled in the 1970s with a new roof added as well as the addition of 9,500 seats. During the 2001/2002 season the pitch was lowered, allowing a further 8,000 seats to be added.

The stadium has a dual capacity depending on the nature of the matches played – for normal Bundesliga matches the capacity is over 42,000, but this falls to around 35,000 for internationals as the terracing has to be converted to seating. Normally the ground has around 32,000 seats. The stadium also houses a museum, and

holds regular tours of the ground which costs €5 for adults and €2.50 for concessions. Plans have been drawn up for a new 50,000-seater stadium a few hundred yards away from the Weserstadion and August 2009 has been pencilled in as a potential opening date, although construction has not begun as of August 2007.

■ Who plays there?

Werder Bremen are now established as one of the most feared teams in German football, after their capture of the domestic double in 2004, and appearances in the Champions League group stages every season since. Their 3–1 victory in the Olympic Stadium in Munich in May 2004 will go down in history as one of the most dramatic games in German football history as it broke Bayern's seemingly unbreakable hold on the Bundesliga title. The team, led by coach Thomas Schaaf, won the title for the fourth time, and the first time since 1993 through the efforts of players like Johan Micoud, Ailton and Miroslav Klose. In the last two Champions League campaigns, the club have made it out of difficult group stages, only to fall against perceived weaker teams in the first knock-out rounds.

The club were originally formed in 1899, and whilst performing well in the North German leagues, they did not taste any glory until 1961 when they beat Kaiserslautern to win the German cup. After failing to be included in the first ever Bundesliga in 1963, the team showed their critics the errors of their ways by winning the Bundesliga

Weserstadion – Bremen (Germany)

title in their first season in the league in 1964/65. Over the next decade the team couldn't find any consistency and actually fell into the second division in 1980. The appointment of Otto Rehhagel as coach revived the club and, under young stars such as Rudi Voller, the team rose again and in 1983 they finished runners-up in the league. In 1988 they took their second Bundesliga title, starting a magical period for the club under Rehhagel which saw a further league championship in 1993, German cup wins in 1991 and 1994 and victory in Europe with the European Cup Winners' Cup title in 1992.

After Rehhagel left the club in 1995, the club struggled to replace him until they decided to promote Thomas Schaaf in 1999. In his first season Werder took the German cup after beating Bayern Munich on penalties. His performance during the remaining seasons to date are of legendary status, and the double of 2003/2004 has proved to be no fluke after another top-two finish last season with Klose, Klasnic and Borowski powering the team forward. Werder are also the highest scorers in German football, as fans have seen the team score four or more goals ten times on average each season, although the loss of Klose to Bayern will be a major issue. Another 3rd place finish in 2007 was fine reward for this exciting side.

■ How to get there

The Weserstadion is located to the south east of the city centre on a reclaimed part of land next to the River Weser.

The stadium is easily reached by public transport, as well as being close to the A1 Autobahn. From the Hauptbahnhof take tram line 10 in the direction of Sebaldsbrücke and alight at Juergen Strasse, or take line 3 in the direction of Weser. The journey should take less than 10 minutes and is free for match ticket holders.

■ Getting a ticket

Last season Werder sold out a number of matches, including the games versus Hertha Berlin, Bayern Munich and Hamburg, but the average attendance was around 39,500 meaning that for matches against the majority of opposition tickets are available. Tickets can be purchased from the stadium on match days, as well online at http://www.werder.de. Tickets range in price from €11 behind the goals to €29 in the upper tiers close to the halfway line. Ticket prices tend to be 10% higher for Champions League matches.

■ Nearest airport – Bremen Airport (BRE)

Bremen Airport is located 3½ kilometres from the city centre. From the airport you need to catch tram number 6 which runs from outside the departures area direct to the central station every 10 minutes. A single ticket costs €1.95 and takes just over 15 minutes. A taxi should cost around €10. **Easyjet** currently fly daily to Bremen from London Luton and **Ryanair** from London Stansted.

The Facts

Name: RheinEnergie Stadion
Address: Postfach 45,
Cologne,
Germany
Capacity: 50,374 including 41,206 seats
Opened: 16th September 1923

■ About RheinEnergie Stadion

The RheinEnergie Stadion, once better known as the Müngersdorfer Stadion, is a 54,000-capacity ground complete with running track, stands set back from the pitch and huge banks of terracing behind each goal. When it was opened in 1975 it was the only completely covered stadium in the country.

The decision to redevelop the stadium was made by the city council in June 2000, and construction started a year later. As with the majority of the other stadiums used in the 2006 World Cup, 1.FC Köln continued to play home games at the ground whilst redevelopment took place. The running track was removed, along with the distant stands behind the goals. In its place a two-tier stadium with seats close to the pitch emerged.

The stadium opened in early 2004 with a friendly played between Germany and Belgium inaugurating the new ground. Some of the original features of the ground have been retained such as the old classic German-styled

buildings to the north of the ground which are the original ticket and club offices. For Bundesliga matches, certain sections of the ground are transformed from seating into terracing, increasing the capacity to 51,000. The new ground is a complete two-tier 'box' stadium, comprising tight stands close to the pitch, and some of the most innovative lighting seen in the world, with four columns that rise from the corners of the stadium to provide both a stanchion for the roof cables, as well as a futuristic column of light. Behind each goal netting protects those in the lower tiers from wayward shots on goal. Last season the club averaged 49,000 – an occupancy rate of over 98%. Leg room is very generous and all seats offer an unobstructed view.

■ Who plays there?

FC Cologne are considered to be one of the mainstays of German football, despite only being formed in 1948. They actually won the first-ever Bundesliga in 1964, thus earning the title 1.FC (the first team), and went on to reach the semi-finals of the European Cup in 1965 before losing to Liverpool. There then followed a period of mid-table stability, punctuated only by a German cup win in 1968, until the late 1970s when a further German cup win was achieved in 1977.

The following season they added a second league title to complete only the third ever league and cup double in Bundesliga history. The season had a bizarre ending, with Cologne and Borussia Moenchengladbach level on points going into the final game separated by goal difference. In their final match, Gladbach thrashed Dortmund 12–0, and felt that they had done enough to take the title. However, Cologne were also on top form and hit St. Pauli for five to capture the league title.

The championship allowed 1.FC Cologne to take their place again with Europe's elite in the European Cup. An excellent run in 1979 saw them reach the semi-final where they lost to eventual winners Nottingham Forest. In 1986 they went one better by actually reaching a European final, when they made it to the UEFA Cup Final against Real Madrid. The Germans headed to Spain in a confident mood, but couldn't live up to expectations and suffered a 5–1 defeat. An academic second leg did restore some pride when a 2–0 victory on the night brought some respectability back to the final aggregate score. True German stars Klaus Allofs and Pierre Littbarski carried on the good work and the team finished as runners-up in both the 1989 and 1990 Bundesliga seasons.

The start of the 1990s coincided with a period of depression over the city's football team, as they slipped further and further down the league, until for the first time in their history they were relegated in 1998. Since then the team has bounced between the two divisions, although a second division championship-winning performance in 2005 capped a great first season in the new stadium, with Lukas Podolski impressing so much that he received a call into the national team for the Confederations Cup.

Unfortunately the 2005/2006 season was all too familiar to the loyal fans. A cracking start saw them sit as high as 4th early in the season before a terminal slump saw them eventually finish second from bottom. Relegation also saw the club wave goodbye to their brightest star Lukas Podolski who was tempted by the money from Bayern Munich. Luck wasn't shining on them in 2006/2007 either as they failed to build on some good mid-season form to finish in mid-table, and thus the fans have another season in the second division of the Bundesliga to look forward to in 2007/2008.

■ How to get there
The stadium is not really walkable from the city centre. Instead, jump on one of the very frequent trams on line 1 which run from Neumarkt to the south of the pedestrian zone in the city centre directly to the stadium. The trams run every 5 minutes in the build-up to matches and take 10 minutes to travel to the RheinEnergie Stadion stop.

The ground can also be reached direct from Köln Hauptbahnhof, by S-Bahn line 6 (direction Horrem) or line 13 (direction Düren) which run every 15 minutes to K-Müngersdorf/Technologiepark. When you get off at K-Müngersdorf you can either jump on one of the special stadium buses, or walk 15 minutes to the stadium down Vitalis Strasse. A taxi from the city centre should take 10 minutes and cost no more than €20.

■ Getting a ticket
Despite the tendency to yo-yo between the top two divisions during the last few years, the club sell out almost every home match. Tickets go on sale six weeks before each game via the website http://www.fc-koeln.de. You can also try to book by phone on 01805 32 56 56. Tickets for the standing terraces behind the goal start from €10 whilst €49 will get you a place in the business club seats. A good seat for the neutral is in the upper east or west stands which start from €35. Last season the club averaged nearly 49,000, despite their indifferent form.

■ Nearest airport – Köln-Bonn Airport (CGN)
Köln-Bonn Airport is located to the south east of the city, and connected directly to the city centre by the S-Bahn line 6 or 13. A single ticket costs €2. From the UK, **Germanwings** fly from London Stansted and Edinburgh, **Easyjet** from London Gatwick, Liverpool and East Midlands, and **HLX** from Birmingham and Manchester.

Signal Iduna Park – Dortmund (Germany)

The Facts

Name: Signal Iduna Park
Address: Strobelallee 50,
              44139 Dortmund,
              Germany
Capacity: 81,264, including 54,000 seats
Opened: 2nd April 1974 Dortmund v FC Schalke 04

■ About Signal Iduna Park

The Signal Iduna Park is a relatively new name for the stadium previously known as the Westfalenstadion. The stadium is the second largest club stadium in Europe, behind the Nou Camp. Whilst the stadium in Barcelona can boast around 10,000 more seats, it cannot match the intensity, passion or vocal support that the 81,000-plus Borussia Dortmund fans create. It also boasts the highest average attendance in Europe – currently at the 77,235 mark. The stadium is impressive – from the sheer size of the Kop, the largest standing area in Europe with space for over 25,000 – to the cliff-like seating around the pitch of the other stands. On a match day, when it seems every fan turns up decked out in yellow and black, the stadium is an awesome monument to Dortmund's finest. For internationals, the capacity is reduced as the Kop has to be converted into seating.

The stadium has come through considerable changes and redevelopments to reach the finished article you see today. It was originally built for the 1974 World Cup, and located next door to the Rote Erde stadion which served as Borussia's home for nearly 70 years. The original 54,000-capacity stadium was seen as one of the most modern and functional in the country at the time.

As Borussia Dortmund's fortunes changed in the late 1970s and early 1980s the need to increase capacity at the stadium became apparent. The first phase of the redevelopment work took place in the early 1990s when the east and west stands were rebuilt. This gave the capacity to over 66,000. After Dortmund became the first German club to win the Champions League in 1997, the south (Kop) and north stands were rebuilt in line with the two other stands. This gave the Westfalenstadion a capacity of over 71,000, including the 25,000 Kop stand.

Still demand outstripped supply and a final redevelopment phase took place in the early part of this century when the four corners were filled in, giving the ground a capacity of just over 81,000.

The stadium is absolutely awesome on a match day. Every seat offers an unobstructed view of the action, although the view from the seats at pitch level takes some getting used to. The stadium has plenty of food and drink outlets both inside as well as outside the stadium. For a good pre-match beer visit the old Rote Erde Stadion next door to meet some of the most fanatical Dortmund fans.

■ Who plays there?

Borussia Dortmund are today viewed as one of the most

successful German teams of the modern era.
Whilst they can certainly claim to be the best supported, their most recent history has not been very promising. A disappointing 7th-place finish in 2004/2005 was a mighty achievement based on the fact that the club suffered crippling financial problems off the pitch which almost saw it enter administration – a fate worse than death for German clubs as it would mean automatic demotion to the regional leagues. Their last major honour was the 2002 Bundesliga title, won on the last day over rivals Bayer Leverkusen and Bayern Munich. Matthias Sammer's team of stars such as Koeller, Amoroso and Ewerthon were soon up for sale as the club suffered off the field from the costs associated with redeveloping the Westfalenstadion.

Such problems were hard to conceive when the club was formed out of a Christian youth organisation in 1909. During the 1920s and 1930s the club was dominated by its neighbours and fierce local rivals FC Schalke. In fact it wasn't until 1949 that Borussia actually made it to their first championship final, although the 3–2 defeat to VfR Mannheim was not the result they had planned. In 1956 Dortmund managed to go one better by winning the championship with a 4–2 victory over Karlsruhe. A year later they retained their title with a comprehensive 4–1 victory over Hamburg. In winning their first title, Borussia entered the first-ever European Cup where, despite a shaky start when they needed a play-off to get past Spora Luxembourg, Borussia eventually reached the 3rd round before losing to Manchester United.

The next major honour that Borussia won was the 1963 German championship – famous for being the last played as an amateur championship by beating Köln 3–1, and thus securing their place in the first Bundesliga of 1963/64. The Rote Erde Stadion was redeveloped during the following season, and fans were rewarded with a first German cup win, beating Aachen 2–0. This gave Borussia entry into the 1965/66 European Cup Winners' Cup where they met holders West Ham in a close-run semi-final. A victory over the Londoners gave Dortmund the impetus to win their first European Cup after beating Liverpool 2–1 at Hampden Park.

The 1970s and early 1980s were a barren time for Borussia Dortmund, coupled with a decline in attendances at the newly redeveloped Westfalenstadion. In a time when no team could dominate the league for more than a couple of seasons at a time, Dortmund couldn't climb the ladder to success. It took until 1989 for the club to make a major final again when they beat Werder Bremen 4–1 in the German cup final. Four years later in 1993, Dortmund managed a sustained run in the UEFA Cup and reached

the final where they met Juventus. The team could not reproduce its form from previous rounds and lost 6–1 over two legs – a result that would be seen as the major motivator for when the teams would meet four years later in the Champions League Final. In 1995 the club won their first Bundesliga championship, and then repeated the feat 12 months later. This gave them opportunity to compete in the newly expanded and revamped Champions League competition. In a great run to the final, including a two-leg win over Manchester United, Sammer's team outplayed Juventus in the Olympic Stadium in Munich to win the title 3–1. The 2002 Bundesliga title was the final honour Borussia Dortmund managed to claim, before the current slide took hold.

■ How to get there

On a matchday the U-Bahn lines 45 and 46 run directly to Westfalenstadion station, located in the south east corner of the stadium. If you have tickets for the north or west stands then it may be easier alighting one stop earlier at Westfalenhallen and walking the 5 minutes or so down Strobelallee to the stadium. From the city centre at Stadtgarten then it is just three stops to Westfalenhallen and four to the stadium stop. From the Hauptbahnhof the U45 line runs direct, taking around 10 minutes. If you are coming by taxi from the city centre then allow 15 minutes and around €10 for the journey.

■ Getting a ticket

Despite the huge capacity, tickets to see Dortmund are often hard to come by. For the big games such as Bayern Munich and FC Schalke 04 tickets rarely go to a public sale, whereas most games will have a small number of general sale tickets which go on sale around three weeks before the match from the club's ticket office, or at http://www.bvb.de. Tickets range in price from €53 for a directors' box seat, to just €12 for a spot on the Kop with the hardcore Dortmund fans. A good ticket for the neutral is in the east stand wings at €32.

■ Nearest airport – Dortmund Airport (DTN)

Dortmund Airport is located 8 miles east of the city. It has one terminal that serves mainly budget carriers such as **Easyjet**, **Air Berlin** and **Whizz**, although its is only Luton's finest that currently serve Dortmund from the UK daily. The easiest way to travel into the city centre is via the special bus service to Dortmund Hauptbahnhof. The journey takes 25 minutes and costs €5 each way. The bus arrives and departs from the bus station opposite the Hauptbahnhof. A taxi is also an option – the 20-minute journey in normal traffic should cost no more than €25.

The Facts

Name: Veltins Arena
Address: Ernst-Kuzorra-Weg 1,
45891 Gelsenkirchen,
Germany
Capacity: 61,482, including 45,173 Seats
Opened: 31th August 2001 Schalke v Borussia
Dortmund

■ About Veltins Arena

The Veltins Arena is the current name for Schalke's futuristic stadium. Since it was constructed in 2001 it has been known under various names including the SchalkeArena and the AufArena. Now the club have signed a multi-year deal with the brewers Veltins to sponsor the stadium.

The stadium was recently graded by UEFA as a 5-star venue. The stadium has a retractable roof, which opens and closes in just 20 minutes – offering complete cover for all spectators. This enables them to host indoor events such as concerts and exhibitions – made easier by the ability to remove the pitch completely in one section, by lifting one of the end seating sections up slightly and sliding it out on casters. The stadium was also one of the first to eliminate the use of cash in the stadium by implementing a chip and pin card. Views are excellent from all seats, with decent leg room and a great view of the huge central TV that hangs above the centre circle.

What makes the stadium even more impressive is that Schalke actually had a perfectly good ground located next door to the Veltins Arena. The Park Stadion was their home from 1974 until 2001, built on the waste from the region's coal mines in time for the 1974 World Cup finals. The club regularly filled the 70,000-capacity stadium, but facilities were basic for the majority of fans, with huge banks of terracing exposed to the harsh Ruhr elements. The reward for the loyal fans was the construction of the Schalke Arena in 2000. However, the Park Stadion still sits idly beside the new Arena, and is now used as a venue for practice matches. Part of the old south terrace has been demolished to make way for a hotel and a conference centre, but plans have still not been drawn up to determine the fate of this old ground, that would put many other current stadiums being used in Europe to shame. The club also has half a dozen training pitches located around the stadiums which are used by the youth academy teams. The venue is renowned throughout Germany as the home of the most passionate fans, and despite their relatively recent barren past the crowd's intensity has not waned at all – last season Schalke averaged 61,341. With a total capacity of 61,524 it had a utilisation of 99.9%, easily the highest in Europe.

■ Who plays there?

Schalke were originally formed under the name of FC Westphalia in 1904, drawing its support and players from the local mining community in the Ruhr valley. In 1924 the club merged with TV Schalke 1877 to become the club as we know it today. Just four years later the club moved into its new Glückauf Kampfbahn ground and fans flocked to one of the most modern grounds at the time in Germany. However, economic conditions in Germany during the early 1930s were dire, none more so than in the Ruhr where unemployment was over 66%. The club's players were drawn from this section of society and so they felt they needed to assist them in making ends meet. The German Football Association ruled these payments excessive and classed them as professional, and suspended them from the German league. In a move of unexpected solidarity, over half of the clubs in the Oberliga threatened to strike in sympathy with Schalke's plight, and so the DFB was forced to allow the club to compete again.

In the next ten years Schalke became the most feared team in German football. They captured their first German championship in 1934, beating the seemingly invincible Nuremberg 2–1, and followed it up with further wins in 1935, 1937, 1939, 1940 and 1942. In 1939 they set the record score for the championship final when they beat Admira Vienna (Austrian teams were allowed to play as Austria had been annexed by Hitler under his Anschluss plan) 9–0. They added a German cup win to these titles in 1937 (and the first-ever double in German history), as well as being runners-up on four occasions between 1935 and 1942.

After the war the club found itself lagging behind Borussia Dortmund in the Oberliga Westphalia, and actually did not compete for any titles until 1955 when they lost the cup final to Karlsruhe. Three years later they claimed their last-ever title when they beat Hamburg 3–0. The match-fixing scandal which rocked the league in 1970 hit the club hard and almost sent them to the wall. The decision to build the new Park Stadion in 1972 for the World Cup gave the club some fresh momentum, but they couldn't translate this onto the pitch. In 1977 they came so close to winning the title when they finished 1 point behind Mönchengladbach, even after they beat a Bayern Munich team fresh from winning their third European Cup 7–0 in Munich.

As the club entered the 1990s they found themselves in the second division, struggling to break the regional monopoly held by Borussia Dortmund. Eventually promotion followed and the momentum saw them finish in the top six for the first time in years and thus gain a place in the UEFA Cup. The club at last found its feet in Europe the following season and in a close two-leg UEFA Cup Final against Inter Milan they captured their first European title. The following season it looked as if they would go all the way until they met Inter again, going down in extra-time in the final.

Two seasons followed where the club fought it out at the top with Bayern Munich and Bayer Leverkusen right up until the last day of the season. With the final whistle sounding on Schalke's 5–3 victory over Bayern's city rivals Unterhaching and Hamburg beating Munich, the celebrations started in the Schalke Arena. However, with the last kick of the season in the fourth minute of injury time, Bayern equalised in the AOL Arena and thus took the title with the slimmest of margins and left the Schalke fans with a lot of egg on their face. There was some

consolation a week later when they managed to win the German cup with a 2–0 win over Union Berlin. The following season they retained the cup after they beat Bayer Leverkusen in the final 4–2. The 2004/2005 season saw the club hanging onto Bayern Munich's coat-tails from just before Christmas, and even saw them top the league for a week in mid-March. However, Munich's reluctance to drop even so much as a single point saw them win the title by 14 points come the end of the season. Last season the club surprised everyone in German football by leading the way from early in the season – finding the kind of consistency that has been missing in the past few seasons. However, a heartbreaking defeat to rivals Dortmund in the second to last game meant that Stuttgart leap-frogged them to claim the title.

■ How to get there
There is currently only one way to reach the stadium by public transport and that is by taking the 302 tram which runs from the Hauptbahnhof to the Arena stop on Schumacher Strasse. On exiting the tram, walk across the bridge and you will be in front of the stadium's concourse. Tickets for the tram can be bought onboard, and a single journey to or from the stadium costs €1.10.

A taxi from the town centre should cost around €15 and take no more than 15 minutes.

■ Getting a ticket
As you will appreciate from a stadium where the average attendance is some 99% of the capacity, tickets are very hard to come by for neutrals. If any are available to purchase they will be put on sale a week before the game on the official website http://www.schalke04.de. You can also try emailing the club as well to plead your case. Tickets range in price from €9 for a standing place behind the goals to €51 in the Tribunes.

■ Nearest airport – Dortmund and Dusseldorf
Gelsenkirchen sits in the middle of the Ruhr valley industrial conurbation. Whilst it doesn't have an airport of its own, it is close enough to both Dortmund and Düsseldorf airports for easy access. Dortmund Airport is located 35 miles to the east of Gelsenkirchen. It has one terminal that serves mainly budget carriers including **Easyjet** from London Luton.

From Dortmund Airport, the easiest way to travel to Gelsenkirchen centre is by the special bus service to Dortmund Hauptbahnhof which takes 25 minutes and costs €5 each way and then catch the hourly S-Bahn line 2 train to Gelsenkirchen Hauptbahnhof. The train ticket will cost €3.70 each way and takes around 25 minutes.

Düsseldorf Airport is the biggest and busiest in the Rhine/Ruhr conurbation. It has its own S-Bahn railway stop, located adjacent to the terminal building, where trains run to the city centre and beyond. To reach Gelsenkirchen then you will need to travel to the latter station and catch an RE3 train. The journey should take around 40 minutes and cost €8. A taxi from the airport to the stadium will take around 35 minutes, and cost approximately €60.

The Facts

Name: HSH Nordbank Arena
Address: Sylvesterallee 7,
22525 Hamburg,
Germany
Capacity: 57,000, including 47,000 Seats
Opened: 2nd September 2000 Hamburg 4 Juventus 4

■ About HSH Nordbank Arena

The HSH Nordbank Arena is the new name for the futuristic stadium that was once called the AOL Arena. The stadium was the first of the 12 stadiums used in 2006 to be completely ready for the World Cup finals when in September 2000 Hamburg played their first ever Champions League match against Juventus.

The Volksparkstadion needed an urgent update, especially when in 1979 the ground was nearly the scene of a terrible accident after overcrowding in the home fans' end, during the championship-winning match versus Bayern Munich, led to a crush which hospitalised over 70 fans. In 1988 after further improvements had been made, the stadium hosted the semi-final of the European Championships when the host nation surprisingly lost 2–1 to a Marco Van Basten-inspired Netherlands.

Ten years later in 1998 a decision was made to completely rebuild the stadium. In just over two years, all four stands were demolished and rebuilt, as well as the

pitch being rotated 90 degrees. When the stadium was eventually completed, UEFA wasted little time in awarding it a 5-star status, thus enabling it to host Champions League and UEFA Cup finals, although this honour hasn't yet been given to the ground. Views are excellent from all stands – although the neutral may want to avoid the north stand lower tier where the hardcore fans congregate on a match day. The club has an excellent museum located at the ground which gives you access to a daily stadium tour at 5pm. The museum is open daily from 10am, although tours only run on non-match days.

■ Who plays there?

The stadium is home to HSV Hamburg who won their first championship in 1928 when they beat Hertha Berlin 5–2. However, they did not reach another major final until 1956 when they lost in their first ever German cup final 3–1 to Karlsruhe. Two championship final defeats in 1957 (to Borussia Dortmund) and 1958 (to Schalke) preceded a championship win in 1960 and then their final honour of the decade, a 1963 cup win over Dortmund led by their talisman Uwe Seeler. In 1976 a 2–0 cup final win over Kaiserslautern started a glorious ten-year period in the club's history that saw them win three Bundesliga titles, two German cups and their first European trophy. The club at last broke its European duck in 1977 when they beat Anderlecht 2–0 in Amsterdam to capture the European Cup Winners' Cup (a defeat in the 1968 final in Rotterdam to AC Milan was their only other appearance in a final to date).

The Cup Winners' Cup success in 1977 led to the club pulling off one of the transfer coups of the decade when they signed Liverpool's star striker Kevin Keegan. With 'Mighty Mouse', as he was affectionately called by the HSV fans, firing in the goals, Hamburg won their first Bundesliga title in 1979 beating Bayern Munich in their last home match to secure the title. The game nearly ended in tragedy though as overcrowding in the Hamburg end led to a serious crush on the final whistle which resulted in over 70 seriously injured fans being taken to hospital.

A year later the club finished runners up to Bayern Munich as well as reaching the European Cup final where they lost 1–0 to Nottingham Forest in Madrid. Keegan was voted European Footballer of the Year (he subsequently retained the title in 1980 as well), crowning an excellent season for the Germans. When Keegan left Hamburg to join Southampton in 1981, the club continued to build a team capable of competing with the best in Europe, led by the German powerhouse Horst Hrubesch (and even Franz Beckenbauer for a short period in 1982). Ernst Happel's team dominated the 1981/82 season and won the league again with games to spare. The team also reached the final of the UEFA Cup where surprisingly they lost over two legs 4–0 to IFK Gothenburg. In the 1982/83 season they retained their Bundesliga title on goal difference from Werder Bremen and managed to sweep all before them on their way to a European Cup Final against Juventus in Athens. In the Olympic Stadium Felix Magath's goal was enough to bring the cup back to Hamburg for the first time.

The last few seasons have been a story of underachievement in the eyes of the fans. With the redevelopment of the stadium many hoped for an improvement in fortune, but this did not happen until the end of the 2005 season when the team managed to reach the UEFA Cup via the Intertoto route. In the 2005/2006 season under the leadership of Thomas Doll the team never fell out of the top three, and were the closest challenger to eventual champions Bayern Munich right up until week 34 of the season when defeat at home to Werder Bremen allowed them to leapfrog them into the automatic Champions League spot. Last season they had to be content with a mid-table finish as the team never found the consistency required to challenge for a UEFA or Champions League spot.

■ How to get there
The only real public transport option from the city centre to the ground is to take an S3 or S21 train from Hauptbahnhof to Stellingen. On exiting the station you have a choice of either a 20-minute walk through the woods to the stadium, or catching one of the shuttle buses that drop you outside the northern gates of the stadium. Travel to and from the stadium is free to ticket holders on match days.

You can opt to get a taxi from the city centre, although the traffic around the stadium is quite bad and so you may find it easier to walk the last 10 minutes or so. A taxi to the stadium from the city centre/St Pauli area should take around 20 minutes and cost no more than €20. After the match taxis can be found outside the indoor arena on the northern plaza.

■ Getting a ticket
Last season the club averaged nearly 53,000 with a number of games sold out. But that shouldn't deter you from trying to get a ticket. As long as you plan ahead you will be able to get a ticket from the official website. Tickets normally go on sale around four weeks beforehand, and range in price from €15 to €60. If time permits, these will be posted to you in England. Online you can choose the exact seat from the virtual stadium. If you want a place in the hardcore element then head for the north lower tier, which is converted to terracing for home matches. If you are in the city, the official fanshop near Rathaus sell tickets until 24 hours before the match.

■ Nearest airport – Fuhlsbüttel Airport (HAM)
Hamburg's main airport is located 9km north of the city centre. It is linked to the city centre by the Airport City Bus which runs every 15 minutes from 6.30am and takes less than 30 minutes to reach the stop outside Hamburg Hauptbahnhof. **Germanwings** fly this route from London Stansted, supplementing the daily flights that **British Airways** and **Lufthansa** make from Gatwick and Heathrow respectively.

Ryanair fly daily from London Stansted to Lübeck Airport (LBC). This tiny airport is around 6km outside the beautiful city of Lübeck some 50km north of Hamburg. A bus runs from the airport to the main station in the city centre, as well as one that goes all the way to Hamburg's Hauptbahnhof. These buses tend to depart approximately 30 minutes after the flights arrive and cost €8 one way.

The Facts

Name: Allianz Arena
Address: Werner-Heisenberg Allee 25,
80939 Munich,
Germany
Capacity: 69,000 All Seater
Opened: 30th May 2005
1860 Munchen v 1.FC Nürnberg

■ About Allianz Arena

The Allianz Arena represents one of the biggest new stadium constructions in Europe in the past 20 years. Many people questioned the need for a new stadium, with the Olympic Stadium still perfectly functional after its original construction for the 1972 Olympics. The stadium was used for the European Cup Final in 1978, when a Trevor Francis header won Nottingham Forest the cup versus Malmö, and more recently as the final venue for the UEFA Champions League Finals in 1993 and 1997. Its capacity of 63,500 makes it an ideal venue for big games, probably the most famous in England being the 5–1 defeat of Germany that England inflicted in September 2001.

A decision was made in late 2001 to build a new stadium to be ready to be used for the opening ceremony in the 2006 World Cup finals. A number of sites were identified, and the local population had the final say with a referendum. The winning site, to the north of the city in Fröttmaning, was cleared in late 2002 and construction began in earnest in early 2003. The stadium was completed, on schedule and within budget, in April 2005, and the first match was played on the 30th May with a match between TSV 1860 Munich and their local neighbours 1. FC Nuremberg in front of a sell-out 66,000 crowd. The stadium represents the first real shared ground in Germany. The Olympic Stadium was actually used

sporadically by TSV 1860 – their fans preferring the intimate surroundings of their training ground in Grünwalder Strasse, which they used throughout the 2004/2005 season, averaging crowds of over 20,000.

Inside the stadium there are two huge screens, situated on the north and south roofs of the stadium, allowing all spectators an unobstructed view of replays, live coverage and messages. All of the seats are offered protection by the translucent roof. If you are in the upper tier, bear in mind that it is over 120 steps up onto the concourse.

The Arena operates a cash-free stadium, like Schalke and the Amsterdam Arena. The unique feature of the stadium is the amazing outside shell which is lit up at night in either blue or red for when 1860 or Bayern are playing, or white for when the national team are visiting, and is visible for miles around like a huge illuminated floating doughnut next to the Autobahn.

■ Who plays there?

Despite both FC. Bayern and TSV 1860 agreeing to enter into a partnership to run the new Allianz Arena, their histories could hardly be more different. TSV 1860 competed with Nuremberg before the Second World War for the crown of Oberliga Süd champions. However, due to bad luck and bad tactics the team only reached the championship final once, in 1931 when they lost to Hertha Berlin 3–2. The team flirted with the top teams during the next decade, and even managed a first trophy in the German cup final of 1942 by beating Schalke 2–0. It wasn't until 1964 that the team finally started to deliver the success they always promised. In that year they won the German cup for the second time by beating Eintracht Frankfurt 2–0. By winning the cup they also gained a place in Europe for the first time. After a storming run to the final of the European Cup Winners' Cup, they met West Ham United (also in their first European campaign) at Wembley Stadium. A crowd of 100,000 saw the

Allianz Arena – Munich (Germany)

Londoners win 2–0. However, the following season 1860 kept the momentum going in the Bundesliga and at last managed to secure the title by 3 points from Borussia Dortmund. And so ended the high points of TSV 1860. Since that summer's day in 1966 they have failed to win a single trophy. They flirted with relegation during the 1970s and early 1980s and then lost their professional status due to financial irregularities. It took nearly ten years for them to regain their professional status in 1991, and just three years later they returned to the Bundesliga. The club retained their top league status until 2003/2004 when relegation came on the last day of the season. In 2006/2007 they found it even harder to make strides up the league, and a mid-table place was disappointing.

The story at FC Bayern couldn't be more different than 1860s. They were amazingly overlooked at the formation of the first professional league in 1963 when the DFB chose TSV 1860 to represent the city. However, with promotion in 1966 they started building a history that few teams in Europe can match. Cup wins in 1966 and 1967 were supplemented by a European Cup Winners' Cup title by beating Rangers in Nuremberg. In 1969 they captured a domestic double, inspired by new young stars in Franz Beckenbauer, Sepp Maier and Gerd Müller, all of whom went on to star for West Germany in the 1970 World Cup in Mexico. Further league titles were taken in 1972, 1973 and 1974, allowing them to enter the European Cup. In 1974 they became the first German side to win the competition after beating Atletico Madrid 4–0 in Brussels. In 1975 as holders, they beat Leeds United in a feisty final in Paris 2–0. A hat-trick of titles was completed in 1976 when they beat St Etienne 1–0 in Glasgow.

Bayern dominated German football during the 1980s with a team that won six Bundesliga titles and three German cup victories. But European glory was just a step too far – especially after a disappointing final defeat to unfancied Aston Villa in 1982 and then again to Porto in 1987. Franz Beckenbauer returned to the club as coach in 1994, and in his first season they reached the Champions League semi-final before being beaten by Ajax. Two seasons later they captured the UEFA Cup by beating Bordeaux 5–1 on aggregate, with Jurgen Klinsmann scoring in every round of the competition. Under new coach Ottmar Hitzfeld, three titles in the last four years of the century was a great return for the team. They almost captured the ultimate prize as well – after leading Manchester United in the Champions League Final 1–0 until the 90th minute, two injury-time goals took the title to the English team. A year later Bayern managed to hold their nerve in a penalty shoot-out against Valencia to win the cup.

Dominance in the domestic league has seen Bayern fail to win the league only twice since 1998, as well as completing three domestic doubles in this time. In the 2005/2006 season they completed another domestic double, although they were pushed hard by Werder Bremen and Hamburg. However, last season their luck ran out as they could not hang onto the coat tails of Schalke, Stuttgart and Bremen, finishing fourth and thus missing out on a Champions League spot for the first time in over a decade.

■ How to get there

The Bavarian government have invested over €150 million in transport links to the stadium which means that transit times from Marienplatz are around 15 minutes on line U-6. The U-Bahn station at Fröttmaning has been upgraded to cope with the demands of the stadium. There is free travel on match days for ticket holders. The ground is a good 10-minute walk from the station – you will be able to see the impressive arena as you exit the station. If you are coming from the Hauptbahnhof then you will need to change at either Marienplatz or Sendlinger Tor. A taxi from the city centre should cost no more than €15 and should take 15 minutes.

■ Getting a ticket

Ticket availability will depend on who you want to go and see. Tickets for TSV games are available right up until kick-off either from the shop in Orlandostrasse, online at http://www.tsv1860.de or from the ticket office located in one of the canyons on the walk up from the station. All seats offer excellent unobstructed views of the action, and even if you are in the back row of the lower tier the pitch doesn't seem too far away. Ticket prices for TSV start from €10 in the converted standing section in the south stand (the north stand is sold out for season-ticket holders). Tickets for the seats are priced at €20, €25 and €30 depending on which tier you are in. You can also buy a seat in the Löwen area, which offers game by game hospitality. For just €149 per seat you get a sit down meal, drinks and a seat in one of the hospitality areas.

For Bayern games the story is completely different. Almost every game is sold out to members and season ticket holders. Any tickets that do go on sale will be via the online box office at http://www.fcbayern.t-com.de. Tickets range in price from €20 for the standing places behind the goals, to €60 for a top seat in the East or West Stand. A good bet for the neutral, and tickets that are more likely to become available, will be in the upper tier, which will cost between €25 and €35. You will find it is easier to get tickets for Champions League and German cup games as these tend not to be included in the season tickets.

■ Nearest airport – Franz J Strauss Munich (MUC)

Munich's Franz-Joseph-Strauss airport is located 25km north east of the city. S-Bahn lines S1 and S8 run direct from below Terminal 1 up to six times an hour, both stopping at Marienplatz and Hauptbahnhof. A single ticket costs €8.80. Taxis cost around €50 to the city centre. The other option is to take the Lufthansa bus that runs from bus stop 2 in the Zentrum area of the Airport. The bus runs every 20 minutes from 6.28am and takes around 40 minutes to reach Hauptbahnhof. Tickets cost €9.50 single or €15 return. The airport is well served by airlines from the UK, currently with **British Airways** from Bristol, Glasgow and Heathrow, **Easyjet** from London Stansted and **Lufthansa** from Birmingham, London City, London Heathrow and Manchester.

Gottlieb Daimler Stadion – Stuttgart (Germany)

The Facts

Name: Gottlieb Daimler Stadion
Address: Mercedesstrasse 87,
70372 Stuttgart,
Germany
Capacity: 55,896, including 51,709 Seats
Opened: 26th July 1933

■ About Gottlieb Daimler Stadion

Anyone who visited Stuttgart to watch a game ten years ago will be hard pushed to recognise the Gottlieb Daimler Stadion now. Originally built in 1933 for the German Gymnastics Festival and named the Neckar Stadium, the ground was a vast open bowl, with high banks of terracing and one covered main stand. In 1950 the stadium hosted the first German post-war international when over 103,000 crammed into the ground to watch the hosts beat Switzerland 1–0.

Very few changes took place to the ground during the next 40 years, until plans were being drawn up for the 1974 World Cup. When the tournament began in 1974 the Neckar Stadium was a splendid 70,000-capacity arena. In 1986 a few more changes took place to the stadium in time for the European Athletics Championships, including the installation of the first colour scoreboard in Germany. The stadium was given the honour of staging the 1988 European Cup Final when PSV Eindhoven beat

Benfica on penalties, as well as staging the first international match played as a unified Germany when Switzerland were beaten 4–0. In 1991 the stadium was handed the honour of hosting the 1993 World Athletics Championships which meant that the ground received its biggest upgrade to date, with a construction of a new roof over all of the stands, and the conversion of the terracing into seating. The stadium also gained its new name at this point in honour of one of the city's most famous sons.

Over the next ten years a few changes were made to the stadium to bring it in line with the criteria laid down for the 2006 World Cup. This included the construction of a second tier in the main stand and a new media centre. The increased capacity meant that the stadium was the fifth largest in the German Bundesliga. The one downside to the stadium is the presence of the athletics track which means fans are that much further away from the action, especially those seated behind the goals. From the outside the stadium looks very impressive. The white oval roof seems to be suspended by thin wires which run around the perimeter. The design of the roof means that there is no need for any pillars in the ground, thus giving all fans unobstructed views. During the 2006/2007 season Stuttgart averaged over 47,000.

■ Who plays there?

Whilst VfB Stuttgart are the current Bundesliga champions, it is only a few years ago that they sat firmly in the underachieving stakes. In fact it took a slice of luck in

Gottlieb Daimler Stadion – Stuttgart (Germany)

2002/2003 for them to finally finish runners-up to Bayern Munich with a record low points tally for 2nd place. In 2006 the team showed real consistency until the final day of the season when they dropped from 3rd in the table to 5th (and thus out of the Champions League spots) after losing to Bayern Munich.

During the period before the Second World War, the biggest team in the city was Kickers Stuttgart, who reached their one and only championship play off in 1908. In 1935 VfB reached the final, losing to Schalke 04 6–4. After the Second World War, under the French and British forces a league for the region was finally set up, when VfB won the Oberliga Süd. In 1950 the club at last claimed their first ever championship with a 2–1 victory over Kickers Offenbach. Two years later over 84,000 people saw VfB claim the title again with a win over Saarbrücken. A year later they reached the final again, this time losing to Kaiserslautern. The team claimed their first German cup win in 1954 with a victory over Cologne, and repeated the feat in 1958.

It was therefore hard to ignore the case for VfB Stuttgart to be omitted when the plans for a professional league were drawn up in 1963. Unfortunately the transition from amateur to professional did not bring success to the team in the remainder of the decade. In fact it wasn't until the mid-1980s when the name Stuttgart re-emerged as a force. A great run of form during the closing rounds of the 1983/84 season saw the team snatch the title – their first since turning professional in 1963. However, success in Europe still eluded the team after a number of campaigns. This was to change though at the end of the decade. After qualifying for the 1988/89 UEFA Cup, they made steady progress through the rounds before meeting a Maradona-inspired Napoli in the final. After a 2–1 defeat in the San Paolo stadium in Naples, expectations were high for the return leg in Stuttgart. However, whether it was the immense support that the Neapolitans brought to Stuttgart or the inspiring influence of Maradona, it was not to be as the Italians held on for a 3–3 draw to take the trophy 5–4 on aggregate.

In 1992 the club won the Bundesliga for the second time and qualified for the new, revamped Champions League. In the first round they met Leeds United. Under the management of Christoph Daum, the team had a real attacking flair and they took a deserved 3–0 lead from the home leg. Back at Elland Road the team crumbled and lost 4–1, but that single away goal proved to be decisive. Or so Stuttgart thought. Leeds discovered that Daum had actually used a fourth foreign player during the match – which at the time was not allowed – and so UEFA were called in to act. In a decision that showed leniency towards the Germans, UEFA declared the game should be replayed. The game was to be played in the Nou Camp in Barcelona, again much to Leeds' chagrin. However, Leeds need not have worried as they ran out 2–1 winners.

Felix Magath was brought in during the 2001/2002 season to try and make Stuttgart a real challenger to the dominance of Bayern Munich. In his first full season the club finished 2nd in the league, their best finish since 1992. A 4th place finish the following season saw Magath's credentials underlined and so it was no surprise that Bayern Munich came knocking to offer him the top position in German domestic football. However, it is 2006/2007 that will be remembered by the fans for a long time, as the club sneaked up on the rails to pip Schalke for the title on the last day of the season. The turning point was in mid-March when the team lost to Schalke. They then went on a run of eight consecutive victories, and coupled with Schalke's defeat at Dortmund, they took the title on the last day of the season.

■ How to get there
The most direct routes to the station are the U-Bahn line 11 to Gottlieb Daimler Stadion, or the S-Bahn lines 1, 2 or 3 to the station of the same name. If you use the S-Bahn from Hauptbahnhof then you need to catch a train in the direction of Esslingen. The journey time for S-Bahn from central station is around 10 minutes. There is also a special match day U-Bahn 16 service that runs direct to the stadium. If you are coming via U-Bahn line 11 then just carry on walking in the direction of travel as you leave the train on Mercedesstrasse. The ground is a 5-minute walk from the U-Bahn station.

■ Getting a ticket
Whilst Stuttgart are considered the third biggest club in Germany, with a large stadium to match, it can often be quite tricky to get a ticket for the Gottlieb Daimler Stadion. Tickets go on sale around three weeks before the game from the ticket shop on Mercedesstrasse – a 5-minute walk south of the stadium. Tickets are also sold around the city in places such as City Music, Easy Ticket and Event Bureaux. Tickets range from €18 for a place in the Kurve with the hardcore fans, to €45 in the Haupttribune. The best seats for the neutrals are in the EnBW Tribune and cost €33. Details can be found on the official site – http://www.vfb-stuttgart.de.

■ Nearest airport – Stuttgart Echterdingen (STR)
Stuttgart's Echterdingen Airport is located 15km south of the city centre. It is linked to the city by the S-Bahn network with both the S2 and S3 lines running direct from the main station to the airport every 10 to 15 minutes. There is also an hourly bus (the X3) that runs from Pfullingen. A taxi to the city centre should cost around €25 and take around 20 minutes. Currently the airport is served by a number of traditional airlines from the UK including **British Airways** from Birmingham, Heathrow and Manchester, **BMI** from Heathrow and occasionally **Hapag Lloyd** from Birmingham, although only **Germanwings** currently fly the budget airline flag from London Stansted.

The Facts

Name: Olympic Stadium
Address: 37 Kifissias Avenue,
             151 23 Maroussi, Athens,
             Greece
Capacity: 72,000 All Seater
Opened: 6th September 1982 Olympiakos v Osters

■ About Olympic Stadium

The Olympic, or the Spiros Louis Stadium to give its full name, proudly hosted the 2007 European Champions League Final, just three years after successfully hosting the Summer Olympics. However, events in Athens in May when Liverpool took on AC Milan did not reflect well for the stadium as security inadequacies led to a number of issues on the night when thousands of ticketless fans were able to access the stadium. The stadium is named after Spiridon Louise who was the winner of the first modern-day Olympic marathon in Athens in 1896. The stadium was originally opened in 1982 for the European Athletics Championships, as well as the 1983 European Cup Final when Hamburg beat Juventus 1–0. Originally it could hold over 74,000 and was often used for the big Athens derbies between Olympiakos, Panathinaikos and AEK – in fact the biggest-ever attendance at the stadium was for a derby between Panathinaikos and AEK when over 74,470 attended. In 1987 it hosted the European Cup Winners'

Cup Final when Ajax beat Lokomotiv Leipzig. The stadium was regularly used by the Athens teams for their home matches during the 1980s, although facilities were basic and the lack of a roof meant that watching games during the hotter months became very uncomfortable. It was also chosen to host the 1994 Champions League Final when a rampant AC Milan featuring Gullit, Rijkaard and Van Basten destroyed Barcelona 4–0.

In the late 1990s a decision was made to award the 2004 games to Athens, and so work started on planning a complete redesign of the stadium – including a roof to be designed by Santiago Calatrava, who had previously designed the Montjuic tower in Barcelona. The work would also see the redevelopment of the seats, although the poor sightlines especially in the lower tiers would not be addressed. In one of the longest ongoing sagas in modern stadium design, the stadium was completed on the 30th July 2004 – just two weeks before the opening ceremony for the Olympic games. The stadium also hosted the Olympics football final between Argentina and Paraguay, as well as the closing ceremony. The stadium hosted its first Champions League match in September 2005 when Panathinaikos played Werder Bremen.

■ Who plays there?

Whilst the stadium has hosted a number of big games, in recent years it has sparodically hosted league games for AEK Athens and Panathaikos, and the very occasional national team friendly, as they prefer the more intimate atmosphere of the Georgios Karaiskakis Stadium. Last season Panathinaikos and AEK Athens used the stadium for Champions League matches.

■ How to get there
The stadium is best reached by Athens' very efficient metro system. The nearest station to the stadium is Irini which is on the Green Line 1 north of the city centre. Plans are under way for a new line which will run in a loop through the city centre at Evangelismos and Panepistimio to a new stadium – named the Olimpiako Stadio. Bus lines A7 and 550 run from the city centre to the stadium at regular intervals. If you are coming direct from Eleftherios Venizelos airport then catch the regular train link to Doukissis Plakentias which is at the end of Blue Line 3. Instead of catching the metro, follow signs for the

overground line that runs to Larissa Station. The first stop on this service is Neratziotissa, which is just one stop north of Irini on the Green Line 1.

■ Getting a ticket
Availability of tickets will depend on the event. Tickets for the Champions League games featuring Panathinaikos and AEK Athens go on sale via their official websites at the start of the qualifying group stages. For AEK Athens games refer to http://www.aekfc.gr, and for Panathinaikos matches go to http://www.poa.gr. Tickets can also be purchase from the club stores in the city centre – including the main one at the old Panathinaikos stadium in Tsoha Street. Ticket prices start from €10, although these seats are in the upper tiers behind the goal, along way from the action.

The Facts

Name: Karaiskaki Stadium
Address: Alexandra Square,
18534 Piraeus, Athens,
Greece
Capacity: 33,300 All Seater
Opened: 6th June 2004

■ About Karaiskaki Stadium

The Karaiskaki Stadium is the newest football stadium in Greece, and opened in time for the 2004 Summer Olympics where it hosted a number of games in the tournament, including one of the semi-finals. The stadium was completely rebuilt for the tournament – it was originally opened as a velodrome for the 1896 Olympic Games. Technically the stadium is in the port town of Piraeus, some 10km south of Athens. It is within a stone's throw of the waterfront and is home to one of the most passionate teams in European football. The ground is very much in the mould of a British stadium – almost identical in fact to the stadium at Leicester City and Swansea City with a complete bowl of four identical stands. Views from all seats are excellent, and leg room is very generous. The provision of a roof over all the seats is also a welcome bonus on those hot Greek late summer afternoons. The stadium is actually named after the Greek hero from the War of Independence who was mortally wounded in the vicinity of the stadium in 1827. However, the stadium is also known for the worst-ever stadium disaster in Greek history when on the 8th February 1981 at the end of the game between Olympiakos and AEK Athens a crush developed at gate 7 where a locked gate led to the deaths of 21 Olympiakos fans who attempted to re-enter the stadium when a late goal was scored. Today, a monument to those who fell can be found outside gate 7 of the new stadium. More details of the fateful events can be found at the Olympiakos museum at the stadium, which is open daily (except Mondays) from 10am and costs €4 to enter.

■ Who plays there?

The Karaiskaki Stadium is home to Greece's most successful team, Olympiakos. Originally formed as a sports society in 1925, the club were an amalgamation of a number of local sporting teams. The club won the first of 34 championships in 1931, and during the next 30 years won the title on 15 occasions, as well as nine national cup finals. However, their run of success did not continue into the 1960s as their rivals AEK Athens and Panathinaikos shared the glory. The club could not cope with this competition so close to home and so they appointed best young coach in the country, Lakis Petropouluos, who built a team to compete both domestically and internationally. In 1973 they won the title again, following it up with successive titles in 1974 and 1975. A brief hiatus saw no further cups come home until 1980 when they won the title in the next four consecutive season. Unfortunately things off the pitch were a problem – new Chairman George Koskotas took the club into serious debt and there was a strong chance the club would go under. After the title in 1986, the club then went nine long years during which they won nothing, and the famous red and white shirts disappeared from European competition, apart from a solitary season in 1992/93 when they reached the quarter-finals of the European Cup Winners' Cup.

In 1996 the club started a rebuilding process and actually won the next seven championships at a relative canter. This run came to an end with a 2nd-place finish to AEK in 2003. The following season they pulled off one of the transfer coups of the season by persuading Rivaldo to join the club. In his first season the club won the domestic double, and repeated the feat the following season. Champions League football thus returned to the town of Piraeus and with a new stadium now full to busting the team played to their full extent in a group containing Liverpool, Monaco and Deportivo La Coruna. In a group where all teams had a chance of qualifying going into the last game, the Greeks suffered heartache as Steven Gerrard's late goal at Anfield pushed them into the UEFA Cup instead of the second round of the Champions League. In the 2006/2007 season the club finished in a disappointing last spot in a group containing Valencia, Roma and Shakhtar Donetsk. However, with the title again in the bag by early April the team must invest in some new stars to replace the likes of Rivaldo, who has departed for city rivals AEK, and to make an impression in Europe. The stadium is also a favoured venue for the national team, where the intimate atmosphere is often seen a twelfth man.

■ How to get there
The stadium is located in the port of Piraeus, 10km south of Athens. The easiest way to reach the stadium from the city centre is via the metro. The nearest station to the stadium is at Faliro – a 5-minute walk from the metro, with the stadium being visible from the exit of the station. Faliro is on the Green Line 1, two stops from the southern terminus at Piraeus.

■ Getting a ticket
Olympiakos are the best-supported team in Greece – attracting an average attendance of over 21,000. However, with a capacity of over 33,000, getting a ticket for most games is not a problem. In the past the games against AEK and Panathinaikos have tended to sell out, although in the past season or so even these have been sold up to the day of the game. In terms of Champions League matches, the availability of tickets will depend on the opponents. In recent seasons games against Real Madrid and Liverpool have sold out in advance. Tickets for all games can be purchased from the website, although this is in Greek. Ticket prices start from €12 for a place behind the goals to €50 in the VIP section. Tickets for Greek national games are sold via the Greek FA website at http://www.epo.gr.

■ Nearest airport – Eleftherios Venizelos (ATH)
Athens's brand new airport opened its runways on the 29th March 2001, and is named after the former Prime Minister of Greece who fought against the Ottoman occupation of Crete in 1896. To get to the city centre you can either use the Athens metro – Line 3 runs direct from the airport – or the Proastiakos suburban rail service. Alternatively buses E92, E93, E95 and E97 also run around the clock to the city centre. Currently the airport is serviced by **British Airways** from London Heathrow, **Easyjet** from London Gatwick and London Luton, **Excel** from London Gatwick and **Olympic** from London Gatwick and Heathrow.

The Facts

Name: Laugardalsvöllur
Address: Laugardal,
             104 Reykjavik,
             Iceland
Capacity: 14,000 All Seater
Opened: 1958

■ About Laugardalsvöllur

The Laugardalsvöllur sits proudly in one of the greenest parts of the city and is part of the complex that includes the botanical gardens, a small zoo and a huge outdoor swimming pool and thermal baths. The stadium was originally opened in the 1950s as home to the national team, and over the course of the past five decades it has been modernised, cumulating in the current version with two smart all-seater stands that run down the side of the pitch. At each end temporary seating is erected for major national games. As the stadium is multi-purpose and doubles up as the national athletics stadium there is a running track around the pitch which means that views from some parts are not good. Also, in the winter when darkness seems to be a permanent feature of the city, the stadium can be very cold, with the wind whipping in from the west.

■ Who plays there?

The stadium is used by a number of teams in the city including KR, Throttur, Fram, and of course the national team. KR have always been considered the first team of Reykjavik, as well as the country as a whole. They were originally formed in 1899, and went on to win the first Icelandic championship in 1912. As a mark of respect to the English influence on the team, they chose to adopt the black and white of Newcastle United, who had won the English First Division in 1912.

The team have won the premier league championship on 24 occasions, the last being in 2003. The club were also the first Icelandic team to take part in European competition when they drew Liverpool in the 1964/65 European Cup. However, an 11–1 aggregate defeat showed the difference in class between the teams. These two games, though, gave the team a taste for European nights and they have regularly returned to European competition. Some highs and lows of their European campaigns include a 16–2 defeat to Feyenoord in the 1965 European Cup Winners' Cup, a 10–0 away defeat to Aberdeen in 1967 and a 7–0 defeat over two legs to QPR in the 1984 UEFA Cup. On the plus side they recorded their first-ever win away from home in 1997 when they beat Dinamo Bucharest 4–1 on aggregate and Slavia Prague the following year.

Fram are today one of the smaller clubs in Reykjavik despite their glorious past and currently play in the second division of Icelandic football after relegation last season. They have started the season on top form and should return to the top division at the end of this season. The club were formed in 1908 and have played in the top flight for much of their history. They have won the Icelandic title on 18 occasions, including an amazing run from 1913 when they won the title ten times in 12 years. In more recent times they took the title in 1986, 1988 and 1990. They have also won the Icelandic cup on seven occasions, including four times in the 1980s.

One of the biggest games in their history came in 1998 when they drew Barcelona in the first round of the European Cup Winners' Cup. In front of a sell-out crowd at the national stadium, the minnows restricted the score to just 2–0. In the second leg in Spain they conceded five and despite losing 7–0 on aggregate they won many friends in Spain. Two years later they won in Europe for the first time in five years, beating the Swedish cup holders Djurgarden 4–1 on aggregate before meeting Barcelona again. With a place in the quarter-finals at

Laugardalsvöllur – Reykjavik (Iceland)

stake, the Icelandic team managed to equalise at one point in the home leg before losing 5–1 after 180 minutes.

■ How to get there
The stadium is a 20-minute walk from the centre of Reykjavik. The easiest way to reach the stadium is to follow the main shopping street, Laugavegur, eastwards, across the main roads of Noatún and Kringlumyrabraut and up the hill. When you reach the junction with Reykjavegur you will see the stadium ahead of you down the hill. A taxi from the city centre will cost around £10.

■ Getting a ticket
Unless there is a big team in town then tickets for any game at the national stadium are available up until kick-off. The last sell-out was for a game versus Italy in 2004 when the attendance was 20,204. Tickets for national team games can be purchased in advance from the website http://www.ksi.is. For a domestic league game

expect to pay no more than 1000ISK for a seat in the main stand.

■ Nearest airport – Keflavik Airport (KVL)
To maximise your budget when coming to Iceland you should use the excellent daily service offered by **Iceland Express** from London Stansted. Keflavik sits on a very flat, moon-like peninsula in the south-west corner of the island. For miles around there is nothing – in fact the 40-minute drive into Reykjavik is probably as close to isolation as you will see in Europe. The island is also served by the national carrier **Icelandair** but expect to pay top dollar for these return flights. The airport is served by a regular bus service into central Reykjavik, run by **Icelandair**, which stops at most of the big hotels in the town centre. The bus journey costs 1000ISK. A taxi will cost 8,000ISK maximum.

The Facts

Name: Stadio Artemio Franchi
Address: Viale Manfredo Fanti 4,
50137 Firenze,
Italy
Capacity: 47,300 All Seater
Opened: 13th September 1931 – Fiorentina v AK Wien

■ About Stadio Artemio Franchi

When the Tuscan sun shines on a lazy Sunday afternoon, there can be few better places to watch football than in the uncovered seats of the Artemio Franchi. Originally built in 1931 by Pier Luigi Nervi who is perhaps more famous for the design of the Nervi hall in the Vatican, the stadium is built entirely of reinforced concrete with a 70 metre tall tower opposite the main stand, called the Tower of Marathon. The stadium was originally called the Stadio Comunale, but was renamed after Fiorentina's president Franchi in 1991.

The stadium is quite strange in design with two single-tier stands that run the length of the pitch, but the stands behind the goal where the Ultras are located are set back in a curve, meaning the views from here low down are not ideal. The main stand, the Preferencia, is covered, whilst the rest of the stadium is exposed to the elements. The stadium hosted three group games in the 1990 World Cup finals as well as the infamous quarter-final tie between a Maradona-inspired Argentina and Yugoslavia. The Florence hardcore fans are located in the Curva Fiesole.

■ Who plays there?

No team can claim to have a more turbulent recent history than Fiorentina (or 'Viola'). Forced to begin again at the lowest level of Italian professional football in the early part of the 2000s, the club managed to climb their way up the pyramid structure, finishing in a Champions League spot at the end of the 2006 season, only to find themselves relegated due to the match-fixing investigation during the summer of 2006. The gods must have been smiling on them though as on appeal the FIGC decided to reinstate the Tuscans albeit with a points penalty, and relegate their arch rivals Juventus.

The original club were formed in 1909, adopting the purple kit from the city's coat of arms. For the first 30 years in their history the club slowly rose up the divisions until they reached the top division in the 1930s. The 'purple' period in the club's history started in 1956 when the team won their first Serie A title, and qualified for the European Cup. After an impressive run to the final, including victories over Grasshoppers and Red Star Belgrade, the Tuscans met Real Madrid, losing 2–0. Another Italian Cup came in 1960, and their subsequent European adventure went one better than in 1957 when they beat Glasgow Rangers over two legs in the inaugural European Cup Winners' Cup Final.

During the 1960s the club won the Coppa Italia and the Serie A title again in 1969, although this was to be their last league championship. In the early 1990s, after another couple of cup final victories, the club were relegated to Serie B. At the time the team revolved around Argentinian legend Gabriele Batistuta, who scored an average 25 goals a season. Batistuta stood by the club after relegation and helped them bounce straight back up. After winning the Coppa Italia in 2000 things looked rosy for the club. Less than 12 months later owner Vittorio Cecchi Gori's business empire collapsed, forcing the team into administration, and essentially bankrupting the club. The following season they had to reform as Florentia Viola in league C2. After winning that league in 2003 with ease,

Stadio Artemio Franchi – Florence (Italy)

the Italian Football Federation somehow decided to promote them directly into Serie B, and also allowed them to buy back their name. At the end of the 2004 season they finished in 6th place and qualified for a promotion play off with Perugia who had finished 15th in Serie A. A 2–1 aggregate win was enough to complete an amazing return back to the big time for the club, only for the events at the end of the 2006 season to once again put them back in trouble. So the team started 2006/2007 with a mountain to climb, but with quality up front in Luca Toni and Adrian Mutu nothing was impossible. In fact the team managed to find safety from relegation before the Ides of March, and a UEFA Cup spot was secured with a final 6th-place finish. However, the club will have to do without the services of Luca Toni in 2007/2008 after he agreed a big-money move to Bayern Munich.

■ How to get there
The stadium is located out to the east of the city centre, a 20-minute walk from the historic central area. There is a very convenient train station, Campo di Marte, located a 5-minute walk away from the ground. Trains run on a match day from the central Santa Maria Novella station four times an hour. Alternatively bus number 17 runs from the central station every 15 minutes on match days.

■ Getting a ticket
Tickets for most games go on sale from the ground (counter 16 at the stadium) from ten days before the game as well as from a couple of local bars – including Stadio in Via de Manfredo Fanti. It is essential to produce ID when ordering. The club's website http://www.acffiorentina.it allows you to buy tickets online, which can then be collected from one of the booths on the north side of the stadium on a match day. Ticket prices range from an astronomical €130 for a seat in the covered Tribuna D'Onore to €18 in the Curva Ferrovia. A good bet for the neutral is a seat on the open Maratona Laterale, which costs €28.

■ Nearest airport – Amerigo Vespucci (FLR)
The small and compact Amerigo Vespucci airport is located 4km to the north of the centre of Florence. A taxi from the airport takes around 15 minutes and costs €15. A regular bus service runs between the airport and the Santa Maria Novella railway station. The only airline that uses this small airport from the UK is **Meridinia** who fly daily from London Gatwick.

■ Alternative airport – Galileo Galilei Pisa (PSA)
Pisa is one of **Ryanair**'s European hubs, with flights daily to London Stansted, Dublin, Eindhoven, Hamburg and Frankfurt Hahn, amongst others. The airport is located 1$\frac{1}{2}$km from the city centre and has its own train station that offers services through to Florence. If you cannot get a train, then there is a regular city bus route 1 runs every 20 minutes to the main station.

Stadio Luigi Ferraris – Genoa (Italy)

The Facts

Name: Stadio Luigi Ferraris
Address: Via De Pra 1,
               Genova,
               Italy
Capacity: 40,197 All Seater
Opened: 12th December 1933

■ About Stadio Luigi Ferraris

The Luigi Ferraris is one of the most recognisable stadiums in Europe as well as being one of the most intimidating. The ground has been the home to Genoa since 1911, and to Sampdoria since they were formed in 1946.

When the old stadium originally opened in 1911, it had a capacity of just 20,000 and was a very simple affair. It was rebuilt completely in the 1930s and was one of the venues used in the 1934 World Cup – hosting a 30,000 sell-out game between France and Brazil. The stadium had further work completed in 1945 to 1948, and as a result crowds close to 60,000 were often seen in the stadium.

When the decision was made to host the World Cup in Italy in 1990 the stadium was completely demolished again and rebuilt in the style of an English ground with stands close to the pitch, and the four distinctive corner towers. In the 1990 finals the stadium hosted games between Scotland, Sweden and Costa Rica as well as the second round game between the Republic of Ireland and Romania. Since both teams were relegated to Serie B in the 1990s, crowds waned, but since returning to Serie A Sampdoria have averaged nearly 20,000 and Genoa around 18,000. Views from the side stands are excellent, although there is a screen that runs around the perimeter of the pitch that does hamper the view in the lower tier.

■ Who plays there?

The Luigi Ferraris is home to two clubs – UC Sampdoria and FC Genoa. Sampdoria's enforced absence from Serie A for four years has now been consigned to the history books, and they are firmly back amongst the top teams in Italy. In the last few seasons they have reacquainted themselves with European football with a place in the UEFA Cup. Sampdoria are actually quite new on the block, having only been formed in 1946 when the Sampierdarenese and Andrea Doria clubs merged. The club then started working its way up the leagues and reached Serie A for the first time in the 1980s. They won their first trophy in 1985 when they captured the Coppa Italia, repeating the feat in 1988 and 1989.

In 1990 the team had their best run in Europe when they made it to the European Cup Winners' Cup Final, beating Dortmund, Grasshoppers and Monaco on the way to a 2–0 victory over Anderlecht. The following season, the club captured their first (and only) Scudetto, with players like Attilio Lombardo, Roberto Mancini and Gianluca Vialli playing a major part in the success. The title also gave them the opportunity to compete in the European Cup for the first time. They found themselves in a group with Anderlecht, Panathinaikos and Red Star Belgrade. The group went to the wire with a winner-takes-all game versus Red Star in Belgrade which the Italians won 3–1 to make the final at Wembley versus Barcelona. In a hard-fought game that went to extra-time, victory was clinched by a stunning free-kick from Ronald Koeman to take the cup back to Spain.

In 1992 Sven Goran Eriksson joined as coach and immediately made some changes to the squad, bringing in players like David Platt, Ruud Gullit and Walter Zenga as he hoped to retain the Scudetto. Unfortunately the money from Milan and Turin ensured that the title wouldn't leave those cities for many years, and the star of Sampdoria started to fade. English players came and went though with regularity, including such well-known names as Des Walker, Lee Sharpe and Daniele Dichio, but success eluded the team. In 1994 they did win their last trophy, the Coppa Italia, for the fourth time. At the turn of the century the team were relegated back to Serie B and only returned to the top division in 2004.

Genoa FC were formed in September 1893, thus making them one of the oldest teams in Italy. In 1898 they played their first game of football versus the crew of HMS Revenge, and just 12 months later they became the first champions of Italian football, repeating the feat in 1900. In the early years of the 20th century they adopted their famous red and blue halved shirts, earning them the nickname Rossoblu. The club continued its dominance of Italian football with four further championships as well as a Coppa Italia in 1937, which was to be their last major domestic honour. The next 50 years were a dark period for the club as they suffered frequent drops into Serie B, and even as low as Serie C in the early 1970s.

The good times seem to have returned in the early years of the 1990s as they were promoted back to Serie A, and even managed a 4th place finish in 1991. The following season they fared well in the UEFA Cup, their first European adventure for many years. Fired on by the goals of Tomas Skuhravy, the club reached the semi-finals of the UEFA Cup, where they lost 4–3 on aggregate to Ajax. On the way to the semi-final they beat Dinamo Bucharest, Boavista, Steaua Bucharest and an impressive 4–1 aggregate victory over Liverpool. In 1996 the team won their only European title, capturing the last-ever Anglo-Italian cup by beating Port Vale at Wembley on their return to Serie B. It took the club two owners, and ten years, to reach the top of Serie B when the club won the second tier in 2005. Unfortunately the joy of promotion soon turned to despair as the club were found guilty of match-fixing in a game versus Venezia and were relegated to Serie C. The club were forced to take their position in the third tier of Italian football in 2005/2006 but did manage to make the end of season play-offs where a 2–1 victory over Monza secured their place back in Serie B. Twelve months later they went one better, securing promotion to Serie A at last.

■ How to get there
The stadium is located to the north east of the city centre, just a 1km walk from Stazione Brignole. On a match day special buses run from the station to the ground, although it is often quicker to walk, following the river bed up to the ground.

■ Getting a ticket
Tickets for matches go on sale around ten days before the matches in a number of outlets throughout the city including Sampdoria Point in Via Cesarea, as well as at the stadium itself. The website http://www.listicket.it also sells them online. On a match day, tickets are on sale up until kick-off from the ticket offices just to the south of the stadium in Via A. De Stefanis. Tickets for Genoa matches cost €30 for a Tribuna Superior ticket, and €14 for a Gradinata Sud ticket. Tickets for Sampdoria matches are more expensive at €20 to €40.

■ Nearest airport – Christopher Columbus (GOA)
Ryanair make the regular journey from London Stansted to Genoa. The airport is also served by **British Airways** and **XL.com Airlines** daily from London Gatwick. From the airport the easiest way into the city centre is to use one of the half hourly buses that run to both Stazione Principe and Brignole. Tickets cost €3.

The Facts

Name: San Siro – Stadio Giuseppe Meaza
Address: Via Piccolomini 5,
20151 Milan,
Italy
Capacity: 85,700 All Seater
Opened: 19th September 1926 –
AC Milan 3 Inter Milan 6

■ About San Siro

Without doubt one of the cathedrals of world football, the San Siro is a magnificent sight when it is full on a match day. The stadium was originally built between August 1925 and September 1926. The first game played in the stadium was actually a Milan derby, with Inter winning 6–3 in front of a capacity crowd of 35,000. Ten years later a second tier was added through funding from the local government, taking the capacity to 60,000. In 1980 the stadium was renamed after the Inter Milan legend Guiseppe Meazza. The stadium then went through a massive upgrade in time for the opening game of the 1990 World Cup finals; the result being an all-seater stadium capable of holding 85,700. The views from most of the seats are magnificent. The stands rise steeply from the pitch, and unlike a number of other big stadiums in Italy, there is no running track. The seats in the lower tier are not the best, with glass screens providing a barrier between the crowd and the players. The middle tier is where the Tifosi are located – to the north end for AC and south end for Inter. All of the seats in the standard areas are the bucket types, with no backs, making them uncomfortable for long periods of time.

However, the atmosphere on a match day builds from hours before kick-off. The fans spend weeks rehearsing their 'presentations' and it is almost a crime to roll up to your seat five minutes before kick-off and miss their wonderful efforts. In Italy, as with a number of other countries in Europe, firecrackers and flares are commonplace. The stadium also has an excellent museum and daily tour that takes place on non-match days from Gate 21 from 10am to 5pm.

■ Who plays there?

The San Siro is home to both Milan clubs, and despite the fierce rivalry between the clubs, the arrangement works very well indeed. In 1899 Alfred Edwards founded the club on some very British traditions, one of which was the actual name – the club were called, and still are today, Milan instead of the Italian Milano. The club entered the national leagues in 1901 and were soon challenging the domination of Genoa, winning the league in that first season as well as in 1906 and 1907.

The following year the club were split on the policy of signing foreign talent, and a number of the players decided to form their own team – which is now known as Internazionale. The pre-war domination of Italian football by the clubs from Turin was beginning to make the league very predictable, but after the Superga disaster, Milan, amongst others, saw an opportunity. In 1950s they embarked on a magnificent few seasons, winning the title in 1951, 1955, 1957 and 1958 as well as a couple of Italian cup victories.

The club became the first Italian team to win a major European trophy when they defeated Benfica in the European Cup Final in 1963. They followed up this success with a European Cup Winners' Cup victory in 1964 and another European Cup title in 1969. They captured their tenth title in 1979, and won the right to wear the star over the badge. Nobody could have foretold what would happen though just 12 months later. The club were dumped out of the European Cup in the first round by Porto, and after a disappointing league campaign, news broke that the club had been heavily implicated in a betting scandal. Their penalty was relegation from Serie A, along with SS Lazio.

Despite coming back up in 1983 the club was floundering. Lifelong fan and media mogul Silvio Berlusconi saw an opportunity to revive the club and took control in February 1986, to start the golden period of Milan. Within 12 months gone were players like Liam Brady, Ray Wilkins and Luther Blissett, and instead new coach Arrigo Sacchi had assembled a team featuring Marco Van Basten, Frank Rijkaard and Ruud Gullit as well as home-grown talent such as Carlo Ancelotti. The title returned in 1988, and the following season they won their third European Cup with a 4–0 victory over Steaua Bucharest. Twelve months later they retained their trophy in Vienna with a 1–0 win over Benfica. In 1992, they responded to the President's call for domination with back-to-back championships in 1992, 1993 and 1994, as well as three consecutive Champions League Final appearances.

The 4–0 demolition of Barcelona in Athens is considered by many as the most complete ever final performance. In 2003, under the control of former player Carlo Ancelotti, they reached the Champions League Final where they met Juventus in Manchester. In one of the most predictable, dull, scoreless draws ever seen, Milan took the trophy on penalties.

The following season the club recruited young Brazilian Kaka, as well as seasoned defenders Cafu and Jaap Stam. The difference was amazing as the team swept all before them to win the Scudetto with weeks to spare. Twelve months later they led 3–0 at half-time in Istanbul versus Liverpool in the Champions League Final. The subsequent 45 minutes are the stuff of legend as the team then conceded three goals to Liverpool and went on to lose on penalties. In 2005/2006 Juventus again proved too strong for Milan, and Ancelotti's team had to make do with 2nd place. They also reached the semi-final of the Champions League.

A 1–0 defeat on aggregate was a bitter pill to swallow, but not as bad as the next few weeks when it became clear that the club were heavily implicated in the match-fixing court case. Initially the club were found guilty and relegated. However, on appeal they were reinstated into Serie A with an eight-point penalty, and still allowed to compete in the Champions League. This in the end caused significant controversy as the team went on to beat Liverpool in Athens to win the trophy again.

Inter are currently the reigning champions of Italy, setting the pace since day one in 2006/2007 – including an amazing run of 19 straight victories. In 2006 the title was handed to them after the match-fixing scandal that saw Juventus stripped of the title and relegated, and Milan docked 30 points. Last season they took advantage of the absence of Juventus, and Milan's and Lazio's points penalties, to lead from the front, dropping just 6 points for their first 13 games and eventually winning the league with a record 97 points, and just one defeat.

The club were founded in 1908. Two years later they won the Scudetto for the first time, taking the title off Milan. The club achieved a second title in 1920, before entering a period best forgotten in their history in the 1930s when Benito Mussolini made the club change its name to Ambrosiana-Inter to rid themselves of the communist-style Internazionale name. Between 1930 and 1942 the club played under this name and they won the championship on three occasions, as well as a Coppa Italia. After they were able to shed their Ambrosiana, Inter went back to winning ways with back-to-back championships in 1953 and 1954. The 1960s came and the club started slowly but in 1963 they captured their eleventh title. The following season they beat Real Madrid in the European Cup Final, repeating the feat 12 months later on home soil versus Benfica. They also won two further championships in 1965 and 1966. The 1970s were a tough period for the club. They were runners-up in the 1972 European Cup Final to Ajax but failed to add to their Scudetos, apart from one in 1980. A couple of Coppa Italia titles were scant reward for a demanding crowd. In 1989 the club regrouped and brought in foreign imports such as Jürgen Klinsmann and Lothar Matthäus.

■ How to get there
The stadium is located to the west of the city centre, close to the outer ring road. The simplest way to reach the stadium is to take the Red Metro line to Lotto, and then walk alongside the racetrack to the stadium. There is a free shuttle bus from Lotto station, but due to the sheer volume of people trying to get on board, and the traffic that makes its way to the stadium on a match day, it is much easier to make the 15-minute walk.

■ Getting a ticket
For most games tickets are available to purchase on the respective clubs' websites – http://www.acmilan.com and http://www.inter.it. Tickets are also available from the respective clubs' shops in the city centre. Ticket prices range from an incredible €270 for a seat in the VIP area to €15 in the second and third tier behind the goal. A really good seat for the neutrals is in the second tier of the Orange level which is €31.

■ Nearest airport – Milan Linate Airport (LIN)
Linate is located close to the city centre and is only 4 miles from the Duomo, and reached by taxi (€15 and 15 minutes) or by bus 73 to the central station every 30 minutes, costing €2. The airport is expanding all the time, as Linate is the preferred choice for **Easyjet** from London Stansted.

■ Alternative airport – Malpensa Airport (MXP)
The main airport for the region, Malpensa, is located close to Lake Maggiore, some 45 miles north west of the city. Only **British Airways** and Alitalia fly into Malpensa from the UK from London Heathrow and Manchester. The best way into the city centre is the train from the airport to Ferrovie Nord railway station in Piazzale Cadorna which runs every 30 minutes from 6.50am every day. Tickets cost €9 each way.

Stadio San Paolo – Naples (Italy)

The Facts

Name: Stadio San Paolo
Address: Pizzale Vincenzo Tecchio,
80125 Naples,
Italy
Capacity: 78,210 All Seater
Opened: 1959

■ About Stadio San Paolo

The San Paolo is one of the great stadiums in Italy,
and is the third biggest behind Milan's and Rome's. It was
originally constructed in the late 1950s, with a huge
renovation carried out in the late 1980s in time to host
some of the most dramatic matches of the 1990 World
Cup finals including the semi-final between Argentina,
led by local hero Diego Maradona, and the host nation.
Previous to this the club played at the Stadio Arturo
Collana in Vomero which is now the home of Internapoli
who play in Serie D. The stadium is a huge bowl, with a
small lower tier, almost completely shaded by the upper
tier that alone can hold over 65,000. The stadium does
have an athletics track which means views are poor from
some seats. In the early part of this century the stadium
was closed on a number of occasions. It lost most of its
roof during some huge storms, forcing the team to play its
games in smaller stadiums in the region. Then in 2001
local flooding caused the stadium to be closed once again.

Apart from the 1990 World Cup finals where the
stadium hosted five games including England's dramatic
win versus Cameroon, it was also used in the 1980
European Championships for three matches including the
third and fourth play-off game between Italy and
Czechoslovakia. With Serie A returning in 2007, the
stadium again hosts the kind of matches that both the
fans and the city deserves.

■ Who plays there?

The long wait appears to be over. After a dark period in
the lower divisions, Napoli are about to return to the top
division of Italian football. Such a return would never have
been considered a few years ago, when the previous
entity, SSC Napoli, fell into bankruptcy and were forced to
play their football in Serie C.

Like many of the famous Italian clubs, Napoli can trace
their history back to an Englishman, William Poths, who
worked on the cruise ships that travelled regularly from
England. Along with a few interested locals, they formed a
sporting club in 1904. In 1912 an Italian faction of the
club broke off to form their own team called FBC
Internaples, later to become AC Napoli. In 1929 the team
were admitted into the national leagues, finishing 5th in
the 1929–30 season. In 1962 they won their first major
trophy, the Coppa Italia, when they beat Spal 2–1 and in
doing so became the first team outside of Serie A to win
the trophy. In 1968, with a young Dino Zoff in goal, the
team recorded their best-ever league position when they
finished runners-up to AC Milan, a feat they repeated in
1975 when they lost the league to Juventus.

In the early 1980s the club found some consistency,
finishing in the top four on each occasion until 1984 when
the new dawn broke for the club. In August 1984 the club
pulled off a world coup – signing Diego Maradona from
Barcelona. Two seasons later they won the domestic
double at a canter, delivering the Scudetto for the first
time. The following season they finished 2nd in the league,
but won their first European trophy by beating Stuttgart in
the UEFA Cup Final. The following season, with Careca
providing the fire-power up front, they won the league
again.

Maradona left in the early 1990s, as too did such
talent as Gianfranco Zola, Paolo Di Canio and Daniel
Fonseca. After their 4th-place finish in 1992, and a
runners-up spot in the Coppa Italia in 1997, the club

entered a spiral of debt and decline and in August 2004 they filed for bankruptcy with debts of €70m. During that summer the club were bought by film producer Aurelio De Laurentiis who vowed to return the club to the big time. Their first promotion was in Serie C1 where an average gate of over 30,000 saw the team dominate the league from day one in 2005/2006. In their first season back in Serie B they have steadily climbed the table, finishing the end of the season in 2nd place and thus returning to Serie A after an absence of more than five years. The current squad includes ex-Chelsea midfielder Samuele Dalla Bona and Paolo Cannavaro. The stadium also welcomes the national team on a regular basis – the last time was in September 2006 when Lithuania were the visitors for a 1–1 draw in front of 50,000 fans.

■ How to get there

The stadium is located in the western part of the city, not too far from the bay side. The view across the bay of Naples to Mount Vesuvius is very impressive. The nearest station to the stadium is Campi Flegri which is seven stops from the centre of the city on the FS Metropolitana line towards Bagnoli. Allow yourself 15 minutes to complete the journey. As you exit the station, the stadium is easily visible up the hill through the trees.

■ Getting a ticket

The stadium rarely sells out these days, although crowds are definitely on the up from the dark days of Serie C and bankruptcy in 2002. Tickets can be bought for most games on the day of the game from the ticket offices on the road up from the station. Away fans are located in the Distinti Curve A, whilst the Napoli Ultras are best avoided in Curve B. Tickets are also sold in the city centre from newsagents and in a number of sports shops from 14 days before home games. Prices start from €20 for a place in the Curve. All ticket purchasers need to be registered with the club and ID needs to be presented to purchase and collect tickets.

■ Nearest airport – Naples International (NAP)

Naples International Airport is located close to the city centre in the district of Capodichino. The airport is served on a daily basis by **BMI** from Manchester and London Heathrow, **British Airways** from London Gatwick, **Easyjet** from London Stansted, and **Thomsonfly** from a number of regional airports including Cardiff, Bristol, Newcastle, Doncaster Sheffield and Birmingham International. To reach the city centre from the airport either take the 3S Line bus which departs every 10 minutes to Piazza Garibaldi, or the Alibus shuttle bus which runs every 30 minutes. Tickets cost €1.

The Facts

Name: Stadio Renzo Barbera
Address: Viale Del Fanta 11,
90146 Palermo, Sicily,
Italy
Capacity: 36,980 All Seater
Opened: 24th January 1932 –
USC Palermo v Atalanta

■ About Stadio Renzo Barbera

The Renzo Barbera is quite unique in terms of Italian stadiums as it is not a communal stadium, and thus the absence of a running track is a bonus for fans. The stadium has one covered stand, with three uncovered areas framed by the huge hills behind the stadium. The stands are two tiered, with both end stands curving away from the pitch. The Curve Nord is where you'll see the flares and the choreographed Tifosi, whilst the away fans are stuck in very basic accommodation in the corner of the north-east stand, almost caged like animals in the zoo – consequently the view from this area is appalling. To access the away end you also have to walk down an unlit and often flooded cage that runs the whole length of one stand. Views from other stands are good, although the seating in many areas is simply plastic seats bolted onto the terraces. Amazingly, after the controversy of the Italian stadiums last season, Palermo was one of the first stadiums to get a safety certificate for its away fans. The stadium initially opened in 1932, and has gone through a number of redevelopments, most recently in time to host group matches in the 1990 World Cup finals. It is named after the former president of the club.

■ Who plays there?

U.S Citia Palermo have spent most of the last 50 years in the lower reaches of Italian football, having experienced underworld interest, bankruptcy and boardroom battles. The club can trace its roots back to 1900, when a group of English sailors started a football team in the city. It would take a number of decades playing in the regional leagues before the club climbed to Serie B, moving to their new stadium to coincide with their first appearance in Serie A in 1932. Since then it has really been a story of regular promotions and relegations and a still empty trophy cabinet. However, fortunes changed in 2002 when the club was taken over by Maurizio Zamperini who injected new funds into the club with an aim to get back to the top league within three years. His goal was reached in two – as Palermo's famous (and unique) pink shirts marched to the Serie B title, thanks in no part to the 30-odd goals from Luca Toni in 2004.

In their first season back in Serie A in 2004/2005, Toni found scoring just as easy and hit over 20 goals for the third successive campaign, as well as being the first-ever player from the club to score for the national team. The crowds also flocked back to the Renzo Barbera in 2004

Stadio Renzo Barbera – Palermo (Italy)

with average attendance reaching over 35,000. Palermo finished the season by qualifying for the UEFA Cup for the first time in their history. They took to European competition easily and had a decent run in the UEFA Cup, beating amongst others Brondby and Slavia Prague before losing to Schalke in the last 16.

They consolidated their league position in the 2005/2006 season, despite losing Luca Toni to Fiorentina and finished in 6th place, but due to the penalties imposed on AC Milan, Juventus and Lazio they found themselves in the final qualifying rounds of the Champions League draw. However, AC Milan's last-minute ruling meant that Palermo were once again relegated back to the UEFA Cup where they made the group stages again, beating West Ham 4–0 on aggregate in round two. They also started the season with a bang and for a time looked the likely challenger to Inter Milan. However, some iffy form after Christmas saw them drop back into the UEFA Cup places again – although this was again exceeding the pre-season expectations.

■ How to get there

The stadium is located 5km north of the city centre, close to the A29 Autostrada in the San Lorenzo area. To get to the stadium from the Stazione Centrale, catch bus number 101 or 107. The nearest suburban station is the Imperatore Federico Stadio which is on the road of the same name just south of the stadium although services from the city centre are infrequent.

■ Getting a ticket

In the 2005/2006 season new ticketing rules were introduced to help fight violence in football stadiums, and so check on the club's website to get the latest regulations before travelling. Tickets can be bought online around two weeks before games at http://www.ticketone.it. Tickets range in price from €27.50 for a Curva Sud ticket to €72 for a top of the range Tribuna Laterale ticket. Tickets can also be bought from a number of Snai outlets in Palermo. Avoid the 'local' derbies versus Messina and Catania which have caused riots and the death of a policeman in 2007. All ticket purchases need to be registered with the club and ID needs to be presented to purchase and collect tickets.

■ Nearest airport – Falcone Borsellino (PMO)

The Falcone Borsellino Airport, named after two anti-mafia judges who were assassinated in the mid-1990s, is located 30km to the west of the city. Buses run every 30 minutes from outside the arrivals hall, terminating at the central station. They cost €4.65 one way. A taxi should cost no more than €40 – it may be best to agree the fare before you commence the journey. **Ryanair** and **Easyjet** fly to Palermo daily from London Stansted and Gatwick respectively.

Stadio Ennio Tardini – Parma (Italy)

The Facts

Name: Stadio Ennio Tardini
Address: Viale Partigiani d'Italia 1,
Parma,
Italy
Capacity: 28,873 All Seater
Opened: 1923

■ About Stadio Ennio Tardini

The Stadio Ennio Tardini is one of the most traditional in Italian football, and could quite easily be mistaken for a stadium in Germany or England due to the design. The stadium was originally built in 1923 and is named after the club's first president. It remains largely unchanged since the end of the Second World War, with the addition of the Curva Sud in the early 1990s the only real development. The stadium is unusual for an Italian ground. It has four stands close to the pitch with no running track. The Tribuna and Distinti stands are covered, with the Curvas being uncovered terraces. Despite its modest capacity, Parma find it difficult to fill the stadium with an average attendance of just 14,000 in the 2006/2007 season. Even the last visit of Juventus, which normally guarantees a sell-out every season, failed to spark the normal interest in the game, with 7,000 seats left unsold.

■ Who plays there?

AC Parma have had a very turbulent few years, which has seen them almost rising to the lofty heights on the national stage, before being a hair's breadth of going bankrupt in 2004 after the collapse of their major financial backer Parmalat. The club were originally formed in 1913 as Verdi FC in honour of one of the city's most famous sons Guiseppi Verdi, although they soon changed their name to FC Parma in early 1914. Their early years were spent yo-yoing between Serie B and Serie C before they managed to gain some stability in the 1950s when they

managed to retain their place in Serie B for the whole of the decade, and even managed their first major honour when they won the Coppa Delle Alpi in 1961.

After a brief spell in Serie D in the late 1960s the club rose again and managed to get promotion back to Serie B in the late 1970s under the guidance of Cesare Maldini. As a prelude to things to come the team developed a number of excellent young players such as Carlo Ancelotti, who today manages AC Milan. However, the team could not find the consistency that would enable them to stay in Serie B, until 1989 when the team at last won promotion to the hallowed land of Serie A.

An opening-day defeat at home to Juventus looked ominous for the blue and yellows, but the team rallied after Christmas and ended the season in 6th place, and therefore qualifying for the UEFA Cup for the first time. At the end of the 1991/92 season, the team finished 6th and overcame Juventus in May to win the Italian cup. Their entry into the European Cup Winners' Cup gave them another crack at some of Europe's finest teams. Early-round wins against Ujpest of Hungary, Boavista and Sparta Prague set up a semi-final clash with Atletico Madrid. An excellent 2–1 win in Madrid propelled the team into the final where they met Antwerp of Belgium. The final was played at Wembley Stadium in front of 40,000 fans who saw the Italians win 3–1.

At the end of the 2002 season the team teetered on bankruptcy due to the implosion of their major backer Parmalat. At the time the club were supported heavily by the company and despite major sales of key players such as Hernan Crespo to Lazio for over £35m, the sudden withdrawal of funding meant the club were plunged into the red, all the while reaching the semi-finals of the UEFA Cup. Last season was all too familiar as they fought a whole season against relegation, finally finishing in 12th place, although only 2 points off the drop. The current squad includes Maurizio Ciaramitaro who was recently signed from Cesena, and Daniele Dessena, the current darling of the Parma tifosi.

Stadio Ennio Tardini – Parma (Italy)

■ How to get there
The stadium is located to the south of the city centre. On a nice day walking is definitely an option – allow yourself around 20 minutes to walk from the centre of the city. The best way to approach the walk is to go down to Palazzo del Commune then turn left onto Strada della Republicca. Follow this road until you reach the Viale San Michelle and then turn right and follow the road to the roundabout. The stadium will then be visible across the main road. If you want to use public transport then buses number 8 and 9 run regularly from the railway station to the stadium in around 15 minutes.

■ Getting a ticket
In the 2005–2006 season new ticketing rules were introduced to help fight violence in football stadiums, and so check on the club's website to get the latest regulations before travelling. Tickets for Parma matches are available via the websites http://www.ticketone.it and http://www.ticketweb.it. You are then able to pick up your tickets from the ticket offices to the north of the stadium. Tickets range in price from €20 in the Curva to €100 in the Preferencia.

■ Nearest airport – Giuseppe Verdi Parma (PMF)
Parma airport is located 3km to the west of the centre of the city. It is close to the A1 motorway that runs from Milan to Rimini. A taxi from the airport to the main station will cost around €10. **Ryanair** are the only carrier to fly here at the moment from the UK, flying daily from London Stansted.

Stadio Olimpico – Rome (Italy)

The Facts

Name: Stadio Olimpico
Address: Via Foro Italico,
00194 Roma,
Italy
Capacity: 82,000 All Seater
Opened: 3rd January 1960

■ About Stadio Olimpico

The Stadio Olimpico is one of the most famous stadiums in European football and has remained relatively unchanged since it opened in 1960 for the Olympic Games. Both tenants had previously played across the Tiber in the Stadio Flaminio, which is now the home of the Italian Rugby team. The stadium is a UEFA 5-star venue, despite the presence of the athletics track and has had the honour of hosting three Champions League/European Cup Finals including the infamous penalty victory by Liverpool against the home team Roma in 1984, and will host the final again in 2009. It also hosted the 1990 World Cup Final between Germany and Argentina.

The stadium is a perfect bowl, with all stands sweeping around in a single tier to form a complete bowl. A roof offers full protection from the elements. The seats in the lower part of the stands are simple bits of plastic bolted onto the terracing, with no back support. The stands have an 8-foot high glass screen protecting the players from the fervent fans, as well as a moat around the running track. The Lazio fans call the Curva Nord home, whilst the Roma fans occupy the opposite end in the Curva Sud. Twice a year the stadium is a riot in more ways than one, when the two teams meet in the Rome derby. On a couple of occasions in recent years events off the field have overshadowed the match, with the derby in 2003 actually being abandoned due to trouble between the rival fans.

■ Who plays there?

The Stadio Olimpico is home to both AS Roma and SS Lazio. Whilst in the past both have had their own stadiums, they have shared relatively happily for over two decades now. AS Roma were formed in 1927 with the merger of a number of local teams. They won their first Scudetto in 1942 whilst the league was weakened due to the effects of the Second World War. However, the club was never mentioned in the same breath as Milan or Juventus and struggled to raise their game above mediocrity. In the early 1980s the team started to improve, with Italian internationals such as Bruno Conti and Brazilian star Falcao providing the spark that had been missing. In 1981 they narrowly finished runners-up to Juventus, although the following season they did manage to win the title for the second time.

In 1983 the club played in the European Cup for only the second time. After beating IFK Göteborg, CSKA Sofia and Hertha Berlin, Roma found themselves up against Dundee United in the semi-finals. The team froze and lost 2–0 in Scotland. However, just a week later they outplayed the Scots in front of a full house in Rome, winning 3–0 to reach the final of the European Cup for the first time and more importantly in front of their home fans. Unfortunately they couldn't overcome a Liverpool side that rode their luck in 120 minutes of football before keeping their nerve in the penalty kicks to win their fourth European Cup.

The club then settled back on a period of mid-table finishes until the turn of the century when under coach Fabio Capello they captured the Scudetto again in 2001, thanks to the goals of home-grown Francesco Totti, Gabriel Batistuta, Cafu and Vincent Candela. In 2004 they finished runners-up in the Serie A, again through the contribution of Totti. They suffered a nightmare though in Europe as they managed only one point from their six Champions League group games, and played behind closed doors for two games due to an incident in the game versus Dynamo Kiev which led to the match being abandoned.

In the 2005/2006 season they were the form team for long stretches. They actually recorded 11 consecutive wins at one point – an Italian Serie A record until Inter went eight games better in 2006/2007. In the end they finished 5th – although the match-fixing ruling promoted them to 2nd and automatic entry into the Champions League. They also reached the final of the Coppa Italia where they lost over two legs to Inter Milan.

Without the distractions of AC Milan and Juventus in 2007, Roma hoped to be challenging for top spot but Inter ran away with the league. They did have the honour though of being the only team to beat them in the league, as well as thrashing them in the Coppa Italia final. In Europe they have performed well enough to qualify in a weak group with Valencia for the knock-out rounds, but were humiliated 7–1 at Old Trafford by Manchester United in the quarter-finals.

Despite taking their name from the region around Rome, SS Lazio were relatively late entrants in the Italian leagues. They were actually formed in 1900 but waited until 1912 to be admitted into the Italian League. In 1927 the plan of the ruling bodies within Rome was to merge all of the local teams into one club that could compete with the giants in the north. Whilst a number of clubs agreed to this, forming the team now known as AS Roma, Lazio refused.

In 1973 they came within a whisker of winning the Scudeto after losing on the final day to Napoli. However, 12 months later they managed to hold onto their lead throughout the season with goals from Chinaglia and won their first title. In 1980 they were forcibly relegated in relation to the betting scandal that engulfed Italian football. Whilst they returned in 1983 to the top league, relegation two seasons later ensured that the club were no longer considered one of the big teams in Italy. In 1987 the club came within a play-off of being relegated to Serie C. In 1992 Sergio Cragnotti took over the club and instigated a massive revival in fortunes for the Lazio faithful. At the end of the 1997 season the club appointed Sven-Goran Eriksson as coach and within 12 months he had taken the team to the final of the UEFA Cup where they lost to Inter Milan.

In 1999 the team again came within one game of winning the championship, with the attacking force of the team being provided by Roberto Mancini, Attilio Lombardo and Pierluigi Casiraghi. The team did win the last-ever European Cup Winners' Cup at Villa Park when they beat Real Mallorca. Twelve months later they achieved the unthinkable and won the double. Eriksson left in 2001 to take up the position as England coach and since then a number of coaches have come and gone, including Dino Zoff and Roberto Mancini. In 2002 Cragnotti was forced to step down due to the financial crisis engulfing his company Cirio, which resulted in a number of big-name players being let go. In 2005 coach Delio Rossi managed to persuade lifelong fan Paolo Di Canio to lead the team, and through his drive and determination he scored 11 goals in 50 appearances to keep them in the top flight. In the 2005/2006 season the team finished in 6th place and thus earned a UEFA Cup spot. However, the outcome of the

match-fixing trial saw Lazio implicated and initially they were automatically relegated and were ordered to start the 2006/2007 season with a points penalty. On appeal, Lazio were re-instated with a 30-point penalty, meaning that they finished in 16th place, just one point above the relegation zone, as well as starting this season with a 3-point penalty and being stripped of their UEFA Cup spot.

■ How to get there
The stadium is located in the northern suburbs of the city, close to the River Tiber. There are a couple of ways to get to the stadium on a match day. Either take the metro line A to Ottaviano and then get bus number 32, or take metro line B to Flaminio then catch tram 225. Both public transport options terminate just east of the bridge over the Tiber. From here it's a 5-minute walk to the stadium. If you are in the city centre before the game then allow at least 30 minutes for either of these options.

■ Getting a ticket
Tickets for a vast majority of the games are available right up until the day before from the ticket windows dotted around the stadium. The only exceptions to this are the derby matches, and the games versus Juventus. For games like these you will need to get your tickets either online from the clubs websites (Lazio's are available from http://www.listicket.it and AS Roma's from http://www.asromacalcio.it) or go to their respective shops in Piazza Colonna 360 (AS Roma) or Via Farini 34 (Lazio).

As with most grounds in Italy, ticket prices range considerably. In the case of the Stadio Olimpico, the cheapest seats are in the Curva Sud and Distinti stands which are €14, whilst you will pay €60 for a place in the Tribuna Monte Mario Sud or Nord. A good bet for the neutral is the Tribuna Tevere, which starts from €30.

■ Nearest airport – Leonardo da Vinci (FCO)
Rome's main airport is located on the coast 30km south west of the city. The main advantage of flying here rather than Ciampino is that the airport is connected to the city centre by an express train service that runs to the central station every 30 minutes with a journey time of 25 minutes. The journey will cost €9 one way. The airport is served by the flag carriers, **British Airways** from London Gatwick and Heathrow, and **Alitalia** from Heathrow. A new airline, **AirOne** has started flying to Rome from London City, and **British Airways** offshoot **BA Connect** fly here from Birmingham International and Manchester.

■ Alternative airport – Rome Ciampino Airport (CIA)
Ciampino Airport was the main airport for the city until 1960 when Fiumicino opened. The airport is served by a number of bus companies who run services to the central station in 40 minutes depending on traffic, costing €8 one way or €13.50 return. There is also a local bus that runs regularly to Anagnina metro station for €1 where you can then take the train into the city. **Easyjet** fly here from Bristol, East Midlands, London Gatwick and Newcastle, and **Ryanair** from East Midlands, Glasgow-Prestwick, Liverpool, London Stansted and London Luton.

Stadio Marc Antonio Bentegodi – Verona (Italy)

The Facts

Name: Stadio Marc Antonio Bentegodi
Address: Piazzale Olimpica,
Via Perloso,
Verona
Capacity: 39,211 All Seater
Opened: 7th August 1963

■ About Stadio Marc Antonio Bentegodi

The Stadio Marc Antonio Bentegodi is one of the classic stadiums in Italy. It is named after a 19th-century Veronese politician and was built in 1963 in a very similar design and look to the stadiums in Naples. The stadium was used during the 1990 World Cup finals, hosting matches between Belgium, South Korea, Uruguay and Spain as well as a second round match between Yugoslavia and Spain. It is a three-tiered elliptical stadium, with a running track around the edge. The roof covers all but the lower tier and views are excellent from most places. The away fans tend to be placed in the north end of the stadium.

Like many Italian stadiums, it is owned by the local council and so is a multi-use venue which means the athletics track is a slight hindrance to watching a game here, especially in the lower tier. The middle tier is used on one side for hospitality seats, although for the rest of the stadium it provides a narrow enclosed seating area.

■ Who plays there?

The stadium is home to Hellas Verona and Chievo. Twenty years ago it would have been unheard of to imagine that the higher-placed club of the two would be Chievo. Their rise to Serie A is now the stuff of legend in Italian football, even more so because of the contrasting fortunes of Hellas. Despite the fact the club were formed in 1929, the team played in local football and amateur leagues until they finally reached Serie C2 in 1986. They stayed in this league for three years, winning promotion to C1 in 1989.

The club consolidated their position in Serie B for the next few years, playing second fiddle to their city rival Hellas Verona who were challenging for the title at the time. However, in 2002 the miracle happened. Chievo were promoted in 3rd place in Serie B. In this first season Chievo finished in 5th place, missing out on a Champions League spot on the last day of the season to Milan, and even leading Serie A for a time over Christmas. To make matters even better for them, Hellas Verona were relegated.

The team under the inspirational Luigi Del Neri went on to successive UEFA Cup spots. At the end of the 2006 season, due to the enforced demotion of Juventus and AC Milan, Chievo found themselves promoted up the league, meaning that they qualified for the Champions League for the first time in their history. However, their European campaign only lasted to September, and then they had to concentrate on keeping their Serie A position – a situation that came down to the last day of the season. Unfortunately, results elsewhere, when any one of half a dozen teams could have actually gone down, did not go in their favour and so they went back to Serie B with Hellas in 2007/08.

If Chievo's recent form is worrying, then Hellas Verona's is positively alarming. Twenty-five years ago Chievo were no more than a Sunday amateur side, playing in the local leagues around the city, whilst Hellas Verona went on to win Serie A in 1985. The team were originally formed in 1903 when a group of students from the University decided to take up the game. They took their name in homage to their classics lecturer – Hellas being the Greek word for Greece. In 1906 the team started playing in earnest against local clubs from Vicenza and the

Veneto, using the historic Roman amphitheatre north of the river as their home ground. After merging with a number of teams from the city, the team were admitted into the professional Serie B league in 1929.

It took them nearly 30 years to reach the top division, merging with Verona's biggest amateur club in the mid-1950s to form the club today known as Hellas Verona. During the 1960s, the team were relegated back to the 2nd division, and it wasn't until the appointment of Swedish coach Nils Liedholm that the team started making great strides on the pitch. In 1968 they returned to the top flight, where they would remain for nearly 25 years.

In the early 1980s coach Osvaldo Bagnoli started to build a squad that would make a serious impact on Italian football. In 1983 they finished 4th in Serie A and again were runners-up in the Coppa Italia after throwing away a 2–0 home win against Juventus to lose in extra time 3–0 in Turin. A year later they reached the final again, this time losing to Roma in the two-leg final. However, the team had had a taste of success and, then with a team featuring players such as Hans-Peter Briegel, Preben Elkjaer and Antonio di Gennaro, the following season they nosed in front of a pack including Torino, Juventus and Inter Milan to capture their first-ever Serie A title. The team therefore had the opportunity to compete in Europe's biggest club competition – the European Cup. A 5–2 win in the first round against PAOK Salonika took them through to an all-Italian tie with holders Juventus. Despite taking the game to the team from Turin for most of the tie, a 2–0 home win in Turin was enough to eliminate Hellas Verona. Unfortunately, the money spent during the club's stay at the top led to problems years later, and in 1991 the club were forced to fold, with crippling debts, only to re-form as Verona FC. The club also dropped down into Serie B with regularity during the 1990s. Despite having players in the team such as a young Adrian Mutu, Martin Laursen and Mauro Camoranesi the club were relegated for the final time in 2002 – but not before Chievo had joined them for a season in Serie A. That final game in spring 2002, which saw Chievo win 2–1, was the last time the teams met. Worse was to follow in 2004 when the team fell into Serie C1 after a disastrous post-Christmas campaign. The club quickly returned to Serie B, where despite a late run of form in 2005 which nearly saw them promoted, they have remained.

■ How to get there

The stadium is located to the south west of the city centre, and is a pleasant 15-minute walk from the Porto Nuova station. Come out of the station and cut across the car park to the left until you reach Viale Andrea Palladio. Then just follow this road all the way north to the stadium, past the bars and cafes. If you are coming from the city centre then head towards Castel Vecchio and then walk southwards down Corso Cavour, through the city walls and across the river until you reach Viale Andrea Palladio. Then turn right and the stadium will be a 5-minute walk away. If you want to use public transport then bus numbers 11,12 and 13 run from the city centre to the stadium via Porto Nuovo station.

■ Getting a ticket

With such a big stadium, and a small supporter base, getting a ticket to see Chievo or Verona is not normally a problem. However, if you want to buy a ticket in advance you can via the clubs' websites. With neither team averaging over 10,000 at the moment, there are no worries being able to get a ticket. The ticket offices at the ground can be found on the west side of the stadium near the officials entrance, and on the east side. Tickets range in price from €10 to €35 for a Tribuna ticket.

■ Nearest airport – Valerio Catulla (VRN)

Verona's small airport is located 6 miles south west of the city and is primarily served by **British Airways** who fly direct to Catullo from London Gatwick, supplementing the daily flights from London Stansted by **Air Italy**. Airport buses leave every 20 minutes from outside the arrivals doors, costing €4, taking 15 minutes to reach the Stazione Porta Nuova. A taxi to the stadium would costs around €20.

■ Alternative airport – Gabriele D'Annunzio (VBS)

Located 30 miles to the west of Verona is the small regional airport of Gabriele D'Annunzio. Whilst it is significantly closer to Brescia (only 4 miles to the south), **Ryanair** prefer to call it Verona on their route map. Buses run direct to Verona from the airport, taking 45 minutes and costing €16. Alternatively, you can get a local bus to Brescia train station and then hop on a regular train to Verona Porto Nuova station.

The Facts

Name: Skonto Stadions
Address: 1a Melngaila Str,
1010 Riga,
Latvia
Capacity: 8,800 All Seater
Opened: 2000

■ About Skonto Stadions

The Skonto Stadions is one of the new breed of stadiums that are appearing at regular intervals in the smaller European cities, such as in Tallinn and Helsinki. The stadium is very similar to some of the grounds you will find in England, and looks like Blackpool's redeveloped Bloomfield Road (well, the parts that have been built so far!). It has four single-tier stands, two of which sweep round to form one stand. The main stand has some small executive boxes in.

Views from the new stands are good and unobstructed, although based on the attendances you are more likely to have two or three seats to yourself rather than worrying about not seeing the action.

■ Who plays there?

The Skonto Stadions is home to both Latvia's most successful domestic club Skonto Riga, and the national team. The amazing thing about Skonto Riga is that they

actually ceased to exist prior to Latvia's independence in 1991. Like most of the clubs in the Baltic states, there was little point in competing against the might of some of the teams from Moscow and Kiev, as well as the distances involved in travelling to away games.

Whilst it was obvious that the capital city needed a team, and a home, many people questioned the amount of money that was poured into the building of the new stadium and the team. When the new Latvian league started in 1991, Skonto Riga dominated the league from day one. They set a world record by winning the Latvian Virsliga every season up until 2004 – a total of 14 successive seasons. During this period they also reached 12 cup finals, winning seven times. However, their monopoly on the honours has now come to an end as they finished 2nd in 2005, and in 2006 they finished 3rd as well as losing in the Latvian cup final – meaning that for the first time in their history Skonto Riga will not be playing in European football in 2007.

The club have produced some of Latvia's most famous players since 1991, including Marian Pahars who played for Southampton, and more recently Arsenal's young centre-back Igors Stepanovs. Their European campaigns have been short and sweet in most instances, as the team have only reached the 3rd qualifying round of the Champions League on one occasion, in 1999, when after a 10–0 aggregate win against Jeunesse d'Esch from Luxembourg they recorded their best-ever victory by beating Rapid Bucharest 5–4 over two games. This set up a mouth-watering tie against Chelsea (although in the days of Ken Bates and not Roman's roubles). After a 3–0 defeat in London, the Latvians held the Londoners to a 0–0 draw in Riga. Last season they participated in the UEFA Cup, exiting at the 2nd round qualifying phase to Molde of Norway.

The national team has been in the doldrums over the past few years after hitting the highs of qualifying for Euro 2004 in Portugal, and they finished bottom of their 2008 European Championship qualifying group. National games played at the Skonto are still very popular with the locals, and most games do sell out, irrespective of the opposition.

■ How to get there
The stadium is located to the north of the old town close to the Krisjana Valdemare main road. It is easily walkable – from the central station head up Stabu Iela for around 1km and you will reach the stadium. A taxi will cost around €5. Bus lines 11 and 33 run past the stadium, as well as tram line 5.

■ Getting a ticket
With an average attendance in the Latvian Virsliga last season of just 700, getting a ticket for any league match in Latvia is not exactly difficult. Skonto regularly attract the season's biggest attendance for the games versus

Metalurgs but even then the stadium is only around a third full. Therefore it is easy to purchase a ticket on the day of the game. Tickets for the main stand cost around €7.

Tickets for the national team games go on sale via the Latvian FA's website http://www.lff.lv or by calling them on +371 6727 2833. Unless the visitors are one of the major teams in the world, tickets can also be purchased on match day. For recent Euro2008™ qualifying games they have got crowds of around 7,500, although the game against Spain was a 10,000 sell-out after temporary seating was installed behind the goal to accommodate demand from locals.

■ Nearest airport – Riga International (RIX)
Riga International Airport is the biggest airport in the Baltic states. It is located 13km south west of the city and the easiest way to reach the city centre is the Express Bus 22a that runs from behind the car park at the main terminal to the Cathedral at Brivibas Boulevard. Journey time is around 20 minutes and tickets cost LVL0.30. A taxi should cost no more than LVL9 but agree the fare before you start. The airport is served on a daily basis from the UK by **Air Baltic** from London Gatwick and **Ryanair** from Bristol, East Midlands, Liverpool, Glasgow-Prestwick and London Stansted.

Rheinpark Stadium – Vaduz (Liechtenstein)

The Facts

Name: Rheinpark Stadium
Address: Rheinpark Allé,
Vaduz,
Liechtenstein
Capacity: 8,000 All Seater
Opened: September 1998 – FC Vaduz v
Kaiserslautern

■ About Rheinpark Stadium

The Rheinpark is one of the most picturesque grounds in the world, sandwiched between the Alps and the River Rhein. On a late summer evening, sitting in the main stand the quality of the football often takes second place to the amazing views. In late 2006 the stadium was finally completed, with four separate stands offering some superb views of activities both on and off the pitch.

With the opening of the smaller stand on the Rhein, the ground gained the necessary UEFA status to hold big internationals – the first of these was the game versus England in the qualifying tournament for the 2002 FIFA World Cup. The stadium was opened in 1998 with a game between FC Vaduz and the then-current German Bundesliga champions Kaiserslautern. Previous to this, the national side played in Eschen-Mauren which is home to FC Balzers who play in the Swiss 4th division. As you would imagine for such a small stadium, it is quite basic.

However, the views from all of the stands are good, and the roofs do provide some protection from the frequent heavy rainfall. Food and drink are provided from stands in the corners of the stadium.

■ Who plays there?

Liechtenstein's most successful club side, FC Vaduz, currently play in the second tier of the Swiss League, the Challenge League, and have come close to promotion to the top division on a number of occasions in the past few years – most notably when they lost the play-off in 2004 and 2005. The club were originally formed in 1932, and were admitted into the Swiss league structure a year later. They have actually played at the top level before, reaching the Swiss 1st division in 1960 and staying there for 13 seasons before relegation in 1973. In 1992 the club were allowed to enter the European Cup Winners' Cup for the first time when Liechtenstein were formally admitted into UEFA. In that first season they lost 12–1 to Odesa of Ukraine – hardly an impressive start. It would be a further three seasons before they would qualify again, and this time they managed to win their first-ever tie, beating Universitate Riga 5–3 on aggregate, before losing heavily to Paris St Germain.

The club have qualified regularly for the UEFA Cup, winning the Liechtenstein cup on no fewer than the last nine seasons. Last season they beat the once mighty Ujpest of Hungary 4–1 in the 1st round before losing on away goals to Basel in the 2nd round. The current squad, under the leadership of Swede Mats Gren, is a mixture of nations, including Argentinians, Brazilians, Portuguese, Mexicans, Germans, French and of course a few home-grown players such as international centre-back Daniel Hasler and Marco Ritzberger.

■ How to get there
From the town centre, the stadium is just a 5-minute walk away. Just follow the road away from the centre at the roundabout (there is only one – Lettstrasse) and the stadium will be visible at the end of the country road. There are no public transport options to get to the ground. The nearest major city is Zurich which is reached within 45 minutes by car along the stunning Lake Zurich road. When you reach the River Rhine on the A13 Autobahn follow the signs for St Gallen until you see the signs for Vaduz. Cross the river at this point via RheinBrück and then around the corner into Zollstrasse. At the mini-roundabout carry straight on into Rheinstrasse and the stadium is straight ahead of you.

■ Getting a ticket
For Swiss league games featuring FC Vaduz you can simply turn up at the ground before kick-off and get in. In fact, on a match day there is an exodus of fans heading northwards to watch games at Bayern Munich and Stuttgart rather than watch the games on offer in the domestic league. Tickets for league matches are either 20CHF for a place in one of the new end stands or 25CHF

for the side stands. They can be purchased from http://www.ticketcorner.com.

For international games, tickets go onto sale seven days before the game from the Liechtenstein Football Association online at http://www.postcorner.li or by calling them on +423 23963 66. For smaller games tickets are sold on the day of the game from the ticket booths at the south end of the stadium. Ticket prices depend on who the opponents are. For a friendly against a low ranked team, such as the one played against Estonia in 2005, the price per ticket was 40CHF to 75CHF. For a game versus a category one team such as Portugal, prices will double. The national association also issue season tickets starting from 150CHF for a set of games – such as they did for the European Championships 2008 qualifying tournament.

■ Nearest airport – Zurich International (ZRH)
Unsurprisingly, Liechtenstein doesn't have its own airport. It does have a railway line that passes through the country with four stops, including one on the southern border at Schaan-Vaduz. It is bordered by Austria and Switzerland, and is just a 10-minute drive from the German border, meaning there are a number of airports within an hour's drive. Zurich Airport is located to the west of the city centre and is one of the easiest airports to reach by public transport in Europe. If you are planning on using public transport to reach Vaduz then you will need to change trains in Zurich and then again at Buchs-Schaan.

The Facts

Name: Amsterdam ArenA
Address: Postbus 12522,
1100 AM Amsterdam,
Netherlands
Capacity: 51,600 All Seater
Opened: 14th April 1996 – Ajax v AC Milan

■ About Amsterdam ArenA

The Amsterdam ArenA was one of the most modern stadiums in the world when it opened its doors in 1996 with Ajax playing a friendly versus AC Milan, after a two-year construction period and a cost of €98 million that was met by the local authorities.

The original plan was that the new stadium would be the centrepiece of Amsterdam's 1992 Summer Olympics bid, but this was won by Barcelona. The stadium was the first in the world to have a fully retractable roof, allowing the stadium to be used as a multi-purpose arena. However, this brought its own problems as the stadium grass failed to grow in the shadow of the roof, and was replaced four times in the first year. Fans enter the stadium at ground level, but the pitch is actually three levels up, with the lower two levels taken up by a car park and a road through the stadium. Therefore, expect a trek upwards if you are in the upper tier, although the stadium does have a number of escalators to take fans up to the

gods. The lowest levels of seating are located around 6 feet above pitch level, so views are excellent, as is the leg room.

The stadium was also one of the first in the world to be cash-free, using the ArenA card, similar to those used by Schalke and Vitesse Arnhem. There are a number of points around the stadium to buy cards, which come in €10, €20 and €50 denominations. Once you have a card then it can be topped up on any future visits. If you have any credit left at the end of the day you can exchange the card back for cash at the same kiosks. The atmosphere in the stadium on a match day is fantastic, with the two huge screens hanging from the north and south ends providing a great view of the action.

■ Who plays there?

The stadium is home to Ajax, one of Europe's most famous clubs. The team were originally formed in 1900 through an amalgamation of a number of local teams to compete as the sole representative of Amsterdam in the newly formed Netherlands Regional Championship. It was nearly 20 years before they won their first title, taking the Dutch national championships in 1918. In 1928 the club moved to its new stadium, the De Meer, and under English coach Jack Reynolds started a remarkable run that saw them capture five titles during the late 1920s and early 1930s.

The club played in their first European Cup in 1957, reaching the quarter-finals. In the late 1960s Dutch coach Rinus Michels took over the team and started a revolution that was to lead to the club being crowned one of the greatest teams Europe had ever seen. He introduced the concept of 'Total Football' – the idea that any player could cover for any position on the pitch, allowing fast attacking play that often overwhelmed their opposition. In the space of ten years the club went from also-rans in their own domestic league to European dominance. During the remarkable three-year period from 1971 to 1973, the club won three European Cups, two European Super Cups, the Intercontinental Cup (becoming the World Club Champions in 1972) as well as two league titles and two domestic cup final victories. In 1982 Johan Cruyff returned to the club, bringing them the double with a team that included a 17-year-old Marco Van Basten and midfielder Frank Rijkaard.

In 1991 Louis Van Gaal took over the reins and oversaw the second coming in terms of European football. He was responsible for blooding players such as Edwin Van Der Sar, the De Boer twins, Edgar Davids, Marc Overmars and Patrick Kluivert. His first success was the UEFA Cup in 1992 when they defeated Torino on away goals. A year later he captured the national championship, giving them entry into the 1995 European Cup. They won a group containing AC Milan, Salzburg and AEK Athens and then had luck on their side in the next round, brushing aside a weak Hajduk Split before beating Barcelona 5–2 in a classic semi-final encounter in the Olympic Stadium in Amsterdam. The final saw the young Dutch side pitched against one of Europe's strongest teams, Juventus. In a tense game in Vienna a late strike by Kluivert was enough to bring the title back to Amsterdam.

The following season their European form was just as impressive in their new stadium, scoring 15 goals, and conceding just one in their five wins at the group stages, before beating Borussia Dortmund and Panathinaikos to reach the final against Juventus again, only to lose on penalties in Rome. The team then dispersed across Europe, and although Van Gaal, and latterly Ronald Koeman, delivered domestic honours with regularity, it was the team from Eindhoven that took over the mantle as the Netherlands' best team. Ajax took the double in 2002 and the title in 2004 but have since failed to make an impression in Europe. Last season they led the table for so long, only to suffer heartache on the final day of the season as they lost the championship on goal difference to PSV.

■ How to get there
The stadium is within walking distance of two railway stations – Duivendrecht and Biljmer. Services run to these stations from the central station platforms 2 and 7b, taking 15 minutes. A ticket to Biljmer costs €3.70 return. If you are coming by metro, then the stadium has its own stop, close to the north and east stands called Strandvliet/ArenA. The station is on line 54 in the direction of Gein. A taxi from the city centre will cost around €20.

■ Getting a ticket
As with all other clubs in the Dutch league, you cannot buy a ticket on match day unless you have a Club Membership card. But fear not. The club reserves a number of tickets that are specifically available for foreign fans. The club also has offers that combine lunch at the training ground (the Toekmost), entry to the museum, an official picture taken on the pitch and a ticket for the game. These packages start from around €95 per person and can be booked direct from the club.

If you are able to get a ticket for a league game then you should not pay more than €40 for a seat in the east or west stands. The average attendance at the ground for league games is close to 48,000 so expect tickets to be available. The ticket office is on the west side of the stadium, close to gate B.

■ Nearest airport – Amsterdam Schiphol (AMS)
Schiphol Airport is one of the busiest in the world. The airport is huge and has a couple of hotels within the terminals, hundreds of shops and its own casino. The airport is served daily from the UK by **Easyjet** from Belfast, Bristol, London Gatwick, London Stansted, East Midlands and Newcastle, **British Airways** fly here from London Heathrow as too do **BMI**. **Jet2** arrive here from Manchester and Leeds Bradford, and **ThomsonFly** have just opened this route from Doncaster Sheffield. Finally, **VLM** fly here from London City. To reach the railway city centre from the airport, head to the railway station under Schiphol Plaza where trains leave every 15 minutes with the journey taking around 15 minutes into central station. A ticket costs €3.60 return and can be bought from the yellow machines.

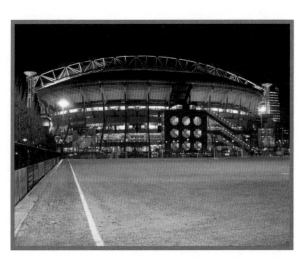

Philips Stadium – Eindhoven (Netherlands)

The Facts

Name: Philips Stadium
Address: Frederiklaan 10a,
5616 Eindhoven,
Netherlands
Capacity: 36,500 All Seater
Opened: 31st August 1913

■ About Philips Stadium

The Philips Stadium is one of the most modern in Europe, and is quite rightly a UEFA 4-star venue. It is also quite unusual in that it is actually not owned by the club, but by their main sponsor. Whilst the ground is now one of the finest club venues in Europe, it is hard to imagine what it looked like when the Philips organisation chose the area as the location of their sports ground in 1919. During the next few years basic facilities were added, and just after the Second World War the ground had seating for around 15,000 people. The stadium was upgraded throughout the successful periods of the 1970s and 1980s, although the funding of Philips was certainly as important in the ability of the club to build the facilities.

The stadium today is similar in design to Anfield. There are corporate facilities galore, with over 1,300 corporate seats and a restaurant that can hold a further 250 people in quite luxurious surroundings. Large heaters inside the roof also ensure that the crowd is kept quite toasty on

those cold Dutch nights. The playing surface looks excellent, and with lots of space in the concourse areas it is no surprise that UEFA chose the stadium to host the 2006 UEFA Cup Final when Seville destroyed Middlesbrough 4–0, as well as being a host venue during Euro 2000.

■ Who plays there?

The stadium is home to PSV Eindhoven who are currently the Netherlands' most successful team, although up until the mid-1970s they were simply a bystander in the Ajax/Feyenoord show. However, the club's success started in 1974 when they won the KNVB Cup. The team captured back-to-back championships in 1975 and 1976, and again in 1978 when they capped off a fantastic period in the club's history by beating Bastia 3–0 to win the UEFA Cup.

The next phase in the club's success came during the late 1980s when a team including such international stars as Ruud Gullit, Ronald Koeman, Soren Lerby and Frank Arnesen won the championship in 1986, 1987, 1988 and 1989. Included in this period was the first ever back-to-back double of 1988 and 1989. The crowning moment of this period though was in May 1988 when PSV beat Benfica on penalties to capture the European Cup.

The club continued to win trophies on a regular basis during the 1990s with such stars as Romario, Ronaldo and Van Nistelrooy scoring regularly for the team. As the club entered the new millennium they had overtaken Ajax as the most successful club in Dutch football history. In 1991 and 1992, with Bobby Robson, they won the Dutch Championship. They won the championship again in 2000, 2001, 2003, 2005 and again in 2006 at a canter under the leadership of Guus Hiddink. They also surprised many people by reaching the semi-finals of the Champions League in the 2005/2006 season, narrowly losing to AC Milan in a close-fought two-leg match. Last season it looked as if their domestic success was going to be broken by Ajax and AZ Alkmaar. Going into the last game of the season they sat in 3rd place, but a strange set of results saw them leapfrog AZ and finish in top spot on goal difference from Ajax. The Champions League campaign wasn't as memorable as 2006 although they did reach the quarter-finals, beating Arsenal along the way before they lost to Liverpool 4–0.

■ How to get there

The stadium is located very close to the city centre, and is best reached by foot. From the Central Station plaza, turn right and simply follow Mathildelaan until you reach the stadium – this should take around 10 minutes. If you have had a few too many Heinekens then you can get either a line 16 or 17 bus in the direction of Veldhoven.

■ Getting a ticket

Since it is complicated for us foreigners to apply for the obligatory Dutch Club Card, PSV offer the possibility to buy tickets without going through this application process. The club reserve a limited number of tickets for overseas visitors for each match, except for the games versus Ajax and Feyenoord, and those played in the Champions League. Tickets can be reserved by emailing the ticket office at ticketoffice@psv.nl or by calling them on +31 40 2 505 505. Ticket prices range from €18.50 behind the goals to €46 for the best seats in the house with padded armrests and under-seat heating.

■ Nearest airport – Eindhoven Airport (Code EIN)

Eindhoven airport is located 5 miles to the west of the city centre. The airport is served by three airlines from the UK. **Ryanair** currently offer two flights daily to Eindhoven. **KLM** offer a twice-daily flight to Eindhoven from London Heathrow and **Euromanx** offer a twice-weekly flight from Southampton. Hermes operates an airport shuttle bus that runs every 15 minutes to the Central Station. Look for bus line 41. The journey takes around 20 minutes. There is also a shuttle bus that runs a twice a day, approximately 45 minutes after the **Ryanair** flights land, to Amsterdam central station costing €30 return.

The Facts

Name:	Euroborg
Address:	Euroweg,
	Groningen,
	Netherlands
Capacity:	19,980 All Seater
Opened:	6th January 2006

■ About Euroborg

When plans were initially published for a brand new multi-purpose stadium in Groningen for the then 2nd division club, many people wondered what the point was. The old Oosterpark stadium, which stood on the same spot as the Euroborg, was a small intimate stadium which had a capacity of just over 11,000 and was known for the closeness of the crowd to the action. However, it was really showing signs of aging in the early part of this century, having been constructed in 1933.

The new stadium was constructed next door to the Oosterpark in late 2004. The 19,980 capacity may have seemed ambitious at first, but last season the stadium was full on almost every occasion, proving that if you do build people will come. It certainly is an impressive venue both inside and out. Around the perimeter of the stadium you will find a health spa, supermarket, Chinese restaurant, cinema and a casino. Inside the stadium is a simple two-tier uniform arena, with a double row of executive boxes

in the upper tier of the main stand. Views are very good from all parts, although the presence of a perimeter fence does hinder the first few rows of the lower tier.

The stadium certainly lives up to its 'Groene' tag with all of the seats a bright-green colour. The concourses are wide and provide plenty of space for people buying refreshments as well as allowing fans to watch the game from behind the seated areas.

■ Who plays there?

The Groene Kathedraal (The Green Cathedral) is the home to one of the Netherlands' most ambitious clubs, FC Groningen. The team weren't actually formed until 1971 but have made massive strides, playing for the majority of their existence in the top flight of Dutch football. Their most famous ex-players are Ronald and Erwin Koeman who were the heart of the side in the 1980s, a period where the club played European football for the first time. Their success has always been very modest – they still have not won a major honour yet – and their best league position was 3rd in 1991.

In 2006 they finished 5th in the league, meaning that they earned the right to fight for Champions League qualification. In a tense match versus Ajax they eventually went down by a single goal. Last season they qualified for the UEFA Cup again, although a disappointing 4–3 defeat to Partizan Belgrade was not the welcome the new stadium was hoped to bring the club. In 2006/2007 the club finished in 8th place and qualified for the UEFA Cup competition, beating Feyenoord and Utrecht in the domestic qualifying competition.

■ How to get there

The Euroborg is located in the south east of the city centre, next to the A7/E22 motorway. The area around the stadium is under development with such amenities as a health spa and casino already constructed, and a hotel due to be added in the next year. From the old town and train station it is a pleasant 20 minute walk. Simply follow Trompsingel eastwards until you reach the bridge over the canal, then turn right and follow Winschoterdiep southwards along the canal. Once you pass under the E22 ring road the stadium will be in front of you. Alternatively, use bus number 20 that runs from the bus station next to the central station and drops you right outside the stadium.

■ Getting a ticket

FC Groningen's attendances have risen dramatically over the past few seasons, coinciding with the upturn in fortune on the pitch. In the 2005/2006 season the rise was over 30% to 15,500, whereas last season the average rose to close to 19,180, meaning that tickets

for most games were in short supply. With European competition returning to the Euroborg again in 2007, tickets will be in demand for most games. This means booking is absolutely essential to avoid disappointment. The club does allow foreign fans to book tickets in advance – contact them at info@fcgroningen.nl. Last season tickets ranged in price from €20 in the Eerste Ring to €40 in the main stand. Tickets for the seats behind the goal were sold out last season to members.

■ Nearest airport – Groningen Eelde Airport (GRQ)

The small Groningen Eelde Airport is located in the village of Paterswolde, 5 miles south of the city. It is served by a handful of operators – **Ryanair** used to fly here but recently cut the route as it was not reaching its strict capacity levels. Currently, **BMI** fly daily from Aberdeen, **VLM** once a day from London City via Amsterdam and **KLM** from Norwich. To reach the city centre from the airport, catch the twice hourly 52 bus that terminates at the central station. A single will cost €2.40 and the journey takes around 40 minutes. A taxi will cost around €30.

De Kuip Stadium – Rotterdam (Netherlands)

The Facts

Name: De Kuip Stadion
Address: Van Zandvlietplein 3,
3077 Rotterdam AA,
Netherlands
Capacity: 51,100 All Seater
Opened: 27th March 1937 – Feyenoord v Beerschot

■ About De Kuip Stadium
The De Kuip, or the Tub, is one of the best-loved stadiums in Europe. It has been used by UEFA for a number of high-profile games – the last being the UEFA Cup Final of 2002 when the home team Feyenoord beat Borussia Dortmund 3–2. It was also host to the final of Euro 2000 when France beat Italy.

The stadium was originally opened in 1937 and soon became a really hostile place for teams to visit. The stadium was expanded during the next 50 years as and when funds were available. After the appalling scenes witnessed during the home leg of the 1974 UEFA Cup final against Tottenham Hotspur, there was real danger that the ground would be closed permanently. However, the local government stepped in and funded a development programme that cumulated when the De Kuip was chosen as the venue for the 2000 European Championships final.

Most of the seats offer an unobstructed view of the action, although the seats directly behind the goal are temporary and so the step rake is not as high as the rest of the stadium, meaning that fans that are shorter than the fans in front may not be able to see very well. However, all of the seats are now offered protection from the (frequent) rain by the new roof. The perimeter fences were taken down in the late 1990s although the moat around the pitch still remains.

■ Who plays there?
Feyenoord have always been the bridesmaids of Dutch football. For so long they sat in Ajax's shadows, waiting for a chance to shine, and then as the team from Amsterdam faded, the PSV machine took over and claimed the crown of top dogs in the Netherlands. That is not to say that the club hasn't had its moments of glory. Without a doubt their most famous achievement was being the first Dutch team to win the European Cup in May 1970 when they beat Celtic in a replay in Milan.

The team were formed in 1908 by a group of poor workers in the south areas of Rotterdam, collectively called Feijenoord. The team was originally called Wilhelmina, after the Queen of the Netherlands, but soon changed it to the now world famous Feyenoord in 1912. The team soon entered the ranks of the amateur leagues, and eventually reached the top division in the early 1920s. They celebrated their first Dutch league title in 1924.

De Kuip Stadium – Rotterdam (Netherlands)

In the early 1970s the team rose to the top of Europe, not only with the European Cup win, but also with the Dutch championship in 1971 and in 1974 they reached the final of the UEFA Cup losing to Tottenham Hotspur in a game remembered more for the off-field events rather than those on the pitch. This game also ended the run of success for the team until the mid-1980s when an aging Johan Cruyff and a young Ruud Gullit inspired the club to a domestic double in 1984. Two further titles during the 1990s were scant reward for a young team who played some exciting attacking football. During the first few years of this century the team found it hard to break the Ajax/PSV monopoly although the fantastic UEFA Cup triumph on home soil in May 2002 was a just reward for a team including Paul Bosvelt, a young Robin Van Persie and the goalscorer extraordinaire Pierre Van Hooijdonk. Ruud Gullit arrived with a great fanfare in 2003 but his reign was characterised by in-fighting and poor on-field discipline. Today, the team has been rebuilt under Erwin Koeman (Ronald's brother) and is trying to win back a championship they last had their hands on over six years ago.

The last few seasons haven't gone too well for the club as they slipped along way behind PSV, AZ and Ajax. A good run in the UEFA Cup was on the cards in 2006/2007, but the club were sensationally thrown out of the tournament in January 2007 after repeated incidents of violence in previous rounds. They finally finished in mid-table and lost out on a chance of UEFA Cup football when they lost a two-leg play off against Groningen.

■ **How to get there**
The stadium is easily reached from most parts of the city centre north of the Maas River. From the central station catch tram number 23 that runs down to Olympiaweg and Stadionweg. Alternatively bus line 49 runs from central station to Zuid station via Olympiaweg. There is also a special match-day train service from the central station that runs about every 15 minutes and takes 5 minutes. If you are in the Zuidplein area then catch bus 72 or 75 to the stadium. A taxi from the city centre will take about 15 minutes on a match day and cost about €15.

■ **Getting a ticket**
Like PSV Eindhoven, the club reserve a number of tickets that are specifically available for foreign fans. To reserve a ticket download an application form from the official website, or email the club at support@feyenoord.nl. Tickets range in price from €25 to €45. A good neutral seat in the stadium is in the Maastribune where ticket prices start from €40.

■ **Nearest airport – Rotterdam Airport (RTM)**
Rotterdam's airport is located next to the A13/E19 motorway that links Rotterdam to Amsterdam Schiphol Airport. It is 5km north of the city centre. **Transavia.com** are the principal budget carrier at the airport and flies twice daily to and from London Stansted. **VLM** run up to four flights a day on the short hop from London City airport. **KLM**'s cityhopper service also departs on weekdays on from London City Airport and London Heathrow. The bus service 33/43 run by RET runs frequently to the central station in about 20 minutes. A single ticket can be bought from the driver for €2.70. A taxi to the city centre will cost around €20.

Estadio da Luz – Lisbon (Portugal)

The Facts

Name: Estadio da Luz
Address: Avenida General Norton De Matos 1500,
Lisbon,
Portugal
Capacity: 65,000 All Seater
Opened: 25th October 2003 – Benfica 2 Nacional 0

■ About Estadio da Luz

There is a misconception that the Estadio da Luz actually means Stadium of Light. Whilst the original Estadio da Luz was an open-air monster of a stadium, the name actually comes from the area around the stadium (Luz). One thing is certain though – the modern version of the stadium is magnificent, one of the best in Europe and is rightly referred to as a cathedral of football. The original stadium was one of the largest in the world with a capacity of 120,000, spread out in a huge bowl with three tiers – very similar in style to the Nou Camp in Barcelona.

During the 1960s and 1970s the stadium often hosted over 100,000 spectators – especially for the matches against neighbours Sporting. The stadium was originally built in the 1950s and opened its gates for the first time in 1954. Originally it was a single-tier stadium with a capacity of 50,000. As the team's success was matched with an increased demand for tickets, the club added a second tier in the 1960s, taking capacity to over 80,000.

In a bold move by the club's directors to prove to the world that they were one of the world's leading clubs, a third tier was constructed during the late 1970s – coinciding with a downwards spiral of the club – but taking the capacity to 120,000.

As the club struggled to compete with Porto, and a resurgent Sporting, the ground fell into disrepair – and often safety decreed that only the lower tier could be open for games. However, in 2001 worked commenced on the building of a new stadium to host the finals of Euro 2004 that had been awarded to Portugal two years earlier. The decision was made to build the new stadium partly on the site of the existing stadium, and so the team continued to play in a strange environment with half of their existing stadium demolished, and a new one going up in its place.

The end result, designed by Damon Lavelle, is a magnificent structure and opened in 2003 when Benfica played Nacional of Uruguay in front of a sell-out 65,000. The stadium is a three-tier structure, and is similar in design to the new Emirates Stadium in London. All of the seats offer excellent views of the action. The new stadium hosted some of the biggest matches during Euro 2004, including the England v France match – which caused significant logistical problems in trying to get 40,000 England fans into a stadium in 20 minutes and of course the final between the home nation and Greece. The stadium has a 4-star rating from UEFA, meaning it can host UEFA Cup Final matches. However, it is now over 14 years since the stadium has hosted a European

Estadio da Luz – Lisbon (Portugal)

final – the last one being the 1992 European Cup Winners' Cup final when Werder Bremen beat Monaco in front of just 16,000.

■ Who plays there?

It is hard to imagine that 40 years ago Benfica were the greatest team in the world. Back-to-back European Cup victories in 1961 and 1962 broke the monopoly of the competition by Real Madrid, and a third victory was only snatched from them by a late AC Milan goal in 1963 and Inter Milan in 1965. The team also took part in the legendary 1968 Final at Wembley, when the rampant Manchester United beat them 4–1 in extra time.

That team, captained by Jose Aguas and starring the legend that was Eusabio, had also dominated domestic football with eight titles in the decade as well as four national cup titles.

The club were formed in 1904 by a group of wealthy sports fanatics who lived along the river in Belem. The principles of the club were laid down so that only Portuguese nationals should ever play for the club (although they did bend the rules to include players from their colonies such as Mozambique and Angola, like Eusebio) – a state that existed right up until the early 1980s. After Porto's surprising league title victory in the first-ever national league in 1935, Benfica took over the mantle as national champions by capturing the next three titles, as well as three further titles in the 1940s and four national cups. Titles followed regularly during the 1950s before the team embarked on their plans to conquer Europe in the 1960s. Unfortunately, the team began losing the plot off the field during the 1970s. Bad administration led to money bleeding out of the club, and despite regularly filling the Stadium of Light with close to 100,000 people, the club faced financial ruin.

In 1983 the club turned to young Swede Sven Goran Eriksson, to lead the club forward. In his first season the club captured a league title as well as reaching the UEFA Cup Final where they lost on aggregate to Anderlecht. In 1986 Eriksson left for Roma, although he was soon tempted back in 1989 after the club had failed to beat PSV Eindhoven in the European Cup Final, where again he led them to the title, and into the European Cup. In one of the most impressive runs to the finals in recent years, they scored 19 goals. In a tight two-leg semi-final, a 2–1 defeat in Marseilles proved to be decisive as the away goal took them into the final in Vienna with their old foes AC Milan. Unfortunately a single Rijkaard goal broke their hearts in that final.

And so the 1990s dawned on a club that played in a stadium that had seen better days, a team that was too old and a leadership team without direction. Eriksson's reign ended soon after he delivered the title in 1991. Despite a deal to sell their TV rights to buy the latest star of the national team, Paulo Futre, there was no money left

in the bank to actually pay anyone else's wages and the team suffered. After a single title win in the middle of the 1990s the most notable incident in the decade was the decision to appoint Graeme Souness as manager. Within 12 months they were floundering in mid-table with a team featuring Scott Minto, Brian Deane, Mark Pembridge, Michael Thomas and Dean Saunders. Crowds started to fall as the tradition of only playing Portuguese nationals was clearly going out of the window. The rise of Porto and Boavista in the north during this period was a bridge too far for President Azevedo and in March 1999 Souness was sacked.

With nothing left to mortgage to rebuild the team, Benfica's saving grace came in the decision to award the European Championships 2004 to Portugal, which meant that the stadium was going to be redeveloped at little cost to the club. On-field changes started slowly first under Italian legend Trappattoni who delivered a championship and national cup in 2005, and more recently under the leadership of Fernando Santos. The team have, however, managed to build on their surprisingly impressive performances in the Champions League in 2005 when they beat Manchester Utd in the final group game to qualify for the knock-out stages. In the 2nd round game versus Liverpool they stunned the reds with a 2–0 win at Anfield, adding to the 1–0 victory in Lisbon to reach the quarter-finals. There they faced Barcelona, who lived up to their billing as favourites by winning easily over the two legs. Current stars of the team include Nuno Gomes, Rui Costa and Giorgos Karagounis but they have failed to make an impact on the domestic scene, as Porto and Sporting have run away at the top of the table, Benfica having to be content with a 3rd place finish last season.

■ How to get there

The stadium is located opposite the Colombo shopping centre, on the intersection of the Avenida General Matos de Matos and Avenida Lusiada. The nearest metro station is Colégio Militar/Luz, which is located in the shopping centre. It is six stops and 15 minutes from Marques de Pombal. A taxi from the city centre will cost around €15.

■ Getting a ticket

With average attendances around 48,000, and a capacity of over 64,000, for most games it is not particularly difficult to get a ticket on the day. Even for the derby matches versus Sporting, and the grudge match with Porto, tickets are available on days running up to the game from the ticket office at the stadium or from one of the club shops in the Colombo shopping centre. Tickets can also be bought online for collection at the stadium. Tickets range in price from €20 for a top-tier seat in the Piso 3 Superior, to €55 in the lower tier in the Bancada PT Comunicacoes or Sapo stands.

Estadio Jose Alvalade XXI – Lisbon (Portugal)

The Facts

Name: Estadio Jose Alvalade XXI
Address: Rua Professor Fernando da Fonseca,
Lisbon,
Portugal
Capacity: 52,000 All Seater
Opened: 6th August 2003
Sporting v Manchester United

■ About Jose Alvalade XXI

The story behind Sporting's stadium development is almost identical to rival Benfica's. A club in terminal decline that couldn't compete on the pitch or an international stage, playing in a soulless arena that had passed its sell-by date. Then the decision was made in December 2001 to award the Euro 2004 championships to Portugal and the rest is history. There were long debates about which stadium should be developed but in the end it was decided that both Benfica and Sporting should have new grounds.

Work commenced on the new Alvalade in early 2002. Originally the plan was to rebuild the existing Alvalade stadium, knocking down each stand in turn, but that proved too problematic at the planning stage. The old stadium was a large bowl-like structure, mostly open air, and had an athletics track around the perimeter that added further to the lack of atmosphere in the ground.

Construction work progressed in a similar way to

Benfica's, with games continuing whilst parts of the old stadium were demolished. The new Alvalade was ready to open its doors less than two years later and in August 2003 a friendly between Sporting and Manchester United inaugurated the stadium. Original plans were for a 40,000-seater stadium, but during the latter stages of planning it was felt that the club would automatically be made to feel inferior to Benfica due to the size of the Estadio da Luz. The stadium consists of four identical two-tier stands, which have a floating roof held up by four yellow columns in each corner which give the stadium a unique look from the outside.

When the stadium is empty one can see the coloured seat mosaics. It was felt that a stadium just filled with green seats, with a green roof and a green pitch may be a bit too much for even the most ardent Sporting fans and so the club introduced a mixture of coloured seats in a random pattern. Sightlines are excellent from all parts of the stadium. The stands are also slightly raised and so even people in the first row get a good view of the action. Since moving to the new stadium average crowds have almost doubled to 30,000 – proving the value in making facilities more pleasant for the fans. The stadium is one of UEFA's 5-star venues and in May 2005 it hosted the UEFA Cup Final when the home team were beaten by CSKA Moscow.

■ Who plays there?

Whilst the rivalry between Sporting and Benfica has

always been one of the most fiercely contested in world football, their list of honours definitely puts them in second place. One single European victory – the European Cup Winners' Cup in 1964 when they beat MTK 4–3 on aggregate is hardly the haul you would expect from one of Europe's greats. They had possibly the best chance they will ever have to double this in 2005 when they won through to the final of the UEFA Cup, to be played on their home ground, but they lost to an impressive CSKA Moscow.

José Alvalade founded the team in 1906, although a team had existed in the area under the name of Campo Grande FC since 1902. They played their first match under the Sporting name in February 1907. Less than a year later the team had adopted the famous green and white kit. Five years later in 1912 the club won its first honour – the championship of Lisbon. In the early 1920s, the first national championship was played, although it wasn't seen as official. However, Sporting took the trophy in Faro with a win over Academica de Coimbra.

The official championship of Portugal began in the mid-1930s and despite Porto and Benfica taking the first few championships, Sporting soon built a team that was the envy of the whole nation. They took their first title in 1941 and then won eight titles in the nine years up until 1958. The team had at last arrived on the domestic scene, but in Europe they found it a bit harder. The team then went on to win championships at intervals of around four years, 1962, 1966, 1970, 1974 and 1980, but again failed to make an impact in Europe. Their best run in the European Cup came in 1982 when they reached the quarter-finals before exiting 2–1 to Spanish champions Real Sociedad. The 1982 championship was to be the last title the club won for nearly 20 years. The next few years were spent sacking coaches at regular intervals, and constant fighting in the boardroom. The team that won that cup in 1995 was littered with star players such as Luis Figo, Jorge Cadete and the two young wide men Dani and Hugo Porfirio.

In 1990 the club was taken over by millionaire José de Sousa Cintra who promised the earth to the members who elected him. His grand plans included a new stadium for the club, and in preparation he made himself very unpopular by clearing the housing developments close to the stadium for his aborted plans. He also decided to sack Bobby Robson from his role as head coach despite the fact they topped the league at the time. His services were soon snapped up by Porto, and less than six months later he led them to a cup final win over Sporting. In 1999, Peter Schmeichel joined the club, and had an immediate effect as the team at last broke their 20-year voodoo by winning the title from Porto. Last season they had to make do with a runners-up spot to Porto, and another shot at Champions League glory.

■ How to get there

The stadium is located next door to the site of the old stadium, in the Campo Grande area of the city. The stadium has its own metro station, Campo Grande, which is located on the Green and Yellow lines. From the city centre it is only six stops and 10 minutes from Marques de Pombal in the city centre. If you are arriving in Lisbon by train, then you will probably arrive at Rossio station close to the riverfront. From here the Green line runs nine stops to Campo Grande in around 20 minutes. If you are coming from the Expo site in the north east of the city then use the Red Line from Oriente, and change at Alameda. There are also a number of buses that run to the stadium including lines 1, 3, 46, 77 and 101. A taxi from the city centre will cost €15, and from the airport around €10.

■ Getting a ticket

With the exception of the local derby game versus Benfica, and the occasions when Sporting actually manage to make it through to the group stages of the Champions League – as they did last season – it is not necessary to book tickets in advance. Tickets for most games go on sale from the club around two weeks before the match. Tickets can also be booked online via the official website. The cheap seats in the upper tiers behind the goal start from €20 for a normal league match, to €35 for a Champions League or a Benfica/Porto match. A seat in the side stands will cost €50 to €90 respectively.

■ Nearest airport – Lisbon Potela Airport (LIS)

Portela is the largest airport in Portugal, serving over 50 airlines. It is located 5 miles from the centre of Lisbon, and close enough to Sporting Lisbon's new stadium that it appears as if planes are trying to land on the futuristic new roof. It is currently served from the UK by the following airlines. **British Airways** and **TAP** fly here from London Gatwick and Heathrow, **Easyjet** from London Luton and **Monarch** from London Gatwick. To travel from the airport into the city centre it is best to catch the regular buses on lines 5 or 22 that run every 15 minutes or so, terminating at Areeiro and Marques de Pombal. Tickets cost €1.20 single.

The Facts

Name: Estadio do Dragao
Address: Avenida Fernão de Magalhães,
1862 Porto,
Portugal
Capacity: 52,000 All Seater
Opened: 16th November 2003 – FC Porto 2
Barcelona 0

■ About Estadio do Dragao

The Estadio do Dragao, 'The Stadium of the Dragons', opened its gates on the 16th November 2003 when Porto beat FC Barcelona 2–0. Like the stadiums in Lisbon, the €100 million construction of the ground was undertaken next door to their previous stadium, known as the Antas. The new stadium is a magnificent structure, designed along the same lines as the Sydney Olympic Stadium, and since copied by the Zentral Stadium in Leipzig, with two huge double-tiered side stands and a sweeping curved roof. The stands behind the two goals have been designed so that another tier could be added, increasing the capacity to over 65,000 if required.

The previous stadium, the Estadio das Antas, was opened in 1952 and held over 50,000 spectators in a huge bowl-like seating area, with two small roofs offering limited protection from the frequent inclement northern Portuguese weather. When Portugal were awarded the

2004 European Championships in 1999, plans were immediately put in place for a new stadium for the team, capable of challenging the stadiums in Lisbon to hold big international matches.

One of the key design features was to be able to quickly move people to and from the stadium – an issue that blighted the Antas stadium. This was achieved by the building of a number of road tunnels under the stadium which link directly onto the main northern ring road, as well as giving the stadium its own metro stop – named Estadio do Dragao. In fact today the transport system has been developed within the city with the Estadio do Dragao stop as a major hub, with lines running from the airport and to Campanhã railway station. The fans soon took to the comforts of their new stadium, and its opening coincided with Porto's amazing run in the Champions League that saw them eventually lift the trophy in Gelsenkirchen. The stadium hosted a number of key matches during Euro 2004, including the shock opening match defeat of the home nation by Greece as well as their semi-final victory over the Czech Republic. Consequently, UEFA have awarded the stadium 5-star status, allowing it to host major European finals.

■ Who plays there?

FC Porto have always been considered one of the big three in Portuguese football. After living in the shadows of the teams from Lisbon for over 40 years, Porto rose during the late 1990s to become one of the most successful teams in Europe. Under the guidance of coach Jose Mourinho, Porto won league titles in 2003 and 2004, as well as the UEFA Cup in 2003 and the ultimate prize, the Champions League, in 2004 before he departed for London and Chelsea.

The club's origins can be traced back to 1893 when one of Porto's biggest wine traders, Antonio D'Almeida, formed a team to play against a rival wine lodge. The team played in the first amateur leagues of Portugal in the early part of the century and won their first honour with a cup win in 1922. They followed this up with another win in 1925 and then again in 1932 before the first national league was launched in 1935. Much to the chagrin of the teams from the capital, FC Porto won the title in the first season. They followed this up with back-to-back championships in 1939 and 1940. As the team entered the 1980s they lagged behind Sporting and Benfica both on and off the pitch. In the mid-1980s Jose Maria Pedroto took over the reigns and delivered immediate results as the team took the title and the Portuguese cup in 1984, and a season later captured the championship again. This allowed them to enter the European Cup, in one of its last seasons before it became the Champions League, for the first time in eight years.

The European Cup run proved to be the turning point for the club. Blessed with an easy draw up to the semi-finals, a 4–2 win over Dinamo Kiev sent them to their first major European final. In a close game, the Portuguese beat Bayern Munich 2–1. The following seasons were a dream for Porto fans. After the European Cup success came the UEFA Super Cup (victory over Ajax over two legs), the World Club Championships (beating Penarol of Uruguay), three more league championships and two minor national cups. In the 1990s under Tomislav Ivic and then Bobby Robson, the team became unbeatable at home, winning the championship in every single year apart from 1991 and 1994, as well as adding cup success on four occasions. European success was a bridge too far during this period, a semi-final defeat to Barcelona in the 1994 Champions League being the closest they came to success.

In 1999 Fernando Santos took over the team and through the goals of Mario Jardel Porto won their fifth consecutive title – a record in Portuguese football. It was to be their last major honour for a couple of years until Mourinho took over in 2002. Under the talismanic young coach Porto set a new level for Portuguese football both at a domestic level and in Europe. The team included players such as Paolo Ferreira, Bennie McCarthy, Deco and Costinha. In 2002 the team started making a mark in Europe with a great run in the UEFA Cup. After a win over Lens in the 3rd round and Denizlispor of Turkey in round four, they drew Panathinaikos in the quarter-finals. After a tense 90 minutes in the second leg in Athens, where Porto overturned a 1–0 deficit, Brazilian striker Derlei hit the winner in the 103rd minute. In the semi-finals, a 4–1 home victory over Lazio set them up for an epic final with

Celtic in Seville. There, despite the inspirational Henrik Larsson, Porto won the game on the Silver Goal, 3–2.

The following season they raised the bar with another championship plus a run to the final of the Champions League after victories over Manchester United, Lyon and Deportivo La Coruna. In Gelsenkirchen the team easily overcame Monaco 3–0, proving a fitting departure for the Chelsea-bound coach. Last season the team were back to their best with a league and cup double, although a disappointing Champions League campaign saw them beaten by Chelsea in the round of 16.

■ How to get there

The stadium has a transport infrastructure to match its impressive stands. When the stadium was built, the pinch point was always going to be how to get the huge crowds in and out of the area quickly and safely. The first consideration was to ensure that traffic exiting and entering the ring road did not impede the normal flow of traffic. This was achieved by a series of exits for each stand, and a number of tunnels under the stadium that filter cars directly into the car parks.

The stadium also had its own metro stop built which ferries fans direct from the Campanhã train station in just 5 minutes. The airport is also linked direct to the stadium by metro – line E (dark blue) makes the 15km journey. The stadium can also be reached by buses 21 and 78 from the city centre.

■ Getting a ticket

The stadium was always built with more supply than demand, meaning it is not difficult to get tickets for any game at the Dragao, including the derby games versus Boavista and the visits of the teams from Lisbon. In fact, the highest ever league attendance at the new stadium was just over 50,000 for the visit of Benfica in 2005. Tickets range in price from €15 for a seat in the Bancada Norte (the Coca-Cola stand) or the Bancada Sul (the EDP stand) amongst the hardcore Porto fans, to the €40 seats in the TMN or PT stands. On match days, tickets can be bought from the ticket offices in the north, east and south stands. To book your seat in advance, the Portuguese section of the website allows you to choose your seat before you buy at http://www.fcporto.pt/servicos/bilheteira.

■ Nearest airport – Francisco Sa Carneiro (OPO)

Porto's modest airport is located 6 miles north of the city. It is named after the Portuguese Prime Minister who was killed in a plane crash here in 1980. **Ryanair** currently serves the airport from Liverpool and London Stansted, as well as **TAP-Portugal** from London Gatwick and Heathrow. To reach the airport you can catch line E of the metro which runs through the city centre to Estadio do Dragao. There is also a regular bus service to the city, running every 30 minutes and costing €1.50.

The Facts

Name: Ghencea Stadium
Address: Bdul Ghencea 35
Bucharest – Sector 5
Romania
Capacity: 27,063 All Seater
Opened: 9th April 1974 – Steaua Bucharest 2
Belgrade 2

■ About Ghencea Stadium

The Ghencea Stadium was a break from the norm when it opened in 1974 as it was one of the first stadiums to open in the Balkans without an athletics track. With stands built close to the pitch it was unique for Romanian football and the fans took to the steep terracing immediately, making the stadium a really intimidating place to visit. Originally the stadium was opened as a 30,000 venue, with around 5,000 standing places behind the goal. These were converted into seating areas in 1991 to make the current capacity just over 28,000. Today the stadium still only has a single roofed stand that sits proudly above the others. Basically the stadium is made up of four uniform single-tier stands, with the main stand having a double row of executive boxes. As of October 2006 the stadium was upgraded to UEFA 4-star level. The club have plans to increase the capacity of the stadium by adding a second tier, which would increase the capacity to around 50,000.

■ Who plays there?

ASA Bucuresti were founded in June 1947 by a group of officers in the Romanian army. Initially the club did not concentrate on football, preferring instead to develop their athletics team. The team were soon renamed as CSCA and they competed in their first major competition, the Romanian cup in 1948. A year later they won the

trophy, beating CSU Cluj 2–1 in the final. The following season, after another name change to CCA (Central House of the Army), they entered the Romanian league and in their first season won the championship, following it up with championships in the next two seasons as well.

In 1961 the club adopted the name Steaua for the first time, which is Romanian for star – the obvious symbol of any team playing under Soviet rule. The club won the championship again in this year, emphasising their dominance in domestic football. They won the championship a further three times during the 1970s before starting to feel pressure from some of the new teams emerging in Romania. At the time money was also very tight within the region, and so investment into football was often ignored. However, money was being diverted into the youth academies which would bear fruits during the 1990s. Under the leadership of Emerich Jenei and Anghel Iordanescu, Steaua began to build a team to compete at the highest level. In 1985 they won the championship at a canter, and so took their place in the 1985/86 European Cup 1st round.

Previous European campaigns had always been short and sweet but with a very kind draw the club managed to overcome Vejle, Honved FC, Kuusysi Lahti and Anderlecht to become the first-ever Romanian side to reach the European Cup Final. On 7 May 1986, in Seville, they met the mighty Barcelona. After a goalless draw over 120 minutes, goalkeeper Duckadam saved all four Barca penalties and in the process delivered the trophy to Steaua. The club followed this up by capturing the European Super Cup by beating Dynamo Kiev in Monaco.

Two seasons later they reached the final again, although they lost to a rampant AC Milan side 4–0. The club continued to dominate domestically with three successive doubles during the late 1980s. In addition, from June 1986 to September 1989, Steaua managed a record 104-match undefeated run domestically, setting a world record for an undefeated stretch. A new breed of

Ghencea Stadium – Bucharest (Romania)

young players started to emerge during the late 1980s with future stars such as Hagi, Popescu, Dumitrescu and Raducioiu playing a bigger part in the team. The team went on another amazing domestic run with six consecutive championship titles between 1992–93 and 1997–98, including three more domestic doubles. The club also made it into the European Champions League group stages on a number of occasions, although two 3rd-place finishes were the best they could muster. As the successful team was broken up again, Steaua needed to regroup and this meant changes its structure from top to bottom.

In came former Italian goalkeeper Walter Zenga as coach who immediately took them to the title again in 2005 and 2006, as well as into the UEFA Cup group stages. They managed to reach the quarter-finals of the competition where they met Middlesbrough, after defeating local rivals Rapid Bucharest in the semi-finals. After a 1–0 home victory, the Romanians took a 2–0 lead at the Riverside and appeared to be coasting to the final in Eindhoven. However, a remarkable Middlesbrough comeback saw them win 4–2 late on and so end Steaua's chances of European glory. Last season they finished runners-up in the league, enabling them to attempt to qualify for the Champions League group stages again under the leadership of Romania's finest-ever player Gheorghe Hagi.

■ How to get there
The simplest way of reaching the stadium is to catch a yellow line 3 metro train to Gorjului which is three stops from Eroilor in the centre of the city. Once you leave the station, you will need to catch a number 41 tram that runs from the left. A single ticket will cost €1.

■ Getting a ticket
The club are currently working on launching a new online portal that will enable fans to book tickets in advance. Until then tickets can only be purchased from the club store in advance. One is also able to book seats for the 'armchair' zone, an area of the main stand that has 700 comfortable seats in an enclosed zone, with air conditioning and a bar. These seats have to be booked in advance by calling the club on +40 21 411 46 56, or by email at contact@steauafc.com. Tickets for other games start from €30 or 100RON for a normal league game in the Tribuna 0, or €15 or 50RON behind the goals in the Peluze stands.

■ Nearest airport – Henri Coandă Airport (OTP)
The Henri Coandă Airport is the largest airport in Romania. It is located in the northern part of the city, known as Otopeni. There are plans to build a new airport in the south of the city at Băneasa which will handle the planned growth of low-cost airlines. The airport currently serves **British Airways** and **TAROM** from London Heathrow. **Wizzair** also fly to Bucharest but use the much smaller Aurel Vlaicu airport located 3km south of the main airport. The airport is located around 11 miles north of Bucharest and is accessed via the RATB express bus route 783 which runs to the smaller Aurel Vlaicu airport on the way to the city centre. Buses run every 30 minutes, and the journey is around 35 minutes. Tickets can be purchased from an RATB booth in the terminal and cost 5RON or €1.50 return.

Dynamo Stadium – Moscow (Russia)

The Facts

Name: Dynamo Stadium
Address: 36 Leningradsky Prospect,
125190 Moscow,
Russia
Capacity: 36,450 All Seater
Opened: 17th August 1928 FC Dinamo v R Kima

■ About Dynamo Stadium

The Russian ground merry-go-round continues at a pace as the Dynamo Stadium is now home to Dynamo Moscow, and new tenants and Soviet champions CSKA Moscow. However, the stadium is now showing signs of age, having originally opened in 1928. Amazingly, considering the harsh climate in Russia, the stadium is completely uncovered, offering no protection from the wind, rain and snow that characterises the Russian season.

One of the most notable things about the stadium is the huge floodlights that seem to have enough light bulbs to light up the whole city, let alone the stadium at night. Seats are of the bolted-onto-the-terrace type, meaning that they have little leg room and the rake of the steps is poor. That said, the stadium does look quite smart in the sunshine, but very miserable when the autumn rains start. The ground has a small athletics track, which pushes the end stands back, adding further drawbacks to fans behind the goal. Very little has changed in terms of stadium feel

and design since the ground was chosen to host the 1980 Olympics football tournament.

■ Who plays there?

The Dynamo Stadium is home to both Dynamo and CKSA Moscow. Dynamo Moscow are traditionally known and hated for being the Russian secret police team, although they can actually trace their roots back to the 1880s when Charles Charnock, an English industrialist based in Moscow, put a factory team together. The team were the premier team of Moscow during the pre-revolution years, winning the Moscow championship from 1910 to 1914. After the Revolution in 1917, the club fell into the hands of the secret police, the Cheka, who were certainly influential in building a formidable team during the early 1920s. In 1936, Dynamo won the first-ever Soviet championship and followed it up with the double in 1937. The club then regularly won the Soviet championship, albeit with some strong rumours of influencing the opposition and officials alike. In 1949 the club's dominance really came to the fore, with six championships between 1949 and 1959. It was during this period that legendary goalkeeper Lev Yashin started his long career with the club. As the interests of the Interior Ministry were diverted away from football to the Cold War in the 1960s, the club's on-field success started to wane. Two further championships in 1963 and 1976 were supplemented by Soviet cup wins on four occasions, as well as a European Cup Winners' Cup final appearance in 1972 when they lost to Glasgow Rangers 3–2.

Since the creation of the new Russian order, the club have one solitary cup final win to their name in 1995. Last season they finished 14th, avoiding relegation by one place. Despite all of their success, in recent years the club has failed to make an impact at all on European football. Whilst during the 1970s and 1980s they were regular starters in the UEFA Cup, Champions League qualification has eluded them.

CSKA Moscow – the former Red Army team – were considered for most of their history as Moscow's third team, behind the mighty Dynamo, and the new billionaires Spartak. However, in recent years, thanks to the money of their own billionaire, Roman Abramovich, and his Sibneft oil company, CSKA have been the team to beat. They have also broken nearly 20 years of European emptiness by becoming the first Russian (as opposed to Soviet) team to win a European trophy when they captured the UEFA Cup in Sporting Lisbon's backyard in 2005. The club were formed in 1911, and in 1923 the Red Army took control of the club, retaining a major shareholding right up until the late 1990s. The golden period for the club came just after the Second World War when they won five Soviet championships and three Soviet cups between 1945 and 1951. After the 1951 season the team fell on hard times as the hold of Josef Stalin took effect on Russian life. Their next championship came in the 1970 season, and then the club had to wait until the Soviet championship in 1991 to capture the title again.

In 2003 the club turned back to former coach Valery Gazzaev and with Roman's money the team was rebuilt on a basis of buying the best Russian players and carefully selected foreign imports such as the Brazilians Vagner Love and Jo who fired the club to Russian premier league titles in 2003 and 2005, and into the Champions League

group stages where they met Arsenal, Porto and Hamburg in a tough group. In the 2007 season, Dynamo had their best campaign for years, finishing in sixth place eventually, whilst CSKA saw their recent domination undone by Zenit St Petersburg who pipped Spartak to the title, relegating CSKA into a UEFA Cup spot for 2008/09.

■ How to get there
The easiest way to reach the stadium is the dark green Metro Line 2 that runs straight through the city to Dynamo Metro stop. The ground is just behind this station. Obviously, on a match day this station may be a bit crowded so it may be wise to use the next stop at Aeroport and then walk back down Leningradsky Prospect. Dynamo station is five stops from Red Square and takes no longer than 10 minutes to complete.

■ Getting a ticket
Ticket prices vary a little depending on whether CSKA or Dynamo are at home. Tickets for a seat behind the Dynamo goal start from just 300 roubles (£6) ranging to 4,000 roubles (around £80) for a VIP seat (although still uncovered!), but will come with all of the trappings of Russian luxury. For CSKA games (excluding the Champions League), tickets start from 200 roubles behind the goal (£4) to 2000 roubles for a VIP seat (£40). Neither team are very well supported in the grand scheme of things. Despite being top of the table for most of the season, CSKA average just 12,000, whilst Dynamo's crowds have dropped to below 8,500. A few games do sell out though, such as the derbies versus Spartak and Lokomotiv. Do bear in mind that CSKA play their Champions League matches at Lokomotiv's stadium across town.

Lokomotiv Stadium – Moscow (Russia)

The Facts

Name: Lokomotiv Stadium
Address: 125 Bolshaya Cherkizovskaya,
107553 Moscow,
Russia
Capacity: 30,100 All Seater
Opened: 1st August 2002

■ About Lokomotiv Stadium

The Lokomotiv Stadium is an oasis in the middle of chaos in terms of Russian football grounds. It was built on the site of the former stadium in 2002, and is a shining beacon of modern design that would not look out of place in the Premiership in England. It has four almost identical two-tier stands, all linked together with a pillar at each corner used to hold the roof up. All the seats are covered and offer protection from the harsh Russian elements, as well as having unobstructed views. Each stand has different colour seats, which helps indicate your stand if you don't understand the Russian script on your ticket. The low roof also helps the crowd generate an excellent atmosphere on match days, especially when the visitors are CSKA or Spartak Moscow.

■ Who plays there?

Lokomotiv are now a serious challenger to the former domination of Russian football by Spartak and CSKA.

A 3rd place finish in 1994 was their highest in the new Russian order, and the following season they went one better by finishing runners-up to Spartak-Alania Vladikavkaz. After a quiet few years the team bounced back into the limelight with a first-ever Russian cup final victory in 1996. In 2002, with the goals of Dimitri Loskov, they finally took their first title, repeating the success in 2004. The following season they led the league almost from day one before a series of strange defeats let in CSKA to take the title and relegate Lokomotiv to 3rd place.

The team have also been one of the most consistent on the European scene out of all of the Russian pretenders. They reached the European Cup Winners' Cup semi-finals in 1998 and 1999, losing to Stuttgart and Lazio respectively. In the Champions League they have had a surprising couple of campaigns. Their first-ever campaign was in 2001/2002 when they finished third in the group stages after coming through the qualifying rounds. In 2002/2003 they were drawn with Bruges, Barcelona and Galatasaray in the Champions League, and managed to sneak second place in a very open group with an excellent win in Turkey. In the second group stage the team only managed to gain a single point from their matches versus Borussia Dortmund, AC Milan and Real Madrid in a group that couldn't really have been any harder. Two years later they pipped Inter Milan into second place behind Arsenal to reach the round of 16. There they met in-form Monaco who won on away goals and then went on to reach the final against Porto. Unfortunately last season's UEFA Cup campaign lasted two matches as the club went out 3–2 on aggregate to the Belgium's Zulte Waregem. They will be hoping to break the CSKA/Spartak rule at the top of the table this season after another 3rd-place finish in 2006, although they did win the Soviet cup.

■ How to get there

The stadium is located in the North East quadrant of Moscow. The area around the stadium isn't what you would call plush, with a market and a few 'budget' supermarkets. The stadium has its own Metro stop on the red Line 1 at Cherkizovskaya, one stop from the north end of the line. From Red Square (Okhotny Ryad) it is eight stops and 20 minutes to the stadium. There is also an overland train station above the Metro – trains here run on the outer Moscow loop line.

There is an alternative route that involved using the purple Line 3 to Partizanskaya (five stops from Red Square), and then a 15-minute walk northwards from the station, passing Izmaylovo market on your way. The final option is a taxi. You can hail down almost any car in

Moscow, and if the driver feels like stopping you can commandeer his car as an unofficial or 'gypsy' taxi. Agree a fee beforehand for the journey but you should not pay more than 200 roubles for the journey from the city centre to the stadium.

■ Getting a ticket

Despite having the best-looking stadium in Moscow, the adage that you should 'Build it and they will come' hasn't quite held true for Lokomotiv. Average attendances at the old ground were always low, reaching at best 6,000, and whilst these have increased to around the 12,000 mark since completion of the new stadium, it still means lots of empty seats each week. CSKA have recently moved their Champions League matches to the stadium and sold out their games versus Hamburg and Arsenal in 2006. Tickets for a Lokomotiv match go on sale online via the website from ten days before a game, or can be bought from the ticket booths on the main road to the south of the stadium. Tickets range in price from 1,400 roubles (approximately £4.50) behind the goals to 6,000 roubles for a seat in the VIP section of the west stand.

Luzhniki Stadium – Moscow (Russia)

The Facts

Name: Luzhniki Stadium
Address: 24 Luzhetskaya nab,
119048 Moscow,
Russia
Capacity: 80,600 All Seater
Opened: 31st July 1980 – USSR v China

■ About Luzhniki Stadium

Whilst many see the National Stadium as a relic of the past, UEFA have decided that it is important enough, and more relevantly, capable of hosting big games still and awarded it the honour of hosting the 2008 Champions League final.

The stadium was originally built as part of the Luzhniki Sports Complex for the 1980 Summer Olympics, and is still the biggest stadium in Russia. It is also one of the few major stadiums in the world that uses artificial grass – although this will have to be replaced for the 2008 Champions League final. The stadium originally had a capacity of 103,000 and has hosted events in the past as varied as show jumping, speedway and ice hockey. In 1982 during a UEFA Cup game between Spartak and HFC Haarlem over 60 people were killed in a stampede caused by a last-minute goal. Initially the Soviet media completely ignored the incident, dedicating no more than a paragraph to it in the local press and even then only

stating there had been a few minor injuries. There is now a small plaque at the stadium commemorating those who died. There is also a magnificent statue of Lenin on the main North Boulevard.

The stadium is very smart-looking from the inside, with seats in three bands of yellow, orange and red. The athletics track does hinder the atmosphere, although the roof means that the noise generated by the home fans in the west end of the stadium can be quite intimidating. The concourse areas are really showing their age though. Views are unobstructed, and at night the stadium roof is lit up from the outside, making the whole area literally shine.

For most league matches, only the north and south stands are open. When Torpedo are at home, the fans are placed in the south stand, with any away fans located opposite. When Spartak are at home, the home fans use the west curve as well. Crowds for most games are not too impressive. Torpedo manage to average just 6,200, whilst Spartak have an average of just under 20,000. In the opening game of the 2006 Champions League Spartak drew a crowd of 75,101 for their game versus Sporting Lisbon.

■ Who plays there?

Spartak Moscow have had a nomadic existence, playing for the last 20 years at Dynamo's stadium, Lokomotiv's old stadium, and now ground-sharing the huge Luzhniki Stadium with Torpedo. Land has been secured for a new

Luzhniki Stadium – Moscow (Russia)

stadium close to Tushino airfield and building should commence in 2007, with a completion date of late 2009.

Up until the introduction of Roman's roubles at CSKA, Spartak were the team of the new Russian Republic. From the start of the first Russian premier league in 1992 until the end of last season, Spartak have won nine titles – although the last one was in 2001. They have also won the Russian cup on three occasions. However, European progress has always eluded them. Finishing 2nd to CSKA in the 2005/2006 season at least gave them opportunity to try to qualify for the Champions League group stages. An unconvincing win over Sheriff in the 2nd round on away goals gave them a tricky tie away at Czech champions Slovan Liberec. A 2–1 victory in the Luzhniki, however, was enough to take them into the group stages for the first time since 2002, where they played Sporting Lisbon, Bayern Munich and Inter Milan in a very tough group. Their European pedigree has been less than successful considering they are Russia's biggest club. Their best performance in any competition has been the semi-final stages which they reached in 1991 in the Champions League, 1993 in the Cup Winners' Cup and finally in the UEFA Cup in 1998.

The club can trace its origins back to the early 1920s. The team won their first championship in 1936 and followed it up with the double in 1939. Further titles followed with regularity until the mid-1970s when the club was relegated. They returned to the top division in 1978, winning the title the following year. In 2000 the club was taken over by oil magnate Andrei Chervichenko who owned the Gazprom Oil Company. Initially funds were made available to strengthen the team, including the likes of Fernando Cavenaghi for over £6.5m from River Plate, although this situation was soon reversed and Spartak became a selling club. Talent that has left the club recently includes Nemanja Vidic, to Manchester United in January 2006.

With so many teams playing at the highest level in Moscow it is obvious that some will attract more media interest than others. Torpedo currently sit in the latter category. The club have had a quiet existence to date, capturing three championships since their inception in 1930, the last one over 30 years ago in 1976. The club had traditionally been the team of the working classes in the south-east of the city, and are named after a car-manufacturing plant that funded the club to some extent for many years. Since the creation of the Russian premier league in 1992, their best finish was in 2000 when they finished 3rd. However, last season they could not find any consistency and finished second from bottom. The team currently play at the huge Luzhniki Stadium, although they only average 6,200 for league matches. However, the same company owns the club as the Luzhniki and so any chances of moving back to their roots at the Eduard Streltsov Stadion are remote.

■ How to get there

The stadium forms the focal point of the whole Sports Complex, and is located on a bend in the Moskva River in the south-west of the city. The closest metro stop is Sportivnaya, which is just to the north of the stadium, almost under the central ring road. From the city centre, it is just four stops by Metro. To the east of the stadium, built on a bridge over the Moskva River, is the newly constructed station of Universitet, which is one stop further down the line from Sportivnaya.

■ Getting a ticket

With over 65,000 spare seats for most Spartak and Torpedo home league games, turning up a few minutes before kick-off is never a problem at the Luzhniki. The ticket windows are located on the left-hand side of the main entrance, at the north end of the stadium. As with most public places in Moscow, terrorism is still a threat and so you will be expected to have any bags inspected as well as going through an airport-style metal detector.

Ticket prices vary according to the game. For a run of the mill 'B' grade league game, a seat watching Torpedo in the south stand costs less than 2,000 roubles (£5), whilst prices are almost doubled for Spartak matches. Spartak recently got over 75,000 for a Champions League match with prices starting from 5,000 roubles – which in terms of average weekly wages in some parts of Moscow is a significant part of their salary.

■ Nearest airport – Sheremetyevo (SVO)

Sheremetyevo was the original Moscow airport and hub for **Aeroflot**, who fly here three times a day from London Heathrow. The airport serves almost 12 million passengers annually and chaos reigns on most days. The easiest route to the city is to take the express bus line from Savyolovsky railway station to Lobnaya metro and then catch a bus. Alternatively you can do what the locals do and use the Marshrutkas (minibus taxis) that run from the terminals to the Metro station at Rechnoi Vokzal at the end of the Green Line 2. If you must get a taxi be prepared to pay upwards of $80 for an hour journey.

■ Domodedovo International Airport (DME)

Located 22 miles south of the centre of the city and linked directly to Paveletsky rail terminal in the city centre by the Aeroexpress, Domodedovo is gaining in popularity and importance each year. Since 2003, the airport has also been home to **British Airways** and **Emirates**. The train station is located at the far end of the terminal – trains run every 30 minutes and a ticket costs 125 roubles each way. Make sure you keep your paper ticket as you will need it to get through the barriers at each end.

Celtic Park – Glasgow (Scotland)

The Facts

Name: Celtic Park
Address: 18 Kerry Street,
Glasgow G40 3RE,
Scotland
Capacity: 60,830 All Seater
Opened: 1892

■ About Celtic Park

Celtic Park is the biggest football stadium in Scotland and the second biggest behind Old Trafford in Britain. It is also one of the best examples of how a traditional stadium can be redeveloped into a truly magnificent arena.

The club have called this area home since 1892. Noted architect Archibald Leitch helped design the main stand during the early part of the 20th century, although for decades after they moved here the stadium was no more than huge banks of earth on which benches were put. These banks were made larger during the 1930s, and it was towards the end of the decade that the record attendance of 92,000 was recorded against Rangers.

The major redevelopment work started in the club's centenary season, 1988. At the time most of the stadium was uncovered and behind the goals the stands curved away from the pitch. Work commenced on rebuilding all the stands, apart from the main stand. The final parts of the ground were finished in 2000, making it an all-seater stadium holding 60,000 people. The huge North Stand, previously known as the 'Jungle', holds almost half of the stadium's capacity, with seats for 27,000. The club are still working on becoming a UEFA 5-star venue, and there are plans being drawn up to demolish the main stand and complete the uniform two-tier stadium which would have a capacity of around 70,000. The stadium today is one of the most atmospheric in Europe when it is full, which it is on most occasions that Celtic play here. The views from most parts of the stadium are excellent, although the walk up to the upper tiers can be hard work. The stadium is occasionally used for concerts, as well as hosting the national team on a number of occasions. Tours are available on a daily basis, but you do need to book in advance by calling +44 141 551 4308. Access to the museum and the tour costs £8.50.

■ Who plays there?

Parkhead, or Celtic Park as it is now more commonly known, has been the home to Celtic for over 100 years. The club are also famous for their huge away travelling fans, which was most evident in the 2003 UEFA Cup Final in Seville when an estimated 80,000 Celtic fans travelled to Spain to try and watch their team play Porto. They have won the Scottish league title on 41 occasions, including five times in the last seven years. Added to this are 47 domestic cups and finally (and in the eyes of Celtic fans most importantly) a European Cup which they won in 1967.

The club were originally formed as a boys' club – set up by Brother Walfrid who was heavily involved in community work with the exiled Irish population in the east end of Glasgow. In May 1888 the club played its first match, unsurprisingly against Rangers. It took the club just four more years to win their first trophy. In the early part of the 20th century under the stewardship of Willie Maley the club began to dominate Scottish football. Between 1904 and 1910 the club won six consecutive titles and went on to win 30 major trophies before the Second World War. In the summer of 1965 the club turned to ex-captain Jock Stein to bring the glory years back to Parkhead. Within ten years he had delivered another 'nine in a row' championships, four domestic doubles and in 1967 they won five trophies, including the European Cup final versus Inter Milan in Lisbon. In 1970 they reached the final again, losing 2–1 to Feyenoord in Milan.

Over the next few seasons, managers came and went with regularity, unable to re-create the standards set by Stein. These included Billy McNeil, David Hay, Liam Brady and Lou Macari. In 1994 the club were almost financially down and out and issued a cry for investment. In came Fergus McCann and his consortium and saved the club from financial ruin. He immediately started on a redevelopment plan of the dilapidated stadium, as well as investing in the team. However, the managerial seat was still seen as a hot potato as Tommy Burns, Wim Jansen and Dr Jozef Venglos could not meet the expectation of the board or the fans. This run of failure cumulated in the appointment of the so-called dream team of Kenny Dalglish and John Barnes in July 1999. Despite having such talent in the team as Paolo Di Canio, Jorge Cadete and Henrik Larsson, the team languished behind the likes of Hearts and Aberdeen going into a seemingly easy cup game versus 3rd Division Inverness Caledonian Thistle. In one of the greatest upsets in recent history, the team from the Highlands beat Celtic 3–1, prompting the famous headlines in the *Sun* newspaper, 'Super Caley go ballistic, Celtic are atrocious'. Barnes was soon on his way, replaced by Martin O'Neill.

The Irishman wasted no time in stamping his authority on the team, and in his first season the club won the domestic treble. The team also started a two-season-long unbeaten run at home, notching up 77 games without defeat. In the four seasons O'Neill was in charge, he delivered the championship three times as well as five domestic cups. The 2003 UEFA Cup Final was probably the pinnacle of O'Neill's time at the club and it was with some surprise that he announced he was standing down for personal reasons at the end of the 2005 season. The club wasted little time in appointing Gordon Strachan to the post. However, his start was nothing short of a disaster. Paired against unknown Slovakian champions ArtMedia in the first round of the Champions League, the team lost

5–0 in Bratislava (they subsequently won the 2nd leg 4–0 to regain some pride), and a few weeks later lost 6–0 to Kilmarnock in the league.

However, by the end of the season all was well as the club won the title. In 2006/2007 the team dominated the league from the word go, and bookmaker Paddy Power actually paid out bets on Celtic winning the league in November! The league was sewn up in April, and a domestic double secured when Jan Vennegoor of Hesselink's goal won the Scottish Cup Final.

■ How to get there
Celtic Park is located 3km to the east of the city centre in one of the regenerated areas of Glasgow. The easiest way to reach the ground by public transport is to catch bus lines 61, 62 or 64 from Argyle Street in the city centre. The nearest train station is Dalmarnock which is on the Motherwell line from Glasgow Central. The station is a 10-minute walk away down London Road.

■ Getting a ticket
Celtic are as well supported today as they were 30 years ago, although the capacity at Celtic Park has been reduced dramatically. With a capacity of 60,000 at the moment, the club play their home matches in front of an average of 58,000. Games against Rangers are always sold out. For the rest you are strongly advised to arrange to purchase your tickets in advance. Tickets can be purchased in advance from the box office on +44 141 551 8653. Some tickets are made available at http://celtic.ticketmaster.co.uk. Tickets range in price from £22 in the upper north, Jock Stein and Lisbon Lions stand. A place in the main stand starts from £25.

Hampden Park – Glasgow (Scotland)

The Facts

Name: Hampden Park
Address: Letherby Drive,
Glasgow G42 9BA,
Scotland
Capacity: 52,000 All Seater
Opened: 31st October 1903 – Queens Park 1 Celtic 0

■ About Hampden Park

Hampden Park is one of the oldest national stadiums still being used, having originally opened on the 31st October 1903. Until the opening of the Maracana Stadium in Rio in 1950, the stadium was the largest in the world, with a capacity of over 150,000. The record attendance at the stadium during the golden period was 149,415 for a game between Scotland and England in 1937. The stadium has set more records in footballing history than any other. It was the first ground to introduce turnstiles in the late 19th century, the first to have an all-ticket match (in 1884), the first to install a public address system and the first to install a press box in 1906. The stadium also holds a number of attendance records apart from the game in 1937. In 1970 over 136,500 attended a European Cup match between Celtic and Leeds United, which is the biggest attendance at a UEFA game.

The stadium today holds just over 50,000 but it is clear that significant amounts of money have been spent

on it to convert it from the crumbling terraces that made up the ground in the 1970s and 1980s. The installation of the roof in 1999 was the final step in the redevelopment of the stadium that saw all four stands demolished and rebuilt. One bad point is the inclusion of an athletics track that does put significant distance between the fans behind the goal and the pitch. The stadium's seats are coloured to depict the St Andrews Flag at either end of the stadium, which is an unusual touch. The final confirmation of the stadium's return to former glories was in 2003 when the venue was chosen to hold the Champions League final between Real Madrid and Bayer Leverkusen, and of course the 2007 UEFA Cup final between Espanyol and Sevilla.

■ Who plays there?

Despite having two other stadiums in the city that hold over 50,000, Hampden Park is firmly the spiritual home of the national team. However, very few people from outside Scotland can believe that it is also the home to Queens Park FC – one of Scotland's oldest and certainly most traditional clubs. The club were also responsible for arranging the first-ever match between an English team and a Scottish team on the 20th November 1872. In the same season the club also took part in the first-ever English FA Cup competition, and in fact actually exited the competition without losing as they couldn't fulfil their commitment to play the replay against Wanderers due to the cost of travelling back down to London. They did make it to the final in 1884 and 1885, finishing runners-up on both occasions.

The club went on to dominate the cup competition north of the border, winning the trophy for three consecutive seasons in 1874 to 1876. The following decade saw them crowned as Scotland's most famous club as they took the cup on a further seven occasions. However, since then they have had little success, as professionalism has taken over the game and consigned the club to the lower reaches of Scottish football. They did reach the Scottish 1st division in 1981, winning the 2nd division title the previous season, although they soon returned to the bottom level. In 2000 they won the 3rd division title although again they were relegated a few seasons later. The stadium has been a firm favourite of UEFA in the past, hosting a number of major finals. It is probably best known for the 1960 European Cup final when a Di Stefano and Puskas-inspired Real Madrid demolished Eintracht Frankfurt 7–3 in front of 130,000 spectators. In 1976 it hosted the final again as Bayern Munich beat Saint Etienne, and of course in May 2007 it hosted the UEFA Cup final between Sevilla and Espanyol.

The stadium is also used for concerts, having played host to the likes of Robbie Williams, Rod Stewart and Oasis, as well as hosting a number of other sports including world championship boxing (Mike Tyson fought his last fight here on British soil), Rugby Union in the 1999 World Cup finals and American football, with the stadium being the home venue to the now defunct Scottish Claymores.

■ How to get there
Hampden Park is located in the south of the city, close enough to be classed as central. It is well served by local transport although on a nice sunny day you could quite easily walk there from the city centre. The nearest station to the stadium is Mount Florida, which is four stops from Central Station. Also close by are King's Park and Crosshill stations. From Mount Florida, exit the station and walk down Bolton Drive straight in front of you. Cross two roads and then follow the road into Somerville Drive. The stadium is on your right. If you want to arrive by bus then Line 31 runs from St Enoch Centre, line 37 from Glasgow Cross and line 75 from Argyle Street.

■ Getting a ticket
Ticket availability will vary depending the category of game you are planning on seeing at Hampden Park.

For matches involving the Scottish national team, the quality of the opponent will certainly have a bearing on price and availability of tickets. The recent qualifying game versus France was sold out in hours, whilst tickets for the game versus Georgia were available up until kick-off. In normal circumstances tickets can be purchased in advance from the stadium ticket office on 0141 620 4000. Tickets are also sold via http://www.ticketmaster.co.uk. Prices vary from game to game, although expect to pay around £30 minimum for a decent seat. The stadium is still the home of Queens Park FC, the only amateur club playing in the top level of British football. They regularly play in front of crowds of less than 1,000 in the huge stadium. A £9 ticket sold on the door will get you a seat (or 20!) to watch them. For cup games, tickets are sold by the respective clubs.

The stadium also runs hourly tours of the museum and the ground. These can be booked by emailing info@scottishfootballmuseum.org.uk. Admission is £8.50 for adults and £4.50 for children.

■ Nearest airport – Glasgow International (GLA)
Glasgow International is slowly becoming one of the busiest airports in the UK, now handling over 9 million passengers a year. It is located around 8 miles west of the city centre. A regular Scottish Citylink bus runs every 10 minutes from outside Arrivals to Buchanan Street. Tickets cost £4.30 single. Alternatively, catch a local bus from bus top 1 to Paisley Gilmour Street, and then catch a train into Central Station. **Easyjet** fly here from Bristol, London Gatwick, Luton and Stansted. **Air Berlin** fly here daily from London Stansted. Other regional operators include **Flybe** from Belfast, Birmingham, Exeter, Manchester, Norwich and Southampton, whilst **BMI** fly here from Leeds Bradford, Birmingham, Cardiff, Manchester and London Heathrow. **British Airways** covers the routes from London Gatwick and Heathrow.

■ Alternative Airport – Glasgow Prestwick (PIK)
Ryanair's version of Glasgow Airport is located close to the Irish Sea in Prestwick. They fly here from Bournemouth and London Stansted on a daily basis. The airport is 30 miles south east of Glasgow, and handles 2.3million passengers a year. The airport, like Shannon, was originally a refuelling stop for transatlantic flights. To reach the city centre, catch one of the regular trains from Prestwick station to Glasgow Central, journey time 44 minutes.

The Facts

Name:	Ibrox Stadium
Address:	Ibrox Stadium, Glasgow G51 2XD, Scotland
Capacity:	51,100 All Seater
Opened:	30th December 1899 – Rangers 3 Hearts 1

■ **About Ibrox Stadium**

Ibrox is one of UEFA's 5-Star stadiums, meaning it has the capacity and facilities to host major European finals, although it is yet to have this privilege. However, unlike other 5-star stadiums such as the Millennium Stadium in Cardiff, the AOL Arena in Hamburg and the Stade de France in Paris, Ibrox still retains many of its original features, including the listed main stand façade.

The original stadium was opened in 1887 with a capacity of just 15,000 against the then English champions Preston North End. Less than 12 years later Glasgow Rangers moved up the road to a newly built stadium that is the present Ibrox. The stadium was mainly constructed of wooden stands and it was here in 1902 that one of the terraces collapsed, killing 26 people. After the war, in 1919 the stadium was redeveloped under the supervision of Archibald Leitch who constructed a stadium which could accommodate close to 80,000 people. Twenty years later over 118,000 attended the Old Firm game against Celtic – a record attendance in Britain for a league match. In 1971 another disaster befell the stadium as a crush developed on a staircase in the game versus Celtic, killing 77 people. Over the next 20 years £50 million was spent on turning the stadium into one of Britain's finest arenas.

Today the stadium is fully enclosed and is similar in feel to Anfield. The main stand is a three-tier affair, capable of holding over 20,000. The view from all sections in the stadium is excellent, with no pillars restricting sightlines. The noise generated by the crowd is also one of the greatest features of the stadium. The stadium can also boast two huge TV screens which replay all the key moments during the game. The stadium has a small museum which can be visited on a daily basis, and can be combined with a mini-tour of the stadium for an appreciation of what makes Ibrox so special. Tickets cost £7 and can be booked on +44 870 600 1972.

■ **Who plays there?**

Ibrox Stadium is the long-term home of Glasgow Rangers, Scotland's most successful club side. The team have won an amazing 51 Scottish league titles, almost 45% of the total championships played. Added to these league titles are a further 31 Scottish FA cup titles and 24 Scottish league cups, making Rangers the most successful club side in the world.

The club were formed in 1872 when a group of players used to meet for an informal match on Glasgow Green. The players soon formed a club and they played their first game against Callendar FC. The club had to wait a further decade before they won their first trophy, although they did reach the semi-finals of the English FA Cup in 1887 when they lost to Aston Villa. In 1899 William Wilton became the club's first manager, and he tasted success immediately as the club won their first seven championship titles between 1900 and 1918. Wilton unfortunately died in 1920, having overseen a period of immense success. His right-hand man was Bill Struth and he continued the glory years for the club with

18 championships and 12 cup victories in his 34-year reign. In 1949 the club won the domestic treble for the first time.

In 1954 Scot Symon was appointed Glasgow Rangers' third ever manager. Domestic success continued, but it was on the European front that the club sought to widen its horizons. In 1957 the club competed in the European Cup for the first time, eventually losing to Nice. Three years later the team managed to progress to the semi-finals, and with a place in the final at Hampden Park at stake the team took on the unfancied Eintracht Frankfurt. In a bizarre two-leg game the Germans ran out 12–4 winners, thus taking their place in the final in Glasgow against the legendary Real Madrid.

In 1961 Rangers reached the Cup Winners' Cup Final, becoming the first British club to do so. In a two-leg match against Fiorentina the Scots lost 4–1. In 1969 Willie Waddell was appointed manager and he oversaw the team's one and only European trophy with a 3–2 win over Dynamo Moscow in Barcelona. Unfortunately, due to crowd trouble, the club did not have the chance to defend their Cup Winners' Cup trophy as UEFA banned them for a season. A few weeks after this triumph, Jock Wallace was appointed as Rangers sixth manager and led them into a new period of domestic dominance.

Wallace started by breaking Celtic's nine-season dominance of the domestic league. He also led the club into the new Scottish Premier Division and immediately stamped the club's authority on the new competition by capturing the domestic treble in 1978. Just a week later Wallace resigned for 'personal reasons' and was replaced by former captain John Greig. However, with cash in short supply, and competition now coming from Alex Ferguson's Aberdeen and the Paul Sturrock-inspired Dundee United, Rangers' dominance waned swiftly. The club reaction was a knee-jerk. They sacked Greig, and tried to lure Ferguson and Dundee United's Jim McLean before turning again to Jock Wallace, then manager of Leicester City.

The next phase in Rangers' history can be said to have commenced in August 1986 when they appointed Graeme Souness as player-manager. Despite a rocky start when Souness was sent off on his debut versus Hibernian, the club soon started recruiting wisely. As English clubs were banned from European competition, Rangers, now funded by new chairman David Murray, were able to attract top English players like Ray Wilkins, Terry Butcher and Chris Woods to form a team that was able to start the domination of Scottish football again. The club matched Celtic's achievements with its own nine-in-a-row between 1989 to 1997, only missing out on the title in 1998 by one win. Souness left the club in 1991 to take over at Liverpool, and was succeeded by Walter Smith who delivered a total of 12 trophies during another successful period which saw the club almost reach a Champions League Final in 1993 by remaining unbeaten during the competition.

In 1998 Dick Advocaat replaced Walter Smith, who had left to manage Everton. The Dutchman was not a favourite of the Ibrox crowd, due to the import of a number of journeymen foreign players such as Andrei Kanchelskis, Michael Mols and Tore Andre Flo. In his first

season the team won the domestic treble, but soon they fell behind Celtic – returning from the 2001 season trophy-less. The Dutchman was replaced in December 2001 by Alex McLeish. The continuation of expensive, poor signings punctuated the limited success that McLeish enjoyed. Names like Dragan Mladenovic, Thomas Buffel, Nacho Novo and Jean-Alain Boumsong were hardly the world-class players that the board had promised. In 2005 the club won a remarkable league title, with Celtic blowing a 5-point lead with just four games to play.

Season 2005/2006 proved to be the final one for McLeish. The league was lost by Easter to a rampant Celtic, and European football was soon over. Whilst it is often viewed as an unsuccessful period in the club's history, McLeish actually won more trophies than his great rival Martin O'Neill at Celtic during the same period. The job of reinvigorating the club fell to Frenchman Paul Le Guen, who had revolutionised Olympique Lyonnais into a domestic powerhouse. Things did not go right from day one for the Frenchman, and after a huge public spat with captain Barry Ferguson, and the team trailing Celtic by 15 points, Le Guen was relieved of duties in January 2007. Again, the club went back to its successful past and reappointed Walter Smith and Ally McCoist as the new management team.

■ How to get there

Ibrox Stadium is located in the south west of the city, close to the old shipyards of Govan. The easiest way to reach the stadium is by underground on the 'Clockwork Orange', as the station of the same name is a mere 3-minute walk from the ground. A return ticket from anywhere in the city costs £2 The stadium is adjacent to the M8, which runs from the city centre to the airport.

■ Getting a ticket

On average Rangers get 49,950 for home games – meaning that tickets for most games are scarce come match day. However, for most games (excluding the Old Firm matches) you can book tickets, and pick them up on the day of the game. The official website contains all the details of when you can book, and the pricing. Tickets can also be purchased by calling 0871 702 1972. Tickets are normally available in the Broomloan or Copland rear stands, which are the cheapest in the stadium and start from £20. Tickets in the main stand upper tier cost from £34.

Stadion Crvena Zvezda – Belgrade (Serbia)

The Facts

Name: Stadion Crvena Zvezda
Address: Ljutice Bogdana 1a,
11000 Belgrade,
Serbia
Capacity: 51,328 All Seater
Opened: 1st September 1963 Red Star 1 Rijeka 1

■ About Stadion Crvena Zvezda

The Red Star Stadium or the Marakana as it has been more affectionately called since it opened is the most famous stadium in the Balkans. It is a traditional Eastern Bloc stadium built as a bowl, with an athletic track and the trademark prominent floodlights. The stadium opened on the 1st September 1963, after the club and national team moved from the FK Novi Sad stadium. Originally the capacity was 75,000. During the next ten years the stadium was expanded to hold 110,000 with wooden benches covering the terraces. The stadium was originally very similar in appearance to the Zentralstadion in Leipzig, and the Olympic Stadium in Kiev. In 1975 the stadium hosted its biggest-ever club game as Red Star played Ferencvaros in the European Cup Winners' Cup semi-final in front of a rumoured 108,000. The previous season the stadium had hosted the European Cup Final between Ajax and Juventus.

In 1976 the stadium hosted the semi-finals and final of the European Championships when Czechoslovakia upset the form guide by beating West Germany in the final. In the semi-final Yugoslavia lost to the Germans after extra time having led 2–0 for most of the game. The final historic game played in the stadium was in October 2005 when the old country of Serbia-Montenegro played their last-ever game against Bosnia-Herzegovina before the country split into two. The stadium has some basic facilities for supporters, although the open bowl shape can make for some quite chilly conditions during winter. The stadium also has a very good museum charting the progress of Red Star. The museum is open daily from 10am and is accessible from the main entrance of the stadium.

■ Who plays there?

The Red Star Stadium is unsurprisingly home to the Balkans' most famous and successful club – Red Star Belgrade, or Crvena Zvezda as they are known. The club are the current Serbian champions after winning the domestic double at a canter from their local rivals FK Partizan. They are also the only club from the former Yugoslavian states to have won the European Cup, which they did in 1991 by beating Marseille on penalties in Bari. The final is one of the least remembered in modern times due to the negative tactics employed by Red Star in playing for penalties, which surprised most observers as they had played so well up until the final, including a 4–1 victory over Glasgow Rangers, 6–0 over Dynamo Dresden and a 4–3 win over Bayern Munich.

Some of the most famous players in Yugoslavian football have pulled on the red and white shirt of Red Star including Siniša Mihajlovic, Robert Prosinečki and Dejan Savićević, all of whom played in that final in Bari. The club won the Yugoslavian championship on 18 occasions, as well as the Yugoslavian cup 12 times. Since the break-up of the country, they have won the Serbian championship on six occasions. Aside from that famous night in Bari in 1991 they also won the World Club championship in Tokyo by beating Colo Colo of Chile 3–0.

For such a successful team it is amazing to think that they were only formed in 1945 after the Second World War had finished by a group of students from Belgrade University. The club were admitted into the Yugoslavian league in 1948, and won the domestic cup in their first season. Since their 1991 European victory, the club has had little luck in UEFA competitions. In 1992 they needed a victory in their last game away in Anderlecht to reach the final again, but a 3–2 defeat coupled with Sampdoria's draw meant the Italians reached the final. Since then they have failed to make it past the qualifying stages, and have been surpassed in achievement by Partizan who have reached the group stages.

■ How to get there

The stadium is located in the south of the city, in the heart of a middle-class residential area, characterised by smart

Stadion Crvena Zvezda – Belgrade (Serbia)

detached houses with swimming pools. It is also close enough to the central station to be walkable. However, tram lines 2, 7 and 9 pass within 200 metres of the stadium from the station if you don't feel like the walk down Nemanjina to the stadium.

■ Getting a ticket

Although capacity is over 50,000, you will rarely see attendances over 7,000 for a league match, but attendances for games against FK Partizan often attract over 30,000. However, whatever the game, you will not have a problem picking up a ticket on the day. Ticket prices start from 20 Dinar for a place in the cheap seats, although it is best to avoid the hardcore Red Star fans behind the goal. For national team games tickets can be purchased in advance from the Serbian FA on +381 11 323 3447, email fsj@beotel.yu or via http://www.tiketservis.com.

■ Nearest airport – Belgrade Nikola Tesla (BEG)

The busiest airport in Serbia is located around 7 miles west of the city centre in the small town of Surčin. **British Airways** and **JAT Airways** both fly daily from London Heathrow to Belgrade. The easiest way to reach the city centre from the airport is by the **JAT Airways** coach which departs every hour to Slavija Square and the central railway station. The fare is 160 Dinars. Alternatively, bus line 72 runs to the station, takes around 25 minutes and costs 35 dinars. A taxi will cost €9 for a fixed fee and should take 20 minutes – only use licensed taxis though.

Tehelne Pole Stadium – Bratislava (Slovakia)

The Facts

Name: Tehelne Post Stadium
Address: Viktora Tegelhoffa 4,
83104 Bratislava,
Slovakia
Capacity: All Seater
Opened: 1947

■ About Tehelne Pole Stadium

Despite the redevelopment of the city of Bratislava as a whole, the national stadium has been cruelly left as a throwback to the communist 1960s. A single two-tier stand dominates the arena and the remaining stand curves away from the pitch – although there is no athletics track. Segregation is non-existent and it is no surprise that when England played here in 2003 there were serious problems in terms of policing, and UEFA fined the Slovakian FA heavily.

The stadium is a classic ex-communist monument. It is so similar in design to the Dynamo Stadium in Moscow – right down to the coloured seats. The ground is located 4.5km north east of the city centre in the Nove Mesto area. During the 2005 Champions League campaign, the pitch bore the brunt of the poor late autumnal weather and became almost unplayable in the game versus Porto. With only one covered stand, a space on the open end is not quite as appealing in the cold wet winter as in the balmy spring and summer.

■ Who plays there?

As well as being the national stadium, the Tehelne Pole is one of only a couple of UEFA-approved venues in the country. This means that any UEFA matches have to be played here – and so in recent seasons the stadium has seen ArtMedia cause a few waves in the Champions League, knocking out Celtic and Porto on their way to a 3rd-place finish in the group stages in 2005. The current situation of Slovan Bratislava could hardly have been worse. The club were founded in 1919 and had a fine record in Czechoslovakian football, winning the league eight times, the last being in 1992. They then won the Slovakian championship in 1993, 1994 and 1995 before winning it for the last time in 1999. After an exile of two seasons in the 2nd division, the team returned to the top division and finished in a creditable 3rd place although they were a staggering 28 points behind champions Zilina. No more than 200 yards down the main road you will find the 13,000 capacity Pasienky Stadium, home to Inter Bratislava. The basic athletics track is notable for its huge towering floodlights that dwarf anything else in the whole area. Like their local rivals Slovan, Inter have gone through some tough times recently although they are now back in the top flight again after a couple of seasons in the 2nd division.

■ How to get there

If you are coming by tram, then you need to get tram 2, 4 or 6. A number of buses also make the journey from the city centre, including 39, 53, 61 and 63. Buy your tickets for any public transport at the yellow dispensers at most transit stops. Remember to stamp the ticket before you board the tram or bus. A day pass will cost you Skr90. A taxi will cost 150Skr (£3.50).

■ Getting a ticket

For all domestic club games tickets are available on the day of the game. Average attendances for Slovakian football are less than 4,000 and so you will have no problem in getting a ticket for a match from either the main ticket office, or direct at the turnstiles. For big European games information on when the tickets go on sale is posted on the clubs own websites.

■ Nearest airport – Milan Rastislav Airport (BTS)

Bratislava's airport is located 8km north east of the city centre and has recently opened its doors to a number of budget carriers. Traditionally it had been used as an overflow to Vienna, located just over an hour away by public transport.. To get to the city centre catch the number 61 bus to the central station – a single ticket costs around 20Skr (50p). A taxi should cost around SKR 400 (£10) but agree the fare before departing. Currently **Ryanair** serves Bratislava from London Stansted, **Easyjet** from London Luton and **Sky Europe** from London Stansted and Manchester.

Estadio Camp Nou – Barcelona (Spain)

The Facts

Name: Estadio Camp Nou
Address: Avinguda Aristides Maillol,
08028 Barcelona,
Spain
Capacity: 98,800 All Seater
Opened: 24th September 1956 Barcelona v Warsaw XI

■ About the Camp Nou

Possibly the most famous stadium in the world, the Nou Camp offers three staggering tiers of plastic bucket seats with very little cover from the Catalonian sun, which doesn't sound like a mecca to most, but all football fans dream of a visit to the stadium. The club moved here in 1956 after years of success playing in the intimidating Les Corts stadium nearby, with an initial capacity of around 90,000.

In 1980 the third tier was added to the stadium, raising both the external height to a massive 49 metres, as well as the capacity to 115,000 in time for the 1982 World Cup finals. In the mid-1990s, in order to increase the capacity once again to compensate for a move to all-seater, the pitch was lowered and further seats were added to the sides of the upper tier. The first event to be hosted in the new UEFA 5-star stadium was the dramatic 1999 Champions League Final when Manchester United snatched victory in injury time from Bayern Munich. So what makes the stadium so special? Certainly if you have been an away fan at the Camp Nou, you won't think much of the view from the away section high up in the gods. However, it is the passion and the history that seeps

through every seat that make the stadium so special.

Visit on a warm, balmy summer night and you cannot fail to be carried away with the locals' passion for the team. Under Frank Rijkaard the good times have returned to Barcelona and now more than ever is a time to get a ticket and sit back and watch the stars perform. The club run daily tours in English, taking in the dressing rooms, dugouts, media room and a photo opportunity with the Champions League trophy. These tours cost approximately €13 and include a visit to the museum. The tours are open from 10am daily, and the last tour is 5.30pm Monday to Saturday, 1.30pm on Sundays.

■ Who plays there?

Despite being one of the most famous clubs in the world, Barcelona's achievements in their 107-year history outside Spain have been relatively modest. All of this seems to be changing with current coach, Dutchman Frank Rijkaard, shaping a team that can compete on the highest stage – a fact borne out by their Champions League final victory over Arsenal in Paris in May 2006.

The club were originally formed by Joan Gamper in 1899. In 1909 Gamper secured the club its first stadium and this coincided with sustained success in the Spanish cup, with eight final victories in his reign between 1908 and 1928. The following season the club won their first of 18 La Liga titles. The bitter rivalry between Real Madrid and Barca began to develop at this time, and was further fuelled by the commencement of the Civil War in the late 1930s that saw Franco's regime favour the Castilian team over Barca. There were a number of events that took place in the next few years that underlined the bitter feelings between the two of them. In the semi-final of the 1943 Copa del Generalissimo, Barca took a 3–0 lead into the second leg of the semi in Madrid. With some farcical refereeing, and some intimidation in the dressing rooms, Barca lost the game 11–1.

After the end of the Civil War the club were forced to rename themselves Club de Fútbol Barcelona and rid themselves of any Catalonian insignia. Despite the efforts of the regime to favour Real Madrid, the club won seven La Liga titles up until 1960 as well as four cup finals. They also won the first-ever Inter-Cities Fairs Cup held in 1958, beating a London XI 8–2 on aggregate. They retained their trophy in 1960, beating Birmingham City 4–1 on aggregate, and again in 1966 by beating Real Zaragoza. In 1961 they became the first team to inflict a European Cup defeat on Real Madrid after more than five years of competition. However, this turned out to be one of the high points of the decade as the huge expansion of the Camp Nou meant that there was little money available to spend on the team. In 1974 the major turning point in the club's history arrived as the world's greatest player, Johan Cruyff, arrived. In his first season at the club the team stole the championship from Real Madrid, capping it off with a 5–0 win in the Bernabeu. Major European success still eluded the team, although in 1979 they won the Cup Winners' Cup by beating Fortuna Dusseldorf, and again in 1982 beating Standard Liege. Cruyff finished his playing career at the club, and would later return as coach. In the meantime they signed teenage sensation Diego Maradona for a world-record fee in 1982. His time at the club was disappointing, with one single Copa del Rey title in 1983 to show for his efforts. In 1985 he moved to Napoli, and the club appointed Terry Venables as manager. 'El Tel' built a solid team, including Scottish international Steve Archibald and delivered the La Liga title in 1985, and a year later almost won the European Cup, the team losing to Steaua Bucharest on penalties in a 99.9% Spanish-supporting stadium in Seville.

The following year Venables brought in Gary Lineker and Mark Hughes to add goals to the flair. Lineker settled very quickly and went on to become the leading scorer in Spain. Hughes had a harder time and returned to Manchester United the following year. In 1988, Johan Cruyff returned to the club as manager, building the 'Dream Team' including Josep Guardiola, Ronald Koeman, Michael Laudrup, Romario and Hristo Stoichkov. The team won successive La Liga titles between 1991 and 1994 as well as beating Sampdoria in the 1989 European Cup Winners' Cup final. In 1992 the club lined up for their second European Cup final at Wembley, again against Sampdoria. A 30-yard free-kick from Ronald Koeman in extra-time was enough to give the trophy to the club.

Despite being the club's longest-serving manager, Cruyff consistently fell out with President Josep Núñez. Eventually, the President had enough and replaced the legend with Bobby Robson. In his one and only season in charge Robson won the Copa del Rey and delivered further European glory with another Cup Winners' Cup victory, this time versus Paris Saint-Germain. Another Dutchman, Louis van Gaal, took over the club in 1998 and delivered immediate results with a team full of flair including Luis Figo, Rivaldo and Marc Overmars. They won the double in 1998, and the La Liga again the following

season. Van Gaal left in 2000 as Núñez lost the presidential election to Joan Laporta, only to briefly return as a stopgap in 2002. The club went through one of the most barren runs in their history, failing to win a single trophy between 1999 and 2005 when Rijkaard arrived on the scene. The Dutchman was soon to make his mark on the squad, moving out some of the older more established players such as Guardiola and Rivaldo and replacing them with the current stars including World Player of the Year Ronaldinho, Deco, Carlos Puyol and Lionel Messi.

In his first season, Rijkaard held off a spirited challenge from champions Valencia to win the La Liga, although defeat to Chelsea in the Champions League last 16 was a bitter pill. Undeterred, they retained their title in 2006, again holding off Valencia and got their revenge over Chelsea in a stormy affair at Stamford Bridge before going all the way to win the Champions League in Paris versus Arsenal. Last season did not go according to plan though. Losing 4–0 to Seville in the European Super Cup in Monaco was not the best start to the season. Their Champions League performances were far from impressive, and a home defeat to Liverpool in the knock-out rounds ended their campaign. In the league, despite some fantastic end of season form, they lost out on their head to head results with arch-rivals Real Madrid as the teams finished level after 38 games.

■ How to get there

The stadium sits between three metro stations – Les Corts and Maria Cristina on line 3 and Collblanc on line 5. The best station is Maria Cristina – leave the station by the Avenida Diagonal exit. Follow the road with the two huge La Caixa towers on your left. When you reach the Hotel Princesa Sofia turn left and walk down Avenida Joan XIII for the stadium.

■ Getting a ticket

Barcelona have around 103,000 members and season ticket holders. For most matches, the number of members who actually attend games ranges from 20,000, up to 98,000 for the games versus Real Madrid. However, there is a process in place whereby members can sell their season tickets back to the club on a match-to-match basis – these are the ones that are then put on general sale by the club. Tickets for games generally go on sale around ten days before the match. If you are a Barcelona club member then you are able to book tickets online via the official website. This link takes you off to the ServiCaixa site that allows you to collect tickets from any of their automated machines in the city. If you are not a member then you can either buy them in person from the ticket office at the stadium (Monday–Thursday 9am to 1.30pm, 3pm to 6pm, weekends 9am to 2.30pm), or by phone +34 93 496 36 00. There are also a number of touts who wait outside the stadium hoping to sell tickets on match days. Ticket prices range from €45 in the third tier behind the goal, to over €100 in the middle tier close to the halfway line. You can also buy Silver and Gold VIP packages that include a meal, drinks, a souvenir gift and a posh seat in the main preferencia. The packages range in price from €140 to €250.

The Facts

Name: Estadio Olimpico Lluís Companys
Address: Passeig Olimpico,
08038 Barcelona,
Spain
Capacity: 55,926 All Seater
Opened: 1927

■ About Estadio Olimpico

Sitting high above the city of Barcelona is the hill of Montjuic, which has been the strategic defensive point for centuries. On top of the hill proudly sits the Olympic Stadium. However, plans have been put in motion to return Espanyol to their own ground after enforced exile for the past ten years playing at the stadium. Their previous ground, the Sarriá, was a homely affair but wasn't up to the increased standards required by La Liga football, despite hosting games during the 1982 World Cup finals. It is hoped that the new stadium, in the Sarriá area of the city, will be ready by the start of the 2008/2009 season.

This new stadium will hold 40,000 fans and is being built to UEFA 4-star standards, making it eligible for UEFA Cup finals – although interestingly the current Olympic Stadium is one of UEFA's 5-star stadiums, meaning it can host Champions League finals. Whilst it is plain to see why Espanyol want to move because of the lack of atmosphere

and crowds for games like Getafe, Santander and Cadiz, the stadium itself is steeped in history and has one of the most magnificent façades in world football. The stadium is most famous for hosting the Olympic Games in 1992. The stadium is far from ideal for football, with the stands set quite along way back from the action. The lack of a roof on three of the four sides also means that the atmosphere is easily lost. For normal league games only the upper tiers of the Lateral and Tribuna tend to be opened. This means that if inclement weather is forecast, demand for the seats in the covered Tribuna rises significantly. The views from all stands are unobstructed – if the weather is good then head for the upper lateral which offers a fantastic backdrop over the west of the city. The stadium also has a small museum tracing the preparations for the 1992 Olympics at the far end to the main entrance.

■ Who plays there?

It is quite ironic that in the last few years the city of Barcelona have had their best seasons in decades – it could be said that the combined success of the two teams in Barcelona moved the city to the top of the pile in the world in terms of footballing power. In 2006, despite finishing in 15th place and only just avoiding relegation by two points, Espanyol got the luck of the draw in the Copa Del Rey, avoiding all of the big teams on their route to a final appearance with Zaragoza in Madrid. There they put their league form behind them and a 4–1 win ensured European football for the team from Montjuic.

Estadio Olimpico – Barcelona (Spain)

The Copa del Rey has been the highpoint of Espanyol's record in Spanish football. They have never won the La Liga, but have captured the King's cup on four occasions. Their first triumph came in 1929, when they beat the mighty Real Madrid with Ricardo Zamora, the national goalkeeper, performing miracles between the posts. Their second win came in 1940, when they again beat Real Madrid, but it was a much weaker team due to the Civil War. In 1988 they had another fine run in Europe, under future national coach Javier Clemente, when they beat both Milan clubs on the way to a penalty shootout defeat in the UEFA Cup Final to Bayer Leverkusen after throwing away a 3–0 first leg lead. By the start of the 1990s, the club had managed to accrue a debt somewhere in the region of £45m, and the sale of their ground in Sarrià was essential to avoid bankruptcy. The move to the Olympic Stadium coincided with new players such as Florin Raducioiu (later to flop badly at West Ham), Jordi Cruyff and Juan Esnaider performing on the pitch, and in the final year of the millennium they captured the cup for the third time, beating Atletico Madrid. Their subsequent travels into the UEFA Cup saw them reach the third round before a 2–0 home defeat to Porto saw them crash out. In the 2004/2005 season they came within one point of making the Champions League, losing out on the last day to Real Betis for 4th spot. The team today has a core of Spanish players as well as star names Walter Pandiani (ex-Birmingham City) and Alberton Riera (ex-Manchester City). In 2007 the team surpassed all expectations in Europe by reaching an all-Spanish UEFA Cup Final where they met holders Sevilla at Hampden Park. In an excellent match, neither side could gain an advantage, and so in a game decided by penalties the team from Andalucía became the first club in UEFA Cup history to retain their title.

■ How to get there
The stadium sits proudly on the Montjuic, overlooking the city of Barcelona and the Mediterranean Sea. Whilst there are a number of options available to fans for reaching the stadium, one of the best ways is by cable car from the port area of the city (Torre de Sant Sebastia), offering magnificent views over the whole area. The stadium is a 5-minute walk back down the hill from the cable car stop. There is also a funicular railway running from Parallel metro station that runs daily until 8pm. Bus numbers 9, 27, 30, 37, 50, 55 and 56 all run from Plaza Espanya if your legs can't manage the walk up past the National Museum (although there are escalators that take out much of the hard work). The nearest metro is Plaza Espanya that is on red line 1 and green line 3.

■ Getting a ticket
Tickets for most Espanyol games are on sale up until kick-off from the two ticket offices on either side of the stadium. If you want to book tickets before you arrive you are able to via the official website http://www.rcdespanyol.com which has a very impressive online booking facility. For a normal league game (i.e. not Barcelona or Real Madrid), tickets for the Lateral Superior (upper tier) are €30, Tribuna Superior (upper tier under cover) €40 and for a place amongst the hardcore Espanyol fans then head for the Gol section where tickets are €25. As a trial, the official tourist office is selling tickets for both Espanyol and Barca games online via its official website (http://www.barcelonaturisme.com) from €25.

■ Nearest airport – Barcelona El Prat (BCN)
The airport is one of the major hubs of the budget airline network with over 100 airlines using it – including **British Airways** from Heathrow and Gatwick, **BA Connect** from Birmingham, **Easyjet** from Bristol, Liverpool, Gatwick, Luton, Stansted and Newcastle. And **Jet2.com** from Belfast and Leeds/Bradford. Currently, the easiest way to reach the city centre is by train from the terminal across the main car park. Trains run every 30 minutes to Sants station with a journey time of 20 minutes. A scheduled bus service from Aerobús runs via Sants, Plaza d'Espanya and terminates at Plaza Catalunya. When the new AVE line is open, there will be a new station at the airport, as well as metro stops on lines 2 and 9. A taxi takes around 25 minutes and should cost less than €20.

Estadio San Mames – Bilbao (Spain)

The Facts

Name: Estadio San Mames – 'La Catedral'
Address: Felipe Serrate,
E-48009 Bilbao,
Spain
Capacity: 39,750 All Seater
Opened: 21st August 1913 – Bilbao v Racing Irun

■ About Estadio San Mames

The San Mames stadium is often referred to as the 'Cathedral of Bilbao', so great is the affection of the city's people for the club. Whilst the crowds have fallen over the years, the atmosphere is still there, and for those big games when Athletic Bilbao play the likes of Real Madrid, Barcelona and the Basque derby with Real Sociedad, the crowd really rise to the occasion.

Athletic average around 37,000, with sell-outs against the big two and the Basque teams a given on a season-by-season basis. The stadium was opened in 1913 and is now Spain's oldest stadium. The stands sit snugly to the pitch, giving the appearance that the fans are almost touching the players. Today the defining feature is the white arch that sits above the main stand (the Preferencia) and can be seen across the city. The home fans congregate in the north stand. The stadium has undergone a number of redevelopments in its 90-year history, most notably the rebuilding of three stands in time for the 1982 World Cup when the stadium hosted England's three group games versus France, Czechoslovakia and Kuwait. More recently plans have been approved to completely rebuild the north, west and south stands, taking the capacity to over 50,000. The views from all parts of the stadium are excellent, although it may be worth avoiding the first few rows as the stands are built below pitch level. The club has a small museum and trophy room that is open to the public and can be accessed through gates 26 and 27 daily

except Monday's. Tours are also available of the stadium four times a day, costing €6.

■ Who plays there?

Athletic Club Bilbao are one of the proudest and most traditional clubs in the whole of Europe. Their identity and principles have not changed at all in their 95-year history despite the game evolving constantly around them. They still stick by their rule that only players with roots traceable back to the Basque country can pull on the famous red and white striped shirts (known as Cantara). They also do not have a sponsor's name on the shirt, which is unheard of in modern football. Finally, they refused to acknowledge their forced name change to Atletico due to pressures of the Franco regime during the 1960s and 1970s.

In fact the club's refusal to change their name is not as a fingers-up salute to the central Castilian ruling of the country – but more to do with their origins. As a major port in the 19th century, Bilbao had many sailors visiting from abroad. One such group, from Sunderland and Southampton, brought the game of football to the region and helped set up the first football club in the city. Of course they decided to adopt the red and white striped shirts of their teams back in England.

In 1902 the team under the name Club Vizcaya entered the Copa del Rey, and beat the famous Barcelona in the final to bring home the trophy. More honours soon followed, including ten further cup titles before the 1920s had finished. In 1930 the club completed a famous league and cup double, and repeated the feat in 1931 and 1933 under English coach Fred Pentland. The club went on to capture further honours, with the league title in 1943, as well as seven more Copa del Ray titles between 1943 and 1958.

With the death of Franco in the 1970s the club began to regain its traditional roots. In 1977, after reverting to the name Athletic Bilbao, the club reached their first

European Final, losing on away goals to Juventus in the UEFA Cup final. The golden period for the club came in 1981 when Javier Clemente was appointed manager. Less than two years later the club won the La Liga title, and followed it up with the league, Copa del Rey and Supercopa titles in 1984. All too recently the story has been one of underachievement. A big fanfare was made of the appointment of Howard Kendall in the mid-1980s but he could not repeat the success he had at Everton. Luis Fernandez had limited success – taking the club to 2nd in 1998 and thus giving them their first shot at the Champions League where they finished bottom of a weak group containing Juventus, Galatasaray and Rosenborg with just one win from six games.

The new millennium has brought troubles on and off the pitch with a string of managers being unable to rise to the high expectations of the home fans. Javier Clemente was brought back during 2005 when the club were bottom of the league, and he worked his magic again to keep them in La Liga to fight another day. For the 2006/2007 season the club promoted from within as Felix Sarriugarte was appointed to the hot seat. However, the move was not very successful as the club struggled for the whole season before results on the last day saw them finish one place, and one point, above the relegation zone.

■ How to get there
The stadium is located close to the city centre, around a 10-minute walk westwards. With loads of bars lining the streets close to the stadium, allow yourself a good hour to get into the mood for the game. Alternatively, the stadium has its own stop on the Sir Norman Foster-designed metro system that is just two stops from Moyua in the centre of the city.

■ Getting a ticket
Tickets go on sale for most home games seven days before the match. Initially tickets are sold to members only from the ticket office at the ground – although it is free to register online to become a member. Tickets are available for most areas of the ground – although the hardcore fans tend to take all the seats in the Fondu Norte. A good bet is a ticket in the Lateral 2nd Gradería, which should cost around €35.

■ Nearest airport – Bilbao International (BIO)
Bilbao's smart modern airport is one of the most pleasing to the eye in Europe, having been redesigned by Santiago Calatrava in 2000. Located in a lush green valley 6 miles north west of the city centre, it is served daily by **Easyjet** from London Stansted as well as flights from London Heathrow operated by **British Airways** and **Iberia**. Bizkaibus 3247 bus runs every 30 minutes from outside the arrivals door to Plaza Moyúa in the centre of town and costs €1.20 each way. A taxi will cost around €18.

The Facts

Name:	Estadio Santiago Bernabéu
Address:	Avenida Concha Espina 1,
	28036 Madrid,
	Spain
Capacity:	80,354 All Seater
Opened:	14th December 1947

■ About Estadio Santiago Bernabéu

One of the most famous stadiums in the world, the Santiago Bernabéu is an awesome sight on a match day. The stands are built close to the pitch and seem to rise up as far as the eye can see. The stadium is equally impressive when it is empty – a uniform of blue seats with the words Real Madrid C.F. The current capacity reflects its all-seater status – a few years ago when terracing was still in place behind the goals, the capacity was regularly over 90,000.

In 1943, Don Santiago de Bernabéu was elected President of the club and he vowed to build the team a new stadium fitting of their position as the best team in Spain. Land was found close to the Chamartin in 1946. The current stadium was officially opened on 14th December 1947 when Real took on the Portuguese team Belenenses. At the time the stadium was built as an open bowl with a capacity of 75,300 and was simply named the Nuevo Chamartin. As the team's success started to spread onto a European stage, the club decided that it should have the finest stadium in Europe. Millions of pesetas were spent in building a third tier to the stadium which took the capacity, when opened, in 1955, to just over 120,000, making it the largest stadium in Europe and one of the largest in the world. The first real test of the new facilities came in the European Cup Final of 1957 when Real Madrid hosted Fiorentina in front of over 124,000 fans.

The stadium went on to host the European Cup Final in 1969 when AC Milan beat Ajax, 1980 when Nottingham Forest beat Hamburg and of course the 1982 World Cup Final. By that time, safety measures had forced the capacity to be reduced to 90,000. In the early 1980s a roof was constructed on three sides. Then a third tier was added to the east stand in the early 2000s which along with the conversion of the whole ground to seating reduced the capacity to the current 80,354. The east stand also went through significant modernisation to its corporate facilities to reflect the status of the club in terms of wealth.

The stadium offers magnificent views, even for those people in the upper tiers. However, be warned that the seating areas are quite steep and it is not wise to jump around too much in the upper tiers. Away fans are located in the north east corner top tier. Giant heaters in the roof provide almost Mediterranean temperatures even on the coldest Madrid nights. The ground is open daily for self-guided tours of the extensive club museum. Check the club website at http://www.realmadrid.com/elclub/tour/portada_eng.htm for more details. The tour costs €9 for adults and €5 for concessions.

Estadio Santiago Bernabéu – Madrid (Spain)

■ Who plays there?

On 9th March 1902, Madrid football club played its first match, with a game between 22 of its members on a ground in Plaza de Toros. In June 1920, the King granted the team his royal patronage and allowed them to become Real Madrid. In 1936 the team won the Spanish cup, beating Barcelona 2–1 in the last final played before the Civil War, which stopped football in the country for over three years. During the early 1950s the team embarked on a programme of recruiting the best players in Europe. 'The Millionaires', as they become known, consisted of world-class players such as Alfredo Di Stefano, Kubala and Ferenc Puskas. In their first season together the team won their first championship in 21 years as Di Stefano's goals saw them beat Valencia to the title. The title meant that Real Madrid were invited to play in the first European Cup competition. The team adapted to a new style of play and in the Parc des Princes in Paris they beat Stade Reims 4–3 to win the first-ever European Cup. A year later in front of over 120,000 home fans the team retained its trophy at the Bernabéu with a 2–0 win over Fiorentina. A third European Cup triumph was achieved a year later as the team beat AC Milan in Brussels. By this point, the team had become the most feared in the whole of Europe, although domestic honours came harder to win during their European triumphs. In 1959 the team replayed their final of 1956 against Stade Reims in Stuttgart, winning their fourth consecutive title with a 2–0 win. Less than 12 months later the team met Eintracht Frankfurt in Glasgow when the forward line including Di Stefano and Puskas dominated the Germans from the first minute, and a 7–3 victory earned Real Madrid their fifth consecutive title. In November 1960 the team lost their first ever European Cup Final as they lost to Barcelona, although this match is tainted by the role played by English referee Leafe who disallowed four Real goals.

The team returned to domestic honours in the early 1960s as Real captured five consecutive titles between 1961 and 1965. They also returned to the European Cup Final in 1962 when they lost to Benfica in Amsterdam and again in 1964 when they lost 3–1 to Inter Milan in Vienna. However, less than two years later the team won the title of champions of Europe again with a 2–1 win over Partizan Belgrade in Brussels. Further league titles in 1968 and 1969 enabled them to become the most feared team in the world.

The 1970s were a low period for the club, capped by the death in 1978 of Santiago Bernabéu. Success on the field saw championships won between 1975 and 1980, with one exception in 1977. After a period of inactivity the team returned to winning ways with new stars like Michel, Hugo Sanchez and Butragueño winning the championship title as well as their first ever UEFA Cup in 1985 beating Videoton of Hungary 3–1, a feat they repeated 12 months later by beating Cologne 5–3. The following season, after a magnificent 5–0 victory against Barcelona, the team won the championship again. In May 2000 the team returned to its favourite European Cup hunting ground, Paris, where they took on Valencia in the first all-Spanish final. Inspired by the creativity of Steve McManaman, Luis Figo and Raúl, the team from the capital ran out 3–0 winners. In 2002 the team celebrated their centenary. Hopes were high for a clean sweep of titles in that year, with a team including 'Galacticos' such as Zinedine Zidane, Ronaldo and Luis Figo. Unfortunately the party was spoilt by Deportivo La Coruna who beat Madrid 2–1 in the Spanish cup final, held in the Bernabéu on the night of their 100th birthday.

The club did gain some consolation with a 2–1 victory in Glasgow over Bayer Leverkusen to capture another European Cup title. Less then three months later they also added their only missing trophy, the European Super Cup, with a 3–1 victory over Feyenoord in Monaco. In December 2002 the team captured their third Intercontinental Trophy with a 2–0 win over the Paraguayans of Olimpia. That season was also memorable for an unlikely title win. With Real Sociedad leading the way for the whole season, it came as a shock to many that they proceeded to throw away the title in the final weeks. On the last day of the season Real Madrid stole the title with a 3–1 victory over Bilbao and thus gave Real Madrid their 29th championship. In the summer of 2003 another Galactico landed at the Bernabéu as David Beckham signed a 3-year deal. In his first competitive game for the club he scored the third goal in a 3–0 win over Mallorca in the Spanish Super Cup. In the past few seasons, the club has had six coaches and players have come and gone regularly. Just when it seemed that 2006/2007 would be another trophyless season, the club stuck at the task in hand and gave Beckham the best send-off he could have hoped for by beating Mallorca on the last day of the season to capture the La Liga title.

■ How to get there

The stadium has its own metro stop, Santiago Bernabéu, which sits on top of Line 1 (dark blue Line) one stop north of Nuevos Ministerios. After the match the station is closed for safety reasons and crowds are either directed northwards to Cuzco, or to the west towards Alvarado and Estrecho stations on Line 2 (light blue Line). The stadium is also well served by buses – lines 14, 27, 40, 43, 47, 120 and 150 make the regular journey from the city centre to Plaza de Lima on the south western corner of the stadium.

■ Getting a ticket

It's actually a lot easier than you think to get a ticket to see Real Madrid. The chances of getting a ticket for the games versus Barcelona or Atletico are slim but you will be surprised at how many tickets are available for the remaining games, especially those in the Champions League. The average league attendance in 2004/2005 was 71,900. The best way to try your luck is to call the ticket hotline +34 902 324 234 to see when and where tickets are available. Normally tickets are on sale to personal callers in the days leading up to the match from the office between gates 1 and 6. Match-day packages are available through http://www.lastminute.com.

The Facts

Name: Estadio Vicente Calderón
Address: Paseo Virgen del Puerto 67
             28005 Madrid
             Spain
Capacity: 57,500 All Seater
Opened: 2nd October 1966 –
             Atletico Madrid 1 Valencia 1

■ About Estadio Vicente Calderón

The stadium has been located on the banks of the River Manzanares for over 40 years, after being inaugurated as the Estadio Manzanares in October 1966. The name was changed in the late 1990s to reflect the contribution to the club of former chairman Vicente Calderón. The stadium also has the honour of being awarded 5-star status by UEFA, meaning that it can hold UEFA Cup and Champions League finals.

The stadium is typical of a number of grounds in Spain, with one main stand set apart from the three other stands. In the case of Vicente Calderón, the stadium is full of rows and rows of alternative red and white seats, mirroring the famous shirts of the team. The main stand is a huge two-tier affair with the only cover from the blistering sunshine, and spans the main ring road. Views from the upper tier are very good, and without a running track in the stadium the feeling of being close to the action is a welcome change. The remaining stands are almost identical to stadiums such as the Camp Nou, Mestalla or Espanyol's Olympic Stadium – very steep and open air, although the atmosphere is not compromised by the lack of a roof at any stage.

■ Who plays there?

The club were founded in 1903 as Athletic Club de Madrid

by three Basque students. Taking their inspiration from their beloved Athletic Bilbao, they bought a familiar red and white striped kit that was to become the club's trademark. At the time they earned the nickname *Los Colchoneros* which literally translates as 'The Mattress Makers', after the red and white striped material that was used to cover mattresses. In 1939 the club merged with Aviacion Nacional, the team of the Spanish Air Force, to form Athletic Aviacion de Madrid. In their first season the club won the Spanish league, retaining their title during the lean years of the Spanish Civil War. By the end of the decade the team had dropped the Aviacion part of the name after all formal military links were severed in 1947. The club went on to win further championships in 1950 and 1951 before earning the opportunity to play in European competition in 1961 when they recorded their one and only trophy by beating Fiorentina over two legs in the 1962 European Cup Winners' Cup final.

In 1966, after winning the Spanish cup, the team lost in the Cup Winners' Cup quarter-finals to Borussia Dortmund. In 1970, now under the control of Jesús Gil y Gil, the club won the title again and looked forward to an extended run in Europe. This time they made the semi-finals before losing 3–1 to an inspired Ajax team who were in the process of conquering Europe. During the 1970s Atletico's haul of three league titles in 1970, 1973 and 1977 was impressive. However, the 1980s proved to be a barren time with only a single Copa del Rey title in 1985. The 1980s were famous though for the number of coaches President Gil y Gil managed to get through. Gil oversaw Copa Del Rey titles in 1991 and 1992 with wins against Mallorca and Real Madrid respectively.

The 1995/96 season dawned with little optimism amongst the loyal fans of Atletico. However, a remarkable run of form up to Christmas saw the team head the league at the half-way point, from Valencia and Barcelona. The team managed to hold its nerve, based on a mean defence that conceded less than a goal a game, to win the league by 4 points. The team, with a midfield inspired by Argentinians Simeone and Caminero, and spearheaded by club legend Kiko, then went on to beat Barcelona 1–0 in the Copa del Rey final to complete an unlikely domestic double.

Unfortunately the team could not build on their success of 1996. Consecutive 5th-place finishes in 1997 and 1998 allowed the club to enter the UEFA Cup again. A run to the semi-finals in 1998 saw the team conquer Leicester City, PAOK Salonika (in an amazing 9–6 aggregate win) and Aston Villa before a narrow 1–0 defeat to Lazio eliminated them. The darkest days in the club's history came in 2000 when they were relegated on the last day of the season, after picking up just nine wins in 38 matches. The season had started so well for the team, with a run to the 4th round of the UEFA Cup before they lost away at Lens late in January 2000. By that time the rot had set in. The team was not short of talent in that season. Inspired by Juninho in midfield at the start of the season, before his move back to Middlesbrough, and with Hasselbaink and club legend Kiko up front, coach Claudio Ranieri could not get the team playing for each other just four years after the team had won the double.

After a 5th-place finish in 2001 the team managed to return to La Liga as champions in 2002. Since then they have finished each season in mid-table. In the 2006/2007 season, with the deadly strike force of Torres and Kezman, expectations were not met with a very disappointing 10th-place finish. 2007/2008 will be a watershed for the club, especially as Torres has now departed for Liverpool.

■ How to get there
The Vicente Calderón is the closest stadium in Madrid to the city centre. The easiest way to reach the stadium on a match day is a 20-minute walk from the Royal Palace down Gran Via de San Franciso towards the river, although the metro is another option. Just hop on line 5 (green line)

southwards to Pirámides station, six stops from Gran Via and then follow the crowds downhill to the stadium. The stadium is also served by a dozen bus routes on a match day, including lines 17, 18 and 23.

■ Getting a ticket
Despite having over 60,000 Socias (members), most games do not come close to selling out. Tickets go on sale around two weeks before the day and can be purchased from the official website, from the ground or from ServiCaixa ATM machines in the city. Tickets range in price from €70 in the Grada Central (main covered stand) to €28 behind the goal in the lower tier. A good bet for the neutral is a seat in the upper tier of the uncovered side stand at €44.

■ Nearest airport – Madrid Barajas (MAD)
Madrid Barajas airport is located 16 kilometres north east of the city centre, and is linked to the city by the newly constructed metro Line 8 (the pink one) to Nuevos Ministerios station. The journey should take 15 minutes. The station at Nuevos Ministerios has been significantly upgraded and it is now possible to check in here for you return flights. The airport is used by **Air Madrid** and **Air Plus** from London Gatwick, **Easyjet** from Bristol, London Gatwick, London Luton and Liverpool, **Ryanair** from Bournemouth, East Midlands and Dublin, **British Airways** and **Iberia** from London Gatwick and Heathrow and **BA Connect** from Birmingham, Manchester and London City.

The Facts

Name: Estadio Manuel Ruiz de L'Opera
Address: Avenida Heliópolis,
41012 Seville,
Spain
Capacity: 55,500 All Seater
Opened: 1929

■ About Estadio Manuel Ruiz de Lopera

The Manuel Ruiz de Lopera stadium could be one of the greatest stadiums in Spain, and even in Europe, if the megalomaniac chairman who named the stadium after himself ever finds the funds to complete it. Originally named the Estadio Benito Villamarin, Betis have played on this ground since 1929. The stadium has always been uncovered – the beautiful Seville weather means that rain is not very common here. Originally built to house less than 30,000, the stadium was adequate for Real Betis's uses until Lopera took over the club in the 1990s and began his expansion plans that seems to characterise all of the building projects in the city. Within two years of taking over the club, the old north and east stands were gone to be replaced by a very smart and modern three-tier stand that wrapped around the corner and held nearly 30,000. This gave the stadium an unbalanced look that survives today, with the old open terrace of the south stand sitting oddly against the new stands and the covered main stand.

However, changes are on the horizon. Lopera recently announced that the south stand would be demolished in late 2007 and the rebuilt one would join up with the north and east stands. Views are unsurprisingly very good, although the back rows of the upper tier are a long way from the action. Quite what the club hope to do with a 70,000-seater stadium when they only attract 38,000 for league games is beyond most reasonable thinking. Whilst the club are rebuilding the stadium they will play games at the Olympic Stadium in the north of the city – itself a white elephant, really only famous for holding the 2003 UEFA Cup Final between Porto and Celtic.

■ Who plays there?

Real Betis Balompié, to give them their full name, were formed in 1907 after a row amongst the players at Sevilla. They adopted their distinctive green kit after one of their founders travelled to Glasgow to watch Celtic play in 1912. They gained their royal patronage ('Real') from King Don Alfonso XIII in 1914. The club's formative years were spent trying to establish themselves in the La Liga, although they did pip rivals Sevilla to the honour of being the first Andalucian club to play in the top league. They won their one and only La Liga title in 1935 and haven't really got close to another one since. The club has won the Copa del Rey on two occasions, in 1977 and again in 2005 when they beat Osasuna in Madrid. They have been runners up on a number of occasions, including in 1997 when they lost to a rampant Barcelona team.

They finished in the Champions League places in 2005. After overcoming Monaco in the qualifying round the club went into a group with Liverpool, Chelsea and Anderlecht. A home victory against Chelsea plus points on their travels in Belgium and Liverpool put them in a position to make the second stages but a final home defeat to Anderlecht saw them finish in third place. Like their neighbours Sevilla, the 1990s were a disastrous time for the club. They made one of the worst transfer deals of all time when they paid £22million for Brazilian winger Denilson, who failed to do anything to justify such an amount in the four seasons he was at the club. The team were then relegated a couple of times, and it was only in 2000 that they forced their way back into the top division. In the last few seasons the team has been forced to look on enviously as Seville have become one of the most feared teams in Europe. In 2006/2007 the team struggled to cope with the intense pressure from the jealous fans who watched Seville's success with envy, and a season-long struggle against relegation was only relieved on the final day when they finished one point above the relegation zone.

■ How to get there

Buses 2 and 34 run from the city centre down Avenida Heliópolis to the the ground. The stadium is also walkable – but allow yourself around 30 minutes from the cathedral area of the city, or 15 minutes from Plaza de Espanya. Whilst the stadium is being redeveloped, the team will play at the Olympic Stadium in the north of the city on the island of Cartuja.

■ Getting a ticket

With an average attendance of 38,000 few games ever sell out – in fact, last season only the derby match was a complete sell out. Tickets for most normal games go on sale ten days before the match from the main ticket office. Tickets range in price from €40 for an upper-tier Fondo (behind the goal seat) to €65 in the covered Preferencia. A good bet for the neutral is the middle tier behind the north goal (Fondu Baja Nord) that costs €45.

The Facts

Name: Estadio Ramón Sánchez Pizjuán
Address: Avenida Eduardo Dato,
41005 Seville,
Spain
Capacity: 55,000 All Seater
Opened: 7th September 1958 – Sevilla FC v Real Jaen

■ About Estadio Ramón Sánchez Pizjuán

The Ramón Sánchez Pizjuán is one of the most atmospheric stadiums in Spain. It was originally opened in 1957, replacing Sevilla's original home, the Estadio Nervion, that was located close to the current ground. At its peak, the stadium held over 60,000 but today, due to safety issues and the conversion to all-seater, it has been reduced to just over 50,000. It is a relatively simple stadium – a two-tiered bowl structure, with steep sides and only one stand covered. The stadium hosted the 1986 European Cup Final between Barcelona and Steaua Bucharest as well as hosting games in the 1982 World Cup finals including the infamous semi-final between West Germany and France. After the 1982 World Cup the land that the club owned around the stadium was sold for development and today it is a strange experience trying to find the stadium within the shopping and residential complex that has been built around it.

The stadium is also used frequently by the national team and is deemed a lucky omen in that they have never lost here in over 20 games. Added to this is the remarkable record Sevilla have in European competition in that they have never lost a European tie at home – a fact that ensured UEFA Cup success in the past two seasons. Average attendances over recent seasons have been over 40,000 but success on the field this season has seen it rise to nearly 50,000. Views from the upper tier are excellent, although the scorching Andalucian sun often makes watching games very uncomfortable.

■ Who plays there?

In light of the last two years of success that the club have experienced, it is difficult to believe that only a few years ago both Seville clubs were regular fixtures in the Segunda division. In the 2005/2006 season the team finally achieved a major honour, beating Middlesbrough in Eindhoven 4–0 to capture the UEFA Cup. They added to this, qualification for the UEFA Cup again, with a 5th-place finish (although they were only two points off 2nd place in the end) and victory in the UEFA Super Cup in Monaco over arch rivals Barcelona. The team kept that momentum going into last season as they led the way ahead of the big three up until Christmas, before finishing in 3rd place. However, they did continue their excellent form in Europe, becoming the first team to retain the trophy after beating Espanyol on penalties in an all-Spanish final.

The club were formed two years before their rivals Betis in 1905, although it took a few years for them to get their hands on their first trophy, beating CE Sabadelll in the Copa del Rey final in 1935. In the 1939 season, the first after the Civil War had ended, Sevilla managed to record some amazing victories, including an 11–1 defeat of Barcelona and a 10–3 victory over Valencia. This form almost delivered them the league title but a draw in their final game against Hercules handed the title to Atletico Aviacion. The following season saw the team 2nd again before a 3rd place finish in 1944. Two years later the club secured their only La Liga title to date, and followed it up a couple of seasons later with a third Copa Del Rey cup, beating Celta Vigo in the final. That Copa del Rey was the last trophy the club won until the UEFA Cup in 2006. In the years in between the club went through a really barren period, trying without luck to buy the title by bringing some expensive imports who failed to deliver the goods. These included Diego Maradona in 1992, as well as Illie Dumitrescu and Bebeto, who failed to deliver anything apart from a UEFA Cup run in 1993. One success was Croatian Davor Suker who scored over 60 goals in less than five seasons with the club.

In 1993, in a bid to stave off bankruptcy, the club sold the lease to the stadium and planned to move across town to the newly constructed Olympic Stadium. Funds were found but the story was the same two years later when the lack of financial guarantees actually led to the club being automatically relegated. However, the Spanish football federation made a dramatic decision that angered many other teams by expanding the league from 20 to 22 teams, thus keeping Sevilla in the La Liga. Less than 12 months later nothing could save them as they finished bottom of the newly expanded league – the only consolation was that Real Betis were relegated as well. The next few seasons were spent bouncing between the leagues until in the early part of this decade they managed to build a competitive team.

■ How to get there
The stadium is situated in the east of the city, outside the historic centre and a 5-minute walk from the Santa Justa railway station. If you are coming from the city centre then you can catch buses C1, C2, 32 and 27 which run to outside the shopping centre. If the club switch a game to the Estadio La Cartuja in the north west of the city, be prepared for a long 30-minute walk from the city centre. The renamed Olympic Stadium sits on the old Expo site north of the Ronda de Circunvalacion ring road, and whilst

an impressive stadium from the inside, it suffers badly from being so isolated.

■ Getting a ticket
Despite Sevilla's meteoric rise to fame over the last two seasons tickets for most games (Betis, Real Madrid and Barcelona excepted) are easy to come by. The ticket office starts selling them from ten days before the match, with prices starting from €30 for a place in the Gol Sur or Norte to €90 for a covered seat in the Preferencia Banco de Pista. Between May and September, temperatures in Sevilla can hit the mid-40s and so it is worth investing more to get one of the limited tickets in the shade, rather than risk sunstroke. Last season Sevilla averaged just over 40,000 for their home fixtures. If Sevilla switch their home games to the Olympic Stadium tickets are sold via the ticket office at the Ramón Sánchez Pizjuán. A couple of seasons ago the club experimented by playing a couple of games here but crowds fell and so they are in no hurry to repeat the experiment.

■ Nearest airport – Aeropuerto de Sevilla (SVQ)
Seville's airport is located 8 miles east of the city. Today, **Ryanair** serves the airport from Liverpool and London Stansted, **GB Airlines** from London Gatwick, **Clickair** from London Heathrow and **Iberia** from London Heathrow. From the airport a bus service runs every 30 minutes to Santa Justa station and on to Palacio de los Exposiciones, with a journey time of 25 minutes. A single ticket costs €2.50, whilst a taxi will cost €25. Another way to reach Seville is by one of the AVE Trains that run every 2 hours from Madrid, with a journey time of less than 2 hours 30 minutes – with an average speed of over 300km per hour.

The Facts

Name: Estadio Mestalla
Address: Avenida se Suecia s/n,
46010 Valencia,
Spain
Capacity: 55,000 All Seater
Opened: 20th May 1923 – Valencia v UD Levante

■ About Estadio Mestalla

When the Louis Casanova Stadium opened in May 1923 it was one of the most modern stadiums in Spain, and indeed was used as the original model for the Bernabéu in Madrid. Now renamed as the Mestalla, it is still possible to see the similarities between the two stadiums, although the sunnier climate means that three quarters of the stadium is still uncovered. The original stadium was a modest 17,000 single-tier affair. A second tier was added during the 1940s as on-field success allowed the club to expand and compete with the big teams from Madrid. In 1954, the roofed main stand opened, taking the capacity to over 45,000.

Very little work was carried out on the stadium until the early 1980s when the ground was chosen as a venue for the 1982 World Cup. The stadium hosted all of Spain's group games including the unpredicted and unwanted draw against Honduras and defeat to Northern Ireland. During the 1990s a tier was added to the east stand,

taking the capacity to its current 55,000. The stands in the upper tier are very steep. Whilst the views are good, you do need to be fit to make the trip to the upper tiers.

The stadium can be quite atmospheric, despite being open to the elements. The stadium is a favourite of the national team, who have an excellent record here. However, the club's time at the Mestalla could be limited as plans have been approved for the Nuevo Estadio Valencia, a 75,000-seater stadium, which could be ready in May 2009.

■ Who plays there?

FC Valencia were formed in 1919 by a group of local students who had heard stories of English football. After a few years of travelling around the city they found roots at the Mestalla, which opened in 1923. The following year they won the regional championship although this was the only trophy won until 1941 when they captured the Copa del Rey, beating Espaynol. The following season they went one step further and captured the La Liga championship for the first time. Two further championships followed in 1944 and 1947 to end the decade as one of the most feared teams in Spain.

The 1950s were a quiet decade although the club did win the renamed Copa Generalissimo in 1953. Ten years later, in 1962, the team entered the Inter-City Fairs Cup for the first time. In a run to the final that included victories over Nottingham Forest (7–1 on aggregate), Inter Milan and MTK, Valencia scored for fun, before beating

Barcelona 7–3. The following year, Valencia retained the title with a 4–1 victory over Dinamo Zagreb and were only prevented from winning a hat-trick of successive titles by a surprisingly well-motivated Real Zaragoza in the 1964 final in the Camp Nou in Barcelona.

In 1970, Real Madrid legend Alfredo Di Stefano joined the club as coach and within nine months he had delivered the title back to the fans in the Mestalla. This turned out to be the last major honour the club won for nearly 20 years, apart from a Cup Winners' Cup victory on penalties against Arsenal in 1980. The other notable event during the 1980s was relegation of the team for the first time after some shocking performances on the pitch. After returning to the top division in the late 1980s the club tried a succession of coaches in an attempt to deliver some consistency. Guus Hiddink took over in 1991 but could only manage a high of 4th place. He was replaced by Carlos Alberto Parreira who had just steered Brazil to World Cup success in the USA.

In 1995 the club reached the final of the Copa Del Rey where they met Deportivo La Coruna in the Bernabeu. After 14 minutes of the game, with Deportivo winning 2–1, torrential rain caused the game to be abandoned, and the result to stand – the shortest ever major final in Spanish history. Parreira was replaced by Luis Aragonés who could not improve performances on the pitch as Real Madrid continued to dominate. Claudio Ranieri was the next to be given the reigns and he did deliver the Copa Del Rey in 1999 with a penalties victory over Barcelona. However, Ranieri never enjoyed a good relationship with the crowd due to his constant desire to change the team (shortly after leaving Valencia he joined Chelsea, where he became known as the 'Tinkerman' because of this reason). Little-known Argentinian coach Héctor Cúper was asked to take over the reigns in 1999 and his blend of attacking football based on two fast wingers (Kily Gonzalez and Claudio Lopez), with an attacking midfield general (Mendieta), coupled with a free-scoring centre forward (John Carew), delivered success in the Champions League. Teams came and left well beaten in Valencia, including victories over Lazio and Barcelona on the way to a final against Real Madrid in Paris. Despite playing well for the majority of the game, it was Madrid who romped to a 3–0 victory. Twelve months later the team were back in the final, this time in Milan's San Siro against Bayern Munich. Again, luck was not on their side and they lost 5–4 on penalties after a 1–1 draw.

Cúper left the following season to join Inter Milan and he was replaced by untested Rafa Benitez. He delivered success within 18 months, with the La Liga coming back to the Mestalla after a 31-year wait. Two years later he won the trophy again, and in Europe captured the UEFA

Cup with a win over Marseille. Benitez's skills were soon spotted by Liverpool and the Spaniard took up the reigns at Anfield in early 2004. Since then the club has gained successive 2nd place finishes in the league, with a team consisting of skill in Pablo Aimar, and strength in Roberto Ayala. Last season they finished in 3rd place, although they will see Champions League qualification as success.

■ How to get there

The Mestalla is based in the eastern suburbs of the city, around a 20-minute walk from the historic centre. From the north of the city catch tram line 4 from Pont de Fusta three stops eastwards to V Zaragoza. From here follow Ave Primado down to the junction with Ave de Catalunya and then you will see the ground. Alternatively, the nearest metro stop to the ground is right by the south stand at Aragon. This is on the new line 5, which extends from line 3 at Alameda. From the Las Arenas beach area, just follow Ave del Puerto from the south end of the beach all the way westwards until you reach Ave de Zaragoza.

■ Getting a ticket

For the majority of games played at the Mestalla tickets are available up until kick-off from the ticket windows in the south west corner of the stadium. Each window sells tickets for different stands, so if it appears from one seller than the game is sold out try other windows. Ticket touts also congregate around these windows. Tickets for most matches go on sale around ten days before the game, both from the ticket windows and from outlets in the city including the official club shop in c/Pintor Sorolla 25 and all Toyota dealerships in the city. Ticket prices range from €80 in the covered Tribuna to €22 in the Grada de la Mar. The latter tickets are open to the elements and it is a long hike to the top tier. At present there is no online ticket booking facility.

■ Nearest airport – Valencia Manises (VLC)

Manises airport is located 8km to the west of the city centre. To reach the city centre from the airport you can catch one of two buses. The Aero bus runs direct to Avenue del Cid every 20 minutes from 6am and costs €2.5 each way. Line 150 runs to the central bus station, making a number of local stops along the way. Tickets cost €1.05 each way. A taxi to the city centre will cost approximately €20. The airport is currently served by **Ryanair** from London Stansted, **Easyjet** from Bristol, London Gatwick and London Stansted, **Thomson** fly from Coventry and **Jet2** from Manchester. It is also served daily by **British Airways** from London Gatwick and Heathrow.

The Facts

Name:	Nya Ullevi Stadion
Address:	Skånegatan,
	401 25 Gothenburg,
	Sweden
Capacity:	43,200 All Seater
Opened:	March 1958

■ **About Nya Ullevi Stadion**

The 'new' Ullevi stadium is the biggest stadium in Sweden. It was originally opened in time for the 1958 World Cup finals, and has since hosted a number of high-profile matches. The stadium is similar in design to newer stadiums built in Mälmo and San Sebastian with two sweeping side stands flowing down to two smaller end stands.

The stadium has an athletics track and was used for the 1995 Athletics World Championships, as well as last year's European Athletics Championships. It is also used for major concerts such as the record-attended Bruce Springsteen concert in June 1985 which nearly caused one of the stands to collapse due to the crowd's dancing. The stadium played host to a number of games in the 1958 World Cup finals, including Brazil versus England, and a 1st round play-off between Russia and England which the Soviets won 1–0. It was also the scene of Wales last-ever World Cup match when they lost 1–0 in the quarter-finals

to eventual winners Brazil. However, the record attendance didn't come during the tournament but a year later when IFK Göteborg hosted rivals Örgryte in front of over 52,000. The stadium hosted the European Cup Winners' Cup Final in 1983 when Alex Ferguson's Aberdeen beat Real Madrid after extra-time in their greatest ever game, and again in 1990 when Sampdoria beat Anderlecht. In 2004 the stadium was used again for a major European final when Valencia beat Marseille in the UEFA Cup Final.

In 1992 the stadium was chosen not only as one of the four host venues for the European Championships but was selected as the final venue. The whole of Scandinavia preyed for a Sweden versus Denmark final at the Nya Ullevi but it was not to be as Germany beat the home nation 3–2 in the semi-finals, before losing to Denmark 2–0 in front of 37,800 in the final. Today the stadium is being used again on a regular basis as the new Ullevi is being constructed next door. Spectators enjoy decent views from the side stands. The hardcore IFK fans congregate on the northwest terrace, although their support is fanatical rather than violent.

■ **Who plays there?**

For many seasons the stadium hardly ever hosted domestic football, as the local clubs IFK Göteborg, Örgryte and GAIS preferred to use the more intimate Gamla Ullevi next door. However, as this stadium is currently being reconstructed, both IFK and Örgryte have taken up residence again. The stadium is also used frequently by the national team, the last occasion being against Liechtenstein in September 2006.

IFK are one of the most successful teams in Sweden, and are the only club to have won European honours when they won the UEFA Cup in 1982 and 1987. Despite a successful start to their history in 1908 when they were champions, it wasn't until young Swedish coach Sven Goran Eriksson took over the team in 1979 that they began to forge a pedigree both at home and abroad. In his first season the club won the Swedish cup, beating Atvidabergs FF. Over the next few season the club won two more Swedish cups as well as the league championship between 1982 and 1984. In that glorious year of 1982 they not only won the domestic double but also the UEFA Cup, beating Sturm Graz, Dinamo Bucharest, Valencia and Kaiserslautern before defeating Hamburg over two legs in the final.

The following season they continued this fine form with another domestic double. In 1986 the team reached the semi-finals of the European Cup, losing on penalties to Barcelona. However, the following season they returned to European triumph by beating Dundee United over two legs to win the UEFA Cup. The club has since won a few honours, including a run of six titles in the seven years between 1989 and 1996 but nothing in the last decade. Champions League football has arrived a few times during the 1990s but that is as far as the good times have gone. Last season's 8th-place finish was considered an embarrassment that must not be repeated.

IFK Göteborg's city rivals are Örgryte IS who are one of the oldest teams in Sweden, tracing their roots back to 1892. Despite their dominance of the game in the early years, they have been without success for a long time. The club went unbeaten for more than four years in the final years of the 19th century, winning ten championships in just 13 seasons up until 1909. Since then a further championship in 1913 was their last honour until 1985. In 2000 the team beat AIK in the final of the Swedish cup final with Marcus Allbäck scoring on the way to a 2–1 victory. Today the club languish back in the 2nd division after relegation in 2006 and are playing their matches at the small Valhalla stadium which is located behind the Ullevi.

Finally, GAIS can be found playing at the Ullevi. The initials stand for the Gothenburg Athletics & Sports Association, and the club were one of the founding members of the Allsvenskan – in fact they actually won the first-ever championship in 1925. Since their Allsvenskan championship win in 1954 they have not won a single honour, although they did lose in the 1987 cup final to Kalmar FF. Last season they narrowly escaped relegation and so this season will be about damage limitation rather than a quest for honours.

■ How to get there

The stadium is located no more than a 5-minute walk away from the central station and so public transport is really not needed. From the station turn left onto Drottningtorget, then right once you get into the one-way system. When this road crosses Ullevigaten turn left and the stadium is 400 metres on the right-hand side. You will pass the construction site of the new Ullevi stadium on the way.

■ Getting a ticket

With over 43,000 places available for each game, the chances of a sell-out are very rare indeed in Swedish football. Last season IFK averaged just over 10,000 per game, and Örgryte just 5,000. Virtually all games played here (including the national team's games) are pay on the door. However, you can purchase tickets in advance from http://www.ticnet.se. Tickets range in price from 90 SKR in the areas behind the goal to 125 SKR in the upper tiers along the side of the pitch.

■ Nearest airport – Göteborg Landvetter (GOT)

The main airport serving Göteborg is located 20km east of the city in the small town of Landvetter. It served over 5 million passengers in 2006 making it Sweden's second biggest airport. The airport is well served by UK airlines including **City Airline** from Birmingham and Manchester, **SAS** from London Heathrow as well as **British Airways**. To reach the city centre from the airport catch one of the Flygbussarna buses that take 30 minutes to reach Göteborg Central Station. A single ticket costs 80 SEK.

■ Alternative airport – Göteborg City (GSE)

Göteborg's second airport is actually more central – located 14km north west of the city. Thanks to the arrival of **Ryanair** in 2005, passenger numbers rose from 10,000 to over 500,000 in one year. The Irish carrier currently flies here daily from Dublin, London Stansted and Glasgow Prestwick. A bus service meets every inbound flight and takes passengers up to the main train station in 20 minutes. Tickets cost 50SEK one way.

The Facts

Name: Olympia Stadion
Address: Mellersta Stenbocksgatan,
Helsingborg SE-250 02,
Sweden
Capacity: 12,625 (9,775 Seats)
Opened: 1898

■ About Olympia Stadion

The Olympia Stadion is one of the most atmospheric stadiums in the Swedish top division. It can hardly be called traditional as it is a mixture of the old and the new and is perched on a hill high above the historic port city of Helsingborg. The stadium was originally opened in 1898 as a multi-sport venue and was further developed during the 1990s when the main stand and east stand were rebuilt, and the athletics track removed.

The stadium is one of the most famous in Swedish football, and unusually the hardcore fans can be seen to congregate in one particular corner on both the terrace and the seated areas. The views from the main stand and the east stand are very good, although the setting sun during the summer months does cause an problem for those seated in the latter. Away supporters are located in the corner of the north stand terrace. Expect lots of coordinated singing and a few ticker-tape showers.

■ Who plays there?

Helsingborgs IF were founded in June 1907 although their formative years brought little joy in terms of success. The club played in the regional leagues until the end of the First World War when they began to dominate Swedish football, but never quite won the honours. All that changed in 1929 when the team at last lived up to their potential by winning the championship. They followed this up by retaining their title in 1930, and went on to win the trophy in 1933, 1934 and 1941 when they completed the domestic double.

After the Second World War ended in 1945, and football returned to Sweden, the club struggled to compete with the big teams, and found themselves on a number of occasions in the 2nd division. They returned in 1993 to herald a new era of success for the club. In the late 1990s the team at last delivered the goods by first winning the Swedish cup in 1998 and the following season the title for the final time. The club have played in Europe a number of times – in fact they played in European competition every season from 1996/97 through to 2002. During that period the most notable success was playing in the Champions League in 2000/2001 when they beat Inter Milan over two legs to qualify for the group stages along with Paris Saint Germain, Rosenborg and Bayern Munich. They will once again return to the UEFA Cup in 2007 after winning the Swedish cup in 2006 by beating Gefle IF 2–0.

The club is managed by a Scot, Stuart Baxter, who has been playing and managing in Sweden since the mid-1980s. Their most famous player, without doubt is ex-Celtic and Barcelona legend Henrik Larsson who promised the club he first made his name with at least one season at the end of his career. He was true to his word, despite turning down an offer to stay at Manchester United where he was on loan during 2006/2007. One notable feature of the team is that they have more sponsors on their kit than a Formula One car – with six different sponsors on the shirt and two on their shorts.

■ How to get there
Most visitors will arrive at the central station which is close to the ferry terminal and adjacent to the bus station. If the weather is nice then the best way to reach the stadium is to walk through the pedestrian area opposite the station, stopping at a few hostelries along the way before taking one of the paths that wind their way up the steep hill. Once you are in the park area, keep heading eastwards and the stadium will come into view behind the houses. The walk from the station takes around 15 minutes. There are a number of buses laid on for the football that run from the bus station.

■ Getting a ticket
Swedish football is enjoying a renaissance, and with the signing of Henrik Larsson Helsingborgs have become a very attractive team to watch, and so tickets can be in short supply for some matches. However, the good news is that it is easy to book a ticket in advance using http://www.ticnet.se where tickets go on sale around six weeks prior to the match. Tickets can also be purchased from the stadium. Ticket prices depend on the opposition, but in general you will pay 105SKR for a place on the terrace for most matches, rising to 145SKR for the game versus Mälmo, whilst a good seat would be 175SKR and 245SKR respectively.

■ Nearest airport – Kastrup Copenhagen (CPH)
Despite being in a different country, Copenhagen is the nearest airport, located 60 miles to the south across the Øresund Bridge. **Easyjet** are the main budget carrier who fly to Copenhagen, flying daily from London Stansted. **British Airways** and **SAS** fly here from London Heathrow. **Snowflake**, SAS's budget brand, fly twice daily from London City. **Sterling** fly three times a day from London Gatwick. From Copenhagen Airport train station under terminal 3 you can catch an hourly train direct to Helsingborg. The journey takes around 75 minutes – but make sure you are in the right carriage as the train often divides at Mälmo Central. A return ticket costs 265DKR.

The Facts

Name: Malmö Stadion

Address: Eric Persson Weg,
Malmö 200 73,
Sweden

Capacity: 27,500 All Seater

Opened: 1951

■ About Malmö Stadion

Anyone who has been on a tour of Swedish stadiums, and to date missed Malmö, would be forgiven for thinking that they had somehow found themselves back at IFK Göteborg's Ullevi stadium. That is because the two venues were designed by the same architect for the 1958 World Cup finals. During that tournament the stadium hosted four games, including the game between West Germany and Argentina that attracted the (still) record attendance of 32,000.

The stadium is certainly unique. There are two almost wave-like stands opposite each other that rise at the half-way line before sweeping down behind the goals where they meet open terracing. The only downside is the presence of the athletics track that does give the feeling of isolation behind the goals. Terracing runs down the side of the pitch opposite the main stand. The stadium will only be in use for another couple of years as the construction of a brand new stadium has started already. The new

stadium, located next to the current version, is due to open in April 2009 with an all-seated capacity of 28,000 and will be one of the host venues for the 2009 UEFA Under 21 Championship.

■ Who plays there?

One of the most famous scenes of football in the 1970s is Nottingham Forest's Trevor Francis diving full length to head in the only goal in the 1979 European Cup Final in Munich. However, few people actually remember that the opponents that day in Germany were FF Malmö in their biggest ever night of football. The Swedish FA recognised this feat by awarding the club the Medal of Honour – the only Swedish club to have gained this. The club were formed in 1910, although it was a number of decades before they managed to reach the top division of Swedish football. Apart from a small blip in 1999, the club have played in the top division for the whole of that time.

In recent years the club have struggled to break the hold on the top of the table that Djurgarden and Göteborg have had – the 2004 championship is the only silverware the club have won in the past 18 years.

Their golden period was during the 1970s when the club won five Swedish championships, five Swedish cups and of course the European Cup runners-up spot. Interestingly enough, Brian Clough declined FIFA's invitation to play in the Intercontinental Cup in 1979, the annual match between the European and South American champions, and so FF Malmö were invited to play against

Olimpia Asuncion of Paraguay instead over a two-leg match, which they lost 3–1.

The club have been managed by a couple of British coaches over the years – Bob Houghton was in charge for the 1979 European Cup Final, whilst Roy Hodgson managed the club for five years during the 1980s when the team enjoyed some domestic success. They were also managed by Tord Grip, Sven-Goran Eriksson's right-hand man, in the mid-1980s. The present team are only too aware of the pressure to win some silverware. The most notable squad members this season are the Finnish legend Jari Litmanen and ex-Charlton Athletic midfielder Jonatan Johansson.

■ How to get there
The stadium is located south of the main city centre, a 20-minute walk from the central station, or 10 minutes from the bus station. Bus number 2 runs close to the stadium, although they get very busy before the game. A taxi from the central station will cost around 75SEK.

■ Getting a ticket
Whilst attendances are on the up at the Malmö Stadion there are still plenty of spaces for those turning up to pay on the gate. The average attendance over the past few seasons has been around the 14,000 mark, making them the second best supported team in the Allsvenskan behind AIK. Tickets can be bought in advanced from the website http://www.ticnet.se. Tickets range in price from 180SEK in the upper tier of the main stand to 105SEK behind the goal on the terraces. At the gate these prices are increased to 200SEK and 110SEK respectively. The main Malmö fans congregate on the terraces of the lower side stand. If you are watching an early evening game then it may be best to avoid the main stand due to problems caused by the setting sun.

■ Nearest airport – Kastrup Copenhagen (CPH)
Despite being in a different country, Copenhagen is the nearest airport, located 15 miles to the west of Malmö across the Øresund Bridge. **Easyjet** are the main budget carrier to fly to Copenhagen, flying here daily from London Stansted. **British Airways** and **SAS** fly here from London Heathrow. **Snowflake**, SAS's budget brand, fly twice daily from London City. **Sterling** fly three times a day from London Gatwick. To get to Malmö from Kastrup airport, catch one of the three trains per hour from the station under terminal 3. The journey time is 23 minutes. A single ticket costs around 130Dkr. A bus also runs from the airport, costing 100DKr.

■ Other airport – Malmö Sturup Airport (MMX)
Ryanair fly into Malmö's small and compact Sturup airport. Despite the fact that the airport is located across the water in Sweden, the completion of the Øresund Bridge means the two countries are now permanently linked. It is 17 miles from the city centre. Buses link the airport to the city centre, taking around 40 minutes.

The Facts

Name: Stockholms Stadion
Address: Klocktornet,
114 33 Stockholm,
Sweden
Capacity: 14,500 All Seater
Opened: 1st July 1912

■ About Stockholms Stadion

After a season playing at the national Råsunda stadium, Djurgarden returned to the Stockholms stadium in 2006. The reason was born out of a disagreement over the ownership of the commercial revenues in the municipal-owned stadium. However, the team still use the national stadium for derby matches with AIK Solna.

The small Stockholms Stadion is best known for being the venue of the 1912 Olympic Games. Many of the unique features are still retained within the stadium – including the listed towers at the east end. Outside, the ivy-clad walls give the impression of a time gone by. In fact the stadium today looks more like its 1912 original due to the renovation work that took place in the mid-1990s. This has been the club's home since 1936, after moving from the Tranesberg Stadium. The present ground still retains the athletics track and is still used for all major track and field events. The stadium consists of a horseshoe double-tier stand, which sweeps around three sides of the stadium, leaving the historic Olympic stands still in existence. The club actually started their playing history in the same area in 1896, with the previous ground, the Idottsparken, their home until they moved to the Tranesberg Stadium in 1910. Views from the side stands are good, although the athetics track does hinder spectators at each end.

■ Who plays there?

Djurgarden were originally formed in 1891, taking their name from the island in the city centre where the founders used to meet. The club played in the lower leagues for a number of seasons before being allowed to compete in the national leagues. In 1904 the club reached the Swedish cup final where they lost to Örgryte. The club did gain revenge over the team from Göteborg eight years later in their next final appearance, thus becoming Swedish champions for the first time.

The club won further championships in 1915, 1917 and 1920 but struggled to compete with the likes of Malmö and Göteborg. In fact it took a further 35 years for the team to win the title again, in 1955, and then followed a golden period with four further cups in a period of nine years. After relegation to the 2nd division in 1981, the club floundered for twenty years. Finally, in 2001, the team managed to find the right on-field formula and at last delivered some success for supporters when they finished 2nd in the Allsvenskan. The following year they went one better and were crowned champions, beating off the strong challenge of AIK and Göteborg. They retained their crown in 2003 and won it again in 2005 to underline their position as Sweden's number one team.

The current team is built around young Swedish talent, with players such as Andreas Johansson and Daniel Sjölund, and coached by Jonas Riedel. Last season the team finished in a disappointing 6th place, and so the club will have to do without European football again in 2007. In fact European football hasn't been too kind to the club. They first competed in the European Cup in 1955–56 when they reached the last eight before losing to Hibernian. In 1964 they met Manchester United in the first round of the UEFA Cup and lost 7–2 on aggregate. In fact, after their win against Grasshoppers in the 2nd leg of their UEFA Cup game in 1965, the club had to wait ten years before they gained another victory, beating Kristiansand of Norway 7–1 in the 1975 UEFA Cup. In 2002 they recorded their best performance to date in the UEFA Cup, reaching the third round after beating Shamrock Rovers and FC Copenhagen before going out 3–1 to Girondins de Bordeaux. Their Champions League debut in 2002 lasted one round as they went out on away goals to Partizan Belgrade, and the following season a

6–3 defeat to Juventus prevented them reaching the lucrative group stages.

■ How to get there

The ground is located close to the red T-line stop at, surprisingly enough, Stadion. It takes around 10 minutes from the central station in the direction of Morby Centrum. As you exit the station follow the subway under the road and then continue for 100 metres, when the stadium will be visible on your right.

■ Getting a ticket

The experiment of moving their matches to the much bigger Råsunda stadium only resulted in thousands of empty seats at each game. Swedish football, like most of the football in Scandinavia, comes a second in terms of popularity to ice hockey, and attendances for almost all domestic matches fail to generate the passion and atmosphere that exists elsewhere in Europe. Therefore, booking of seats really isn't required. Tickets can be booked from the ticket hotline on +46 77 1707070 or http://www.ticnet.se. The average attendance last year was just under 13,000, although as some games were held in the national stadium the figure does not give a true reflection of the gates at the Stockholms stadium. Tickets range from 150SEK for games at the Stockholms to 375SEK to the derby games with AIK and Hammarby.

■ Nearest airport – Arlanda Airport (ARN)

Arlanda is the main airport for Stockholm and is served by both **British Airways** and **SAS** flying from London Heathrow. The airport is linked to the city centre by the Arlanda express train that runs from the terminal in less than 25 minutes every 15 minutes. The train costs 360SEK for a return ticket. A taxi would take around 45minutes and cost close to 500SEK.

■ Alternative airport – Skavsta Airport (NYO)

Skavsta Airport is 50 miles to the south west of Stockholm, close to the town of Nyopking. **Ryanair** are expanding Skavsta as another European hub. They provide a bus to meet all incoming flights, which takes around 2 hours to reach the central bus station in Stockholm for 100SEK single or 150SEK return.

Stade St Jakob Park – Basle (Switzerland)

The Facts

Name: Stade St Jakob Park
Address: Gellerstrasse 235,
4052 Basle,
Switzerland
Capacity: 33,200 All Seater
Opened: 25th April 1954

■ About Stade St Jakob Park

When it was announced that the joint bid from Austria and Switzerland had been successful in hosting Euro2008™, the city council in Basel wasted no time in drawing up plans to provide a stadium that would be a key part of the plans.

Similar in nature to the stadiums at Berne and Geneva, the outer shell of the stadium is hidden on one side by a shopping centre, but inside the stadium is very much as you would expect from the Swiss – compact, neat and efficient. It is very British in design – four stands close to the pitch and excellent sightlines. Behind each goal there are identical two-tier stands, with a screen perched on the roof. The south stand's upper tier is smaller as there is a double-layer of executive boxes here. The north stand is a three-tier affair, with the roof sloping up at the corners.

The concourses are the only problem – they are quite cramped and during half-time it can be a bit of a struggle to move from one side of the stand to another. The stadium has recently been awarded UEFA 4-star status.

In June 2008 the stadium will host the following games in the European Championships:

Match 1 – Saturday 7th June – 18.00 – Switzerland v Czech Republic
Match 10 – Wednesday 11th June – 20.45 – Switzerland v Turkey
Match 17 – Sunday 15th June – 20.45 – Switzerland v Portugal
Match 25 – Thursday 19th June – 20.45 – Quarter-final 1
Match 27 – Sateuday 21st June – 20.45 – Quarter-final 3
Match 29 – Wednesday 25th June – 20.45 – Semi-final 1

■ Who plays there?

Fussballclub Basel are currently the biggest and best-supported club in Swiss football. In terms of honours, they have won 11 national league titles – more than any other club – and seven cups. They have also had more success in Europe than any other Swiss team, most recently under Christian Gross in 2002 when they beat Celtic, Liverpool, Deportivo La Coruna and Juventus on their way to the knock-out stages of the Champions League. These victories all came at home, and reinforced the fact that the club have become almost unbeatable in Basel. On the 13th May 2006 the team lost a league match here for the first time in over 3½ years – an amazing run of 59 games. Unfortunately this game was decided by a last-minute winner by FC Zurich which handed the team the title from the grasp of FC Basel.

The club had modest success in their early years, winning the title in 1953 for the first time. Their most successful period came in the late 1960s and early 1970s when the team won five titles in seven seasons, as well as two Swiss cups. They returned to success in the early 2000s when Christian Gross joined the club after his unsuccessful spell at Tottenham Hotspur. He delivered the domestic double in 2002, and followed this with league victories in 2004 and 2005. Unfortunately last season, despite starting again as favourites, they allowed FC Zurich to break away at the top of the league and 2nd place was their only reward for a season's hard toil.

■ How to get there

The stadium is located in the east of the city, hemmed in by the train line and the motorway. It is almost the demarcation point between the centre and the suburbs. The stadium is walkable – certainly from the area close to the main station it is no more than 30 minutes away. On a match day special football shuttle trains run from the central station to a stop behind the north stand every 15 minutes. Alternatively you can catch tram number 14 that runs through the centre of the old town – from Markplatz to St Jakob is 8 stops or around 11 minutes away – tickets cost CHF3 each way.

■ Getting a ticket

Domestic football in Switzerland is not necessarily the most passionate affair. Attendances tend to be quite low, and the big four of Young Boys, FC Basel and the two Zurich clubs fail to attract on average more than 50%

stadium utilisation, meaning that tickets are always available on the day. FC Basel are the best-supported team at present in Switzerland, with an average attendance of 20,000. However, with a stadium that can hold over 30,000, sell-outs are exceptionally rare. Tickets can be purchased from the kiosks around the stadium on a match day, or if your German is good via the official website. If you are buying from the UK then you will need to pick the ticket up on the day of the game from the Fanshop on the west side of the stadium. Ticket prices range from 20CHF to 50CHF. The 'hardcore' fans are located in the east lower tier. A good seat for the neutral is in the north stand upper tiers.

■ Nearest airport – Basel Mulhouse Airport (BSL)

Now this is a strange concept. An airport that can lay claim to being in two different countries. Basel (Swiss) Mulhouse (French) Airport has been designed to allow customs and immigration into both countries – once you find yourself in the baggage reclaim hall you will see clear signs either directing you towards French (and German) customs, or Swiss customs. If you are heading for Basel city centre then follow the Swiss signs. The number 50 bus leaves from directly in front of the terminal building every 30 minutes and the CHF3.60 tickets can be bought from the machines at the bus stop. The bus runs to the main station in around 20 minutes. Currently the main budget airline serving the airport is **Easyjet** with daily flights from London Luton and Stansted. **British Airways** fly here from London Heathrow on a daily basis, and **Swiss Airlines** from London City.

Stade De Suisse – Berne (Switzerland)

The Facts

Name: Stade de Suisse
Address: Papiermühlestrasse 71,
CH-3022 Bern,
Switzerland
Capacity: 32,000 All Seater
Opened: 18th October 1925

■ About Stade de Suisse

The Stade de Suisse, or to give it its proper name, the Wankdorf, is one of the elite stadiums in Europe that can lay claim to have hosted a World Cup Final, when in 1954 it staged the game between West Germany and Hungary, forever known as the 'Miracle of Berne'. In 2008 the big time will return to the stadium as the Stade de Suisse will host group matches in June 2008.

The stadium is certainly very smart and befitting for such a redevelopment. It is a complete two-tier 'box' ground, with each stand almost identical. This means that views are pretty standard from wherever you are sitting. Leg room is also very reasonable. One of the unusual things about the stadium is the next generation artificial surface that is used. Certainly the look and feel of the pitch is very different to the old-style Astroturf pitches. In terms of other facilities for fans, the concourses are very wide, and there are plenty of concession stands. There are also two large screens that sit on the roof of the stands

behind each goal, allowing everyone in the stadium a view of the screens.

The original stadium, the Wankdorf, opened in 1925 and was built as a new home to the Young Boys Berne team. It was initially built with a capacity of 20,000 but was soon expanded during the next decade as the team started to make progress. When Switzerland were chosen to hold the 1954 World Cup finals, the stadium was expanded to hold 64,000. Facilities were pretty basic – one covered main stand and three open terraces – and this remained in place until the stadium hosted its last game in July 2003, before construction started on the new stadium.

As with a number of other stadiums in Switzerland there is a shopping centre incorporated into the stadium, with the south side of the stadium having a real multi-purpose feel with shops, cafes and restaurants that are located on the wide outer concourse area. The stadium will host the following games during the European Championships:

Match 6 – Monday 9th June – 20.45 – Netherlands v Italy
Match 14 – Friday 13th June – 20.45 – Netherlands v France
Match 21 – Tuesday 17th June – 20.45 – Netherlands v Romania

■ Who plays there?

Tracing their roots back to 1898, Young Boys are one of the oldest professional clubs in Switzerland. When the first national league started in the early part of the century, it was only a matter of time before the club rose to the forefront in Swiss football – capturing a trio of championships in 1909, 1910 and 1911. Originally the club had been formed as a football club, but in 1925 the club incorporated a number of other sports to become a true sporting club – reflected in the change of name to Young Boys Berner Sports Club. This change of name coincided with the move to the new Wankdorf sporting complex in the north of the city which has been their home every since.

The club were regular winners of the national championship over the next few decades to cement their position as Switzerland's top club. After the championship in 1929, and a subsequent first Swiss cup victory in 1930, the club went through a barren spell, during which they had to wait nearly 25 years for another major honour. Under the influence of Albert Sing, who was to lead the club for nearly 14 years, the team broke their domestic drought with a championship in 1957, going on to win the title for four successive seasons. Again the club could not build on this success and within a few seasons they had returned to mid-table mediocrity, falling behind the likes of Servette, Grasshoppers and rivals FC Basel.

The club won their final title in 1986, and a cup victory the following season has proved to be the final honour won by the club. Their European pedigree has been limited to the occasional UEFA Cup outing, although in 1988 they did reach the European Cup Winners' Cup quarter-final. Last season they did not find the consistency needed and the best they achieved was a 3rd-place finish behind FC Zurich and FC Basel – something that does not befit a team playing in such palatial surroundings.

■ How to get there

The stadium is located in the north area of the city, close to the main railway line and the Autobahn A6. On a match day special buses run from the train station (Bahnhof) direct to the stadium, which complement the route number 20 which runs every 5 minutes. A special shuttle train also runs from the Bahnhof to the Wankdorf station – taking less than 5 minutes to make the journey.

■ Getting a ticket

Last season Young Boys averaged around 17,000, meaning there were 15,000 spare seats on match day. The hardcore fans, as much as they get hardcore in Switzerland, are based in the east lower tier. Tickets can be purchased online from the website https://ticket.stadesuisse.ch. You can also reserve tickets via email at ticket@stadedesuisse.ch or by phone +41 31 344 88 77. Ticket prices start from CHF 20 in the lower tier behind the goal to CHF 50 in the upper tiers along the side of the pitch. A good bet for the neutral is the lower side tiers which are CHF 34. Tickets go on sale on the day of the game from the windows on the corner of all stands. Internet bookings are collected from the south west corner kiosks.

Tickets for every match at Euro2008™ have been sold out for many months, and now the only way of getting tickets is by applying through one of the competing nations' football associations.

■ Nearest airport – Berne Belp Airport (BRN)

Berne's small airport is located in the small village of Belp, 6 kilometres east of the city. It is only served by four scheduled airlines, and the daily service from the UK is provided by **Darwin Airline** from London City, although **Flybe** offer flights on some days from Birmingham International and Southampton. From the airport you can catch the bus to Bern railway station that runs every hour and costs CHF15. Alternatively, catch the local bus to Belp station for CHF3 and then get the train into the city.

The Facts

Name: Stade de Genève
Address: Route des Jeunes,
1203 Geneva,
Switzerland
Capacity: 31,000 All Seater
Opened: 16th March 2003

■ **About Stade de Genève**

Located quite a way to the south of the city in the suburb of Lancy, the new Stade de Genève is shoehorned between the La Praille shopping and entertainment complex, the main railway line and an industrial estate. It was opened in March 2003 for FC Servette, after it was deemed that their previous ground in Les Charmilles was too small to be a venue for the Swiss bid with Austria to stage the European Championships in 2008.
When the two countries were awarded the games in 2002, a suitable site was found for the 30,000-seater stadium and work quickly commenced.

The stadium offers excellent unobstructed views from all sections, although there are perimeter fences in the stands behind the goals. Hanging down from the roof at the back of the south stand is a huge TV screen which can be seen by everyone, even if it means craning your neck in the seats underneath it. The concourse areas are wide and spacious, meaning that overcrowding is kept to a

minimum. The stadium has a real atmosphere to it like some of the new English grounds such as Southampton's St Mary's Stadium and Coventry's Ricoh Arena. It has one stand that is noticeably bigger than the others, with the roof curving down to meet the end stands but little has been done or incorporated to make it have a unique feel. The city's government has big plans for the whole development – in fact the presence of FC Servette as tenants is almost forgotten. The first big match the stadium hosted was the friendly between Argentina and England in November 2005. The stadium will host the following matches in June 2008:

Match 2 – Saturday 7th June – 20.45 – Portugal v Turkey
Match 9 – Wednesday 11th June – 18.00 – Czech Republic v Portugal
Match 18 – Sunday 15th June – 20.45 – Turkey v Czech Republic

■ **Who plays there?**

Once viewed as the powerhouse of Swiss football, FC Servette have flown the flag of Geneva proudly on a domestic and a European stage for many years. However, off-the-field developments in the opening of the brand new Stade de Genève have seen the club plunge into despair on the pitch. The once famous club, Swiss champions in 1999, now ply their trade in the lower levels of Swiss football after bankruptcy in February 2005 meant enforced relegation.

Stade De Genève – Geneva (Switzerland)

Just three seasons ago the team finished in 3rd place in the Swiss Super League, qualifying for the UEFA Cup. The club were originally formed in 1890, and was a regular league championship winner during the early years of the century. By 1930, when the league became professional, Servette had won the championship six times. In the next 30 years the club became the most famous in the country with further titles in 1933, 1934, 1940, 1946 and 1950. After winning the title in 1961 the club gained a place for the first time in the European Cup. A 7–1 first round win against Hibernians of Malta was followed by a narrow 5–4 defeat on aggregate to the Czech side Pribram. The following season they went out at the preliminary round stage on away goals to Feyenoord.

The golden period for the club came in the mid-1970s. In 1979 the club achieved an unparalleled domestic quadruple when it won the league championship, the Swiss cup, the league cup and the Alpine cup. They nearly made it five honours but fell at the quarter-final stage in the European Cup Winners' Cup to Fortuna Dusseldorf. A few more honours were captured in the 1980s including a further league title in 1985 and a Swiss cup in 1984. Glory in Europe was still absent for the famous maroons, although defeat to Alpine rivals Sturm Graz on aggregate in the 1999 Champions League final qualifying round could have been so different, as the group draw saw the Austrians in a group with Marseille and Manchester United.

■ How to get there
The stadium is located to the south of the city centre in the Lancy area. Trams 12 and 13 run from the centre of Geneva to close to the stadium. The trams terminate at Bachet de Pesay, a 5-minute walk to the south of the

stadium. The journey from the city centre should take around 20 minutes. There is a direct bus from Cornavin station on matchdays – Route D runs about every 10 minutes and takes 20 minutes, dropping you off opposite the stadium's east stand. From the airport there is an easy if time consuming way to reach the stadium via bus 18 which runs every 20 mins from outside Arrivals to stops close by Lancy-Pont-Rouge. Allow 40 mins for this journey in match-day traffic. A taxi from the airport to the stadium will cost around CHF40 (£22).

■ Getting a ticket
If you are planning on coming to town to see a Servette match then you don't have to worry about buying tickets in advance. With average crowds of less than 2,000 and a capacity of 30,000, you have a choice of quite a few seats! If you are in town to watch an international match or one of the numerous friendlies that are played at the stadium, tickets can be purchased online from http://www.resaplus.ch.

■ Nearest airport – Geneve-Cointrin (GVA)
Geneva airport is located 3 miles to the west of the city centre. The easiest way to reach the city is via train from the airport station to Cornavin station, journey time is 7 minutes. Bus number 10 also does the trip to downtown in 20 minutes. A taxi would cost around CHF35. The main UK carrier who serves Geneva is **Easyjet**, who have their main European hub here. They offer daily flights to over 20 destinations including Belfast, Bournemouth, Bristol, Doncaster, Liverpool, East Midlands, London and Newcastle. The airport is also served by **British Airways** from London City and Heathrow, as well as national carrier **Swiss**.

Letzigrund – Zurich (Switzerland)

The Facts

Name: Letzigrund
Address: Herdernerstrasse,
Zurich,
Switzerland
Capacity: 30,000 All Seater
Opened: 22nd September 2007

■ About Letzigrund

The new stadium in the western suburbs of Zurich represents the ambition of the Swiss football authorities in creating a real legacy from the 2008 tournament. Zurich has always had a fierce rivalry between FC Zurich and Grasshoppers, and so the authorities had a really difficult job deciding whether to develop either stadium or simply build a new one. In the end they chose to completely rebuild the Letzigrund, home of FCZ since 1925.

The new stadium opened with the Zurich derby in September 2007 and is certainly one of the most distinctive being used in the tournament in 2008. It has been primarily designed as a multi-purpose venue so there is an athletics track but the stands have certainly been designed to support football as well. Spectators enter the stadium from wide concourses at the top of the stands, that is the pitch is built some way below ground level. All views are unobstructed and there are two large TV screens on the north and south stands. The most unique feature of

the stadium however are the floodlights. In total there are 32 floodlight spikes which pierce the roof and act both as supports as well as lighting.

The stadium will host the following matches during June 2008:

Match 5 – Monday 9th June – 18.00 – Romania v France
Match 13 – Friday 13th June – 18.00 – Italy v Romania
Match 22 – Tuesday 17th June – 20.45 – France v Italy

When the Letzigrund stadium is complete in 2007, attention will turn to the Hardturm stadium and it will be completely redeveloped as a 30,000 all-seater football-only stadium. Currently the Hardturm has a capacity of 17,700. The stadium is a strange affair with three stands joined together in a similar shape to Nuremberg's Frankenstadion.

■ Who plays there?

The rivalry that exists in Swiss football can never be called bitter, but in Zurich it is the closest you can get to a real derby. The two clubs have existed for over 80 years, separated geographically by the main railway line, but recent events have thrown them together – initially at the Hardturm whilst the new Letzigrund is being constructed, and then when Stade de Zurich is being built in 2008, and then when the two clubs move into FC Zurich's Letzigrund.

Grasshopper Zurich are the most successful of the two, winning the Swiss championship on 27 occasions to

FC Zurich's 11 occasions. However, the balance of power currently lies with the latter as they have won back-to-back championships in 2006 and 2007. They also have a better European record, reaching the European Cup semi-finals in 1964 and 1977.

Grasshoppers were formed in 1886, making them one of Switzerland's oldest clubs, and they dominated some of the early Swiss seasons by winning the championship on four occasions by 1905. Their golden period came during the 1990s when sponsorship monies funded an expansion of the team to include such players as Shaun Bartlett, Hakan Yakin and Christian Sforza, and coaches including Leo Beenhakker and Ottmar Hitzfeld. During this period they won six Swiss championships in an eight-year period as well as two Swiss cups. However, it did take them four attempts to get past the preliminary rounds before they reached the group stages of the Champions League in 1995. They finished bottom of a group featuring Ferencvaros, Ajax and Real Madrid. The following season they faired slightly better, finishing 3rd in their group ahead of Rangers but behind Ajax and Auxerre. Since then they have had to make do with the occasional UEFA Cup campaign, although they can claim the Intertoto Cup as an honour in 2006.

FC Zurich were formed ten years later in 1896 and spent many years in the shadow of their city rivals. In fact up until 1963 they only had two Swiss championships in terms of honours. However, during the 1960s they dominated Swiss football, registering the title in 1963, 1966 and 1968 as well as two Swiss cups during this period. In 1963 they entered the European Cup for the first time and surpassed all expectations by reaching the semi-finals, beating Dundalk, Galatasaray and PSV before losing 8–1 to Real Madrid. The club then went through another period of domination under Timo Konietzka during the 1970s, winning the Swiss cup in 1972 and 1973 before capturing back-to-back titles in 1974 and 1975. In 1976 they won the domestic double for the first time. The following season they enjoyed another great run in the European Cup, beating Glasgow Rangers, TPS and Dynamo Dresden before losing to eventual winners Liverpool in the semi-final.

Apart from a couple of honours in the 1980s the club had to wait until the stewardship of Lucien Favre before they tasted honours again, winning the 2006 title with an injury-time goal against champions-elect FC Basel that resulted in some ugly scenes on the pitch in Basel. Their subsequent Champions League campaign only lasted 180 minutes as the team lost 3–2 on aggregate to Salzburg in the qualifying rounds. After last season's championship win the team will be hoping to fare better in Europe and reach a Champions League group-stage spot for the first time.

■ How to get there

The Letzigrund is located in the western fringes of the city, adjacent to the main railway line. The new stadium will have enhanced public transport access, although for some of the big games during the 2008 European Championships it may be quicker to walk to the stadium by following Badenerstrasse all the way down from

Wersstrasse in the old town. The walk should take around 20 minutes. Tram line 2 runs at regular intervals down Badenerstrasse to the Letzigrund, with the tram stop on the south east corner of the stadium.

The nearest train station to the Letzigrund and the Hardturm is Hardbrücke which is one stop from the central station. For the former, head southwards across the railway bridge and take third right into Bullingerstrasse and the stadium is 400 metres away. For the Hardturm, head north out of the station and take the first major left into Pfingstweidstrasse for the stadium.

■ Getting a ticket

In terms of getting tickets for domestic matches, you will have no problems getting in on the day of the game. FC Zurich are the better supported of the two clubs but they still only average gates of 10,000 even when playing at the Hardturm. The most popular match is the Zurich derby but even this does not sell out. Currently tickets can be purchased in advance from http://www.ticketcorner.com or by calling 0848 800 800 (from Switzerland only) and cost 20CHF for the Kurves behind the goal, to 50CHF for a seat in the main stand. Tickets on the day can be purchased from the numerous kiosks around the stadium.

■ Nearest airport – Zurich Kloten Airport (ZRH)

Zurich airport is located 7 miles outside the city centre in the area known as Kloten. The airport is Switzerland's largest and includes daily flights from the UK with **CityJet** from London City, **British Airways** from London Gatwick and Heathrow, **Easyjet** from London Gatwick and Luton, **Helvetic** from Manchester, **Swiss European** from Birmingham, London City and Manchester and of course **Swiss International** from London Heathrow. To reach the city centre, head down to the railway station which is located in the building opposite the main terminals. Trains run to the Hauptbahnhof every 15 minutes in less than 10 minutes and cost 6CHF each way.

Şükrü Saracoğlu Stadium – Istanbul (Turkey)

The Facts

Name: The Şükrü Saracoğlu Stadium
Address: Fenerbahçe Tesisleri,
           Kadiköy, Istanbul,
           Turkey
Capacity: 50,500 All Seater
Opened: 1908

■ About Şükrü Saracoğlu Stadium

There has been a stadium on this site since 1908 when the government built a small stand here for Union Club, a team made up of English students. The stadium grew over the next few years to be the most important in Istanbul until the Taksim stadium opened in 1923.

In 1929 Fenerbahçe moved in and immediately began the task of renovating the ground – in fact in 1944 the stadium was the largest in Turkey with a capacity of 25,000. Further expansion to 40,000 took place over the next few decades, although a decision to move to all-seater in 1995 reduced this to 25,000. Funding was secured in 1999 to increase the capacity to over 50,000, and the stadium was renamed the Şükrü Saracoğlu Stadium. In 2002, as part of the failed bid by Greece and Turkey to host Euro2008™, the stadium was granted a 5-star status by UEFA, thus enabling it to host major finals – a feat it will fulfil by hosting the 2009 UEFA Cup Final. The stadium is very impressive – a two-tier bowl of a stadium

with yellow and blue seats throughout. It is a very British style stadium – similar to a bigger version of St Mary's in Southampton. Sightlines are excellent and in keeping with the fanatical support of the Turks the intimate surroundings make the match-day experience awesome. The stadium is also the preferred choice for the national team and all bar one of the qualifying games for the 2006 World Cup were played here, as too was the infamous play-off game versus Switzerland when trouble on and off the pitch led to a stadium ban for the country.

■ Who plays there?

Fenerbahçe, or the 'Yellow Canaries', are today the biggest club in Turkey. They are managed by Brazilian legend Zico, who has taken the club to the top of the Super Lig after last season's disappointing 2nd place. The club can trace their history back to 1899 when a team was formed as a sports club – at the time football was banned within the Ottoman Empire. It was a further ten years before football was allowed, and the club entered the regional leagues. In 1959 the first Turkish national league was formed, and the club went on to win this inaugural title, as well as further titles in 1961, 1964, 1965 and 1968. The club also won a number of Turkish cups. In the 1970s the club finished in the top two on all bar one occasion – taking another four titles.

The club has continued its excellent domestic form since, with a total of 16 titles and four cups to date. However, despite the recruitment of such world-class coaches as Guus Hiddink, Jozef Venglos, Carlos Alberto Parreira and Christoph Daum, European success has been very thin on the ground. The highlight of 30 years of European football was a 1–0 victory at Old Trafford in 2003 a Champions League qualifying match although a year later the teams met again in the group stages with Manchester United running out 6–2 winners. The Turks did gain some revenge in the return leg with a 3–0 victory which took them into the UEFA Cup. Last season the priority was to regain the domestic title they last won in 2005, and despite a brave challenge from Besiktas amongst others, the championship was secured in late May.

■ How to get there
The stadium is located on the Asian side of the Bosphorus and so a trip on the river is almost a necessity. Take a boat from landing number 2 at Eminönü to Kadiköy harbour then bus 4 to the Dere Agzi bus stop on the canal. From here the stadium is a short 5-minute walk away. The nearest railway station is at Söğütlüçeşme, a 5-minute walk from the stadium.

■ Getting a ticket
Tickets for most games can be purchased via Biletix (http://www.biletix.com), which is a Ticketmaster company, three weeks before the game. Tickets range from 45YTL in the Tribunes, to 150YTL in the main stand upper tier. A good seat for the neutral is the Fenerium stand which start from 60YTL. The club averages 40,000 – some 10,000 less than capacity. The derby games against Besiktas and Galatasaray normally attract close to capacity although tickets can still be purchased in advance using the above method. On a match day tickets are sold from kiosks on each corner of the stadium.

The Facts

Name: Inönü Stadium
Address: Kadirgalar Cadassi,
Istanbul,
Turkey
Capacity: 32,100 All Seater
Opened: 19th May 1947 – Besiktas v AIK Solna

■ **About Inönü Stadium**

Any stadium that has been described by the legendary Pele as the 'most beautiful stadium in world' must be worth a visit. The stadium was designed by Italian architect Paolo Vietti Violi and has retained the feel and features of the city itself. The stadium is in the heart of the Domlabahçe Palace area of Istanbul.

It originally opened in 1947 and is named after the second President of Turkey. The stadium's special views come from its location close to the Bosphorus River and the Dolmabahçe Palace – one of Istanbul's most beautiful buildings. The stadium certainly has a unique look with three sides covered – two identical side stands that have one staggered tier, and one covered stand which dominates the stadium that sits high above the rest of the ground. At the far end (the Bosphorus end) is a smaller open-ended stand. Views from the higher tiers are fantastic, both in terms of the football and the surrounding scenery.

■ **Who plays there?**

Whilst Beşiktaş JK are the oldest sports club in Turkey, dating back to 1903, they have not enjoyed the success of their city rivals Galatasaray and Fenerbahçe – winning 12 titles and six Turkish cups, the last of which was in 2003. However, the club does have one honour that has never fallen on the other Turkish clubs – namely that in May 1952 the whole of the Turkish national team for a game versus Greece came from the club. To honour this achievement, the club are allowed to fly the Turkish flag alongside their own, as well as incorporate it onto their own emblem.

The team really rose to power in the late 1950s – winning their first championship in 1957 and then winning it again twice in the next three years. In the 1960s the team won three more championships, although the decade will be remembered for the club actually averaging a new coach every season. The team then went over 15 years without another title, as their cross-city neighbours hoarded the honours. They did win a couple more in the late 1980s including the domestic double in 1990 and again in 1994. However, the team seem to be cast as perennial bridesmaids, finishing runners-up nine times since the mid-1980s. Their European adventures have also been brief. A run to the quarter-finals of the European Cup in 1987 may seem impressive, but they only actually played one tie before that as APOEL of Cyprus refused to play in Turkey. A 5–0 defeat in the first leg of the quarter-final to Dynamo Kiev was not a memorable night for the club.

They did qualify for the group stages of the Champions League in 2003, where they were drawn in a group with Chelsea, Sparta Prague and Lazio. The club managed a 2–0 win at Stamford Bridge, the last European home defeat suffered by Chelsea, and going into the last game of the group sat in second place. However, a 2–0 defeat at home to Chelsea and Sparta's 1–0 win versus Lazio saw the club pushed into the UEFA Cup, where they lost 5–2 to Valencia. Last season they played second fiddle to Fenerbahçe for most of the season, having to console themselves with the runners-up spot and the qualifying rounds for the 2007 Champions League.

■ How to get there

The stadium is close enough to Taksim Square to be walkable – a 10-minute stroll towards the river along Gümüşsuyu Avenue will see you at the stadium gates. Alternatively, if you need to use public transport you can get a ferry from the Asian side direct to the landing at Besiktas from Üsküdar and Kadiköy. A dolmus taxi should cost €2 from Taksim.

■ Getting a ticket

Tickets for most games can be purchased from Biletix (http://www.biletix.com), which is a Ticketmaster company, three weeks before the game. Tickets range from 45YTL in the open stand to 150YTL in the main stand upper tier (Numarali). A good seat for the neutral is the Kapali stand, priced 60YTL. The club averages around 27,000, some 5,000 less than capacity. The derby games against Fenerbahçe and Galatasaray normally attract close to capacity, although tickets can still be purchased in advance using the above method. On a match day tickets are sold from kiosks on each corner of the stadium.

■ Nearest airport – Ataturk International (IST)

Ataturk airport is the busiest airport in Turkey, handling 21 million passengers in 2006. It is located 9 miles southwest of the city. The airport is served by a number of airlines from the UK. **Atlasjet** fly from London Stansted and Manchester, **British Airways** from London Heathrow and **Turkish Airlines** from Manchester and Heathrow. There are a number of public transport options to and from the city centre. The easiest is the metro link called Hafif Metro. A journey to the city centre should take an hour and cost €2. Alternatively you can catch one of the Havas airport buses that run to Taksim Square in 45 minutes. Finally, a taxi to Taksim will take around 35 minutes and should cost no more than €20.

■ Alternative airport – Sabiha Gökçen (SAW)

Istanbul's second airport is located on the Asian side of the city 30km from the city centre. The airport is expanding in terms of airlines – **Easyjet** became the first UK-based airline to start flying here from London Luton. To reach the city centre from the airport use the Havas buses which run every 30 minutes to Taksim and take an hour. A taxi will cost YTL45/€35.

Olimpiyskiy Stadion – Kiev (Ukraine)

The Facts

Name: Olmpiyskiy Stadion
Address: Vul Chervonoarminska 55,
Kiev,
Ukraine
Capacity: 83,450 All Seater
Opened: 12th August 1923

■ About Olimpiyskiy Stadion

The national stadium of Ukraine is one of the biggest in Europe today, and when the country formed part of the Soviet empire was the flagship of the country, and even considered as the venue for the 1980 Summer Olympics before a decision was made to build the Luzhniki in Moscow.

The stadium was over ten years in the planning, and even when opened in 1923 it was not really used and in fact was completely rebuilt just 15 years after opening. In 1941 the stadium reopened as the 50,000-capacity Red Stadium. Unfortunately the reopening coincided to the day with the German invasion of the city, and so the reopening was postponed until 1948 – although the city's council agreed to honour the tickets purchased some seven years before! In the 1960s the stadium, renamed the Kiev Central Stadium, was expanded to accommodate over 100,000, although facilities were very basic – simple wooden benches and no roof were the order of the day. More work was carried out in the late 1970s in readiness for the 1980 Olympics, which saw the stadium host a number of the football matches.

Apart from a lick of paint nothing really changed in the stadium during the period before and after the 1991 Ukrainian declaration of independence. In 1996 the stadium was renamed the Olimpiysky (the Olympic), although it has also been refered to as the Tsentralny (Central), Respublykanskyi (Republic) or even the Lobanovsky after Dynamo's great manager.

A final redevelopment was completed in 1999 when the capacity was reduced to 83,450. The stadium today is a vast bowl – similar to stadiums in St Petersburg and even pre-Olympics in Athens. A running track does mean that you are quite a way from the action, but views are still good. The lack of a roof does lead to some wet and chilly nights. On the rare occasions that the stadium has been full in the last 20 years the atmosphere is one of the best in eastern Europe. The decision to allow Ukraine and Poland to host the European Championships in 2012 will almost certainly see a huge redevelopment of the stadium, and the possible addition of a long-awaited roof.

■ Who plays there?

The Olimpiyskiy is used for Ukrainian national home matches, as well as high-profile games featuring Dynamo Kiev. Dynamo's home stadium, the Lobanovsky Dynamo, is located a 10-minute walk from the stadium. In the last decade the stadium has hosted some big European nights for Dynamo, none more so than the Shevchenko/Rebrov-inspired run to the Champions League semi-final in 1999 when the team beat Panathinaikos, Arsenal and Real Madrid before losing 4–3 on aggregate to Bayern Munich.

The history of Dynamo Kiev is remarkable as they rose from formation as an amateur team in 1927 to arguably the greatest Soviet team ever. Despite being part of the Soviet police social society, the club never had the same level of paranoia about it as other such teams in Berlin and Moscow. In fact it wasn't until just before the Second World War that the club began to rise in stature. By 1941 the team had earned a reputation as the strongest in Russia, and so when the Nazis invaded, in a move to crush local morale a series of matches against the famished and weakened team were arranged by the Germans. Kiev beat all comers, including the Luftwaffe team, which resulted in many of the players being imprisoned in hard-labour camps.

After the war the club continued to impress in the Soviet leagues. They won their first Soviet title in 1961, before capturing a hat-trick of titles between 1966 and 1968. In total under the Soviet banner the club won 13 championships, nine Cups and three Super Cups. The club also became the first Soviet team to win a European trophy when they won the UEFA Cup Winners' Cup in 1975, repeating the feat in 1986. When the Soviet Union was dissolved in 1991 Kiev became the strongest team within Ukraine. With little or no opposition in the newly formed Ukrainian league, Kiev won every title between 1993 and 2001. They subsequently won it again in 2003 and 2004 before having to be content to play second fiddle to Shakhtar Donetsk in 2005 and 2006. Under inspirational coach Valery Lobanovsky, who originally joined the club in 1973, a number of young stars were developed before moving on to prominence abroad. Not only was there Andriy Shevchenko and Serhiy Rebrov, but some of the stars of the early 1980s including current national team coach Oleg Blokhin, Andrei Kanchelskis, Oleg Salenko and Oleg Mikhalichenko.

■ How to get there
The stadium has its own metro stop, called Respublykanskyi, which is two stops south on the blue metro line from Khreshchatyk. You can also get to the stadium within a 10-minute walk of the metro stop on the green line at Palats Sportu.

■ Getting a ticket
With Dynamo's failure to make it into the Champions League in recent years, the number of games played at the stadium have been restricted to the national team, although these have also been played away from the capital recently. The recent games against Georgia and Scotland have sparked some interest when over 50,000 were in the stadium for both games. Tickets for most games go on sale from the stadium concourse around a week before the game. They are also sold from a small kiosk close to the entrance of Palats Sportu metro station.

■ Nearest airport – Boryspil State Airport (KBP)
The main international airport of Ukraine is located 29km east of the city centre. It is served by mainly national flag carriers, including **British Airways** from London Heathrow and **Ukraine Airlines** from London Gatwick and Heathrow. You can also get their via Riga with **Air Baltic** from London Gatwick. Regular buses run to and from the city, terminating at the central railway station. A taxi will cost around 100UAH to the city centre.

PHOTOGRAPHY CREDITS

All photographs in this book are owned by GTC Media Ltd, except the following, to which we are grateful for giving us permission to reproduce them in this publication.

http://www.worldstadiums.com

Lyon – Stade Gerland
Djurgarden – Stockholms Stadium
Parma – Stadio Ennio Tardini
Athens – Karaiskaki Stadium
FC Seville – Ramon Sanchez
Real Betis – Ruiz de Lopera
Atletico Madrid – Vicente Calderon
FCC Napoli – San Paolo Stadium
Dynamo Kiev – Olympic Stadium
Red Star Belgrade – Red Star Stadium
Steaua Bucharest – Stadium Steaua
Reykjavik – Laugardalsvöllur Stadium

Also a big thank you to Dennis Woods for providing the pictures for Levski Sofia and Skonto Riga, Jarrod Billard for the pictures from Hampden Park, Jamie 'the Postman' Wyatt for Stamford Bridge, Rick Hooper for the Olympic Stadium in Athens, Mark Bode for Celtic Park and Ibrox and Joe McCrory for the pictures from Valencia's Mestalla, De Kuip in Rotterdam and the Vanden Stock in Brussels.

Finally, thanks to Mr Stephens for donating his picture of the Stade Vélodrome from that wonderful day in English rugby history that today seems so long ago, and to Phil 'The Hammer' Brown for going out of his way to take some pictures of Kiev when he should have been working.

The pictures of Stade de France® are credited to architects Michel Macary, Aymeric Zublena, Michel Regembla and Claude Constantini.